Toward Understanding Women

Virginia E. O'Leary

Oakland University

Brooks/Cole Publishing Company
Monterey, California

A Division of Wadsworth Publishing Company, Inc.

Printed in the United States of America

10 9 8 7 6 5 4 3 2

Library of Congress Cataloging in Publication Data

O'Leary, Virginia E   1943–
    Toward understanding women.

    Bibliography: p. 203
    Includes index.
    1. Women—Psychology.   2. Sex role.   I. Title.
HQ1206.074   155.6′33   77-5103
ISBN 0-8185-0228-2

Production Editor: *Fiorella Ljunggren*
Interior Design: *Jamie S. Brooks*
Cover Design: *Sharon Marie Bird*

Chapter opening photographs for Chapters 1, 3, 5, 8, and 9 (right) by Charlene Depner; for Chapter 4 by Ronald D. Hansen; for Chapters 6, 9 (left), and 10 by Chris Payne. Chapter 2 photograph reprinted by permission from K. L. Moore, *The Developing Human,* 1974, W. B. Saunders Co., Philadelphia. Chapter 7 photograph courtesy of P. Toples.

In loving memory of Morgan,
this book is dedicated
to our son, Sean.

Preface

In 1971 I taught an advanced undergraduate seminar entitled "The Psychology of Women." Nine students enrolled in the course—seven women and two men. We spent an exciting semester reading and discussing psychology's construct of the female. A year later the chairperson of my department suggested that I shift the focus of the course to the sophomore level and open it up to a broader range of students. I did, and this book grew out of my experiences teaching that course.

Six years have passed since the publication of the first textbooks on the psychology of women. In the intervening years there has been a virtual explosion in the number of books and empirical studies aimed at increasing our psychological knowledge about and understanding of women. This book represents my effort to assess and integrate the current state of knowledge about the nature and origins of the behavior of women.

I have pulled together empirical evidence from a variety of fields and perspectives. Although the focus of the text is on women, comparative data on men have been included in an attempt to determine the origins of those biological, psychological, and cultural factors that differentiate or are believed to differentiate the sexes.

The topics covered are broad and the issues complex. I have presented the material in a fashion that should be readily comprehensible for students with only a limited background in psychology. But I have also neither avoided nor oversimplified issues, so that the information could be of value to advanced students as well.

In many ways this is a personal book. My understanding and interpretation of the literature have, I know, been influenced by my perspective as a feminist social psychologist and as a woman. Within that perspective I have tried to present the material objectively. I hope I have succeeded. My use of personal examples throughout the text is intended to be illustrative only; I do not regard my "female experience" as normative, and it should not be interpreted as such.

I am indebted to Algea O. Harrison, who authored the chapter on Black women. Her careful review and insightful interpretation of the psychological literature relevant to Black women represent an invaluable addition to the scope of the book.

This book could not have been completed without the support of a great many people. Among the students at Oakland who read and commented on chapters, tracked down references, and helped check them for accuracy, I would particularly like to thank Cheryl Depner, Jim Donoghue, Larry Helgar, Christine Kassa, David Lewis, and Judy Pearson. Jean Kyriazis prepared the chapter summaries. Ranald D. Hansen's thoughtful comments and encouragement were deeply appreciated. A special thank you goes to Charlene E. Depner, who, as a former student, a research colleague, and a friend, was always available to suggest a reference, discuss an idea, and offer constructive criticism and who even took most of the photographs. Helen Poole cheerfully typed and retyped chapters and was particularly supportive on days when I was discouraged.

The staff at Brooks/Cole, particularly Bill Hicks and Fiorella Ljunggren, were both helpful and patient. The assistance of Consulting Editor Lawrence Wrightsman was invaluable. He is a respected colleague whom I have come to regard also as a valued friend. Janis Bohan of Metropolitan State College, Kay Deaux of Purdue University, and Elizabeth Douvan of the University of Michigan reviewed the manuscript and offered many helpful suggestions.

On a more personal note I am grateful to my family, particularly David, who knew I could, and Sean, who was willing to share Mom with The Book.

Virginia E. O'Leary

Contents

Toward Understanding Women

Chapter One

Introduction

When I entered college in 1961 I eagerly enrolled in a course in introductory psychology. On the first day of class my professor defined psychology as the "science that studies the behavior of *man* [italics mine] and other animals" (Hilgard, 1957, p. 2). He then outlined the goals of this "young" science as the understanding, prediction, and control of behavior. By the end of the semester I was hooked; I wanted to be a psychologist. I naively assumed that the use of the word "man" in my professor's definition of psychology was generic. It was not until my second year of graduate school that I began to discover how naive my assumption had been.

During a seminar discussion of the puzzling results of a classic experiment in social psychology, I observed that the study had been conducted by a male experimenter and that the subjects were all female. The only other woman student in the class nodded in agreement. The professor was incensed at the audacity of my observation. He made it quite clear that in his view there was a distinction between good scientific thought and post-hoc explanations that were both trivial and biased. Later that day I overheard him remark to a colleague that if he had his way women would not be admitted to graduate school. This occurred almost ten years ago, and things have begun to change.

The resurgence of the women's movement in the last decade has focused the attention of the entire society on the necessity for reevaluating both the role of women in contemporary society (Sherif, 1976) and the validity of the traditional assumptions about the nature and origins of behavioral differences between women and men. Participation in feminist organizations has raised the consciousness of many American women and encouraged them to challenge the view that women are by definition the "second," the "weaker," and the "inferior" sex.

As a social movement the "new" feminism has confronted those in power with the inequities inherent in a political and economic system that has relegated women to the status of second-class citizens. As Sherif so aptly observes, "in calling for equality of the sexes, the women's movement is ultimately calling for changes in the basic structure of every known society—the relationship between men and women" (Sherif, 1976, p. 389). And the system has begun to recognize the issues raised by feminist women and men as legitimate. There are some indications that change is occurring, but progress is slow.

For example, the media have begun to respond to pressures to portray women as individuals in their own right. Mary Tyler Moore is single and successful. Maude ran for the state senate despite Walter's vehement protests. Even Edith Bunker recently refused to give up her volunteer work as a Sunshine Lady in order to have Archie's dinner on the table at 6:00 sharp.

The number of life-style alternatives available to contemporary women has increased. Career women, once portrayed as cold and castrating, are now depicted as vital and exciting. The children of working mothers are no longer assumed to be deprived. If a woman is denied a job because of her sex, she has legal recourse.

As the women's movement has matured, many of its goals have become recognized as acceptable, worthy, and even conventional (Mednick, Tangri, & Hoffman, 1975). The impact of feminist thought and action has not been limited to the public arena or to the lives of individual women and men; it has stimulated and vitalized the study of human behavior as well.

Historically, psychology as a discipline tended to be male-dominated and male-oriented (Unger & Denmark, 1975). Psychologists (most of them men) advanced theories of human behavior and attempted to verify these theories empirically in studies using male subjects only (Carlson & Carlson, 1961; Dan & Beekman, 1972; Weisstein, 1971). The exclusion of female subjects from research was justified on a variety of grounds including the greater variability (or inconsistency) of female responses, the practical difficulties in obtaining a sufficient number of subjects to allow the researcher to analyze sex differences, and the investigators' lack of interest in sex differences in areas where they had been demonstrated to exist (Prescott & Foster, 1974). Perhaps the best-known example of the male bias in psychology is in the area of achievement motivation, where the existence of sex differences has long been recognized (McClelland, Atkinson, Clark, & Lowell, 1953) but, until recently, seldom explored (Horner, 1968; Mednick et al., 1975).

Traditional psychology has not completely ignored the issue of sex differences. Indeed, the investigation of such differences was subsumed (and legitimized) under the heading of differential psychology (the study of individual differences). As Parlee (1975) has recently noted, however, the range of problems included under this title was primarily limited to studies of intellectual abilities and (adult) personality characteristics. Even when sex differences were examined, there was a tendency to view male responses as normative and to explain female "differences" in terms of the "male model." Furthermore, such investigations have typically been considered to be peripheral to the mainstream of social-psychological and personality research (Parlee, 1975). As a traditionally trained social psychologist, I was taught to view sex differences as a nuisance variable to be controlled, not investigated.

In 1971 two texts were published that were devoted exclusively to the psychological study of women. Courses in the psychology of women were already being offered (most of them taught by women) on a number of campuses. The availability of two new textbooks in the area provided the impetus for the introduction of many more such courses into the graduate and undergraduate curricula of many institutions. Interest in and knowledge about women has expanded rapidly in the last six years, and the subject of woman has begun to attain a respectable position as a field for scientific study and scholarly analysis.

In 1974 the American Psychological Association formally recognized the growing scientific and professional interest in the study of women when its Council of Representatives approved the formation of the Division of the Psychology of Women. A year later a chapter on "The Psychology of Women" (Mednick & Weissman, 1975) was included in the 1975 edition of the Annual Review of Psychology under the heading "Special Topics." There remain psychologists who would argue that the study of women is peripheral to the traditional business of psychology. But a set of laws and theories applicable to less than half of the population does not constitute good science. As Parlee (1975) suggests, the time has come to develop a "body of knowledge that is more relevant to a scientific understanding of women's behavior and experience" (Parlee, 1975, p. 131).

The focus of this volume is on understanding women. As we have suggested, the systematic exclusion of female subjects from psychological research has severely limited our understanding of human behavior. Therefore, we would be compounding this kind of error if we were to restrict our attention to women exclusively.

Of course, some of the unique aspects of the female, such as menstruation and pregnancy, are biologically determined. But behavioral and experiential differences between the sexes cannot be explained on the basis of biology alone. The behaviors of girls and boys, of women and men are differentially influenced by environmental factors as well. Neither explanation alone can adequately account for the complexities of sex differences in human behavior. Rather, biological and cultural factors interact to produce those behaviors and experiences generally regarded as more characteristic of one sex or the other. Only by viewing the experience and behavior of women (and men) within the biological and social-psychological contexts in which they occur can we move toward understanding women.

Overview

The biological bases of sex differences are established before birth. In Chapter Two we will review the embryological development of sex differences, outlining the origins of genetic, hormonal, and structural differences between the sexes. Then we will attempt to relate these differences to behavioral differences between females and males of the same species. Among lower animals the relationship between biology and behavior appears direct. But human behavior is more complex than that of lower animals. Although the acquisition of certain sex-typed behaviors such as aggression may be a result of sex-linked biological predispositions, it is generally agreed that socialization plays a critical role in the development of patterns of behavior considered more characteristic of women than of men.

Chapter Three focuses on three general theoretical approaches that have been used to explain the development of sex roles. The psychoanalytic approach relies on the Freudian concept of identification; social-learning theories focus on the role of reinforcement in establishing behaviors that are appropriate for one's sex role; and theories of cognitive development stress the importance of defining oneself as either female or male. A single theory of sex-role development that accounts for the observed differences (and similarities) between females and males has yet to be proposed. However, each approach provides a theoretical basis for evaluating the significance of those psychological differences between the sexes that have been established empirically.

Until recently it was widely assumed that the obvious and universal biological differences between females and males were paralleled by clearly delineated psychological differences. Under closer scrutiny, however, a number of the postulated differences between males and females have been identified as social myths rather than as scientifically verifiable facts. In Chapter Four we will review the research in four areas (verbal ability, visual-spatial ability, mathematical ability, and aggression) in which the existence of sex differences has been fairly well established. Then we will consider several areas, such as passivity and dependency, in which sex differences have been postulated but empirical support has been equivocal at best. Finally, we will examine several areas in which postulated sex differences have not withstood the test of time and additional study.

Our society values striving, accomplishment, and success. Yet, women, who constitute over 50% of the population, have failed to pursue occupational goals that require intellectual competence and leadership ability. Chapter Five is devoted to an exploration of why women have failed to achieve positions of status and power, the earmarks of American success.

Because stereotypical conceptions of women and men are so widely shared, it has been easy to assume that they reflect real differences between the sexes. In American society men are "supposed" to be masculine and women are "supposed" to be feminine; neither sex is "supposed" to be much like the other. Only recently has the possibility that a given individual might possess *both* stereotypically masculine and stereotypically feminine traits been acknowledged. Such individuals are labeled androgynous. In Chapter Six we will review the literature on sex-role stereotypes and examine the influence of adherence to these stereotypes on women's definitions of themselves and of their roles. Rapidly accumulating evidence suggests that androgyny is associated with behavioral flexibility and psychological well-being.

Much of the available empirical literature relevant to our understanding of women is based on studies of middle-class White women, many of whom are college educated. Relatively little is known about female behavior and experience within other racial, ethnic, socioeconomic, or even cultural groups. In Chapter Seven Algea Harrison reviews the psychological literature on one such group, Black women.

The impact of sex-role socialization on women's behavior is perhaps most dramatically illustrated in recent studies of female sexuality. In Chapter Eight we will examine the literature on female sexuality, beginning with a review of female reproductive anatomy and the physiology of the sexual-response cycle. We will then consider the sexual behavior of both heterosexually and homosexually oriented women as a social-psychological phenomenon.

Although the social role of women as traditionally defined emphasizes wife and motherhood, the demands and responsibilities associated with these roles shift across the life cycle. In Chapter Nine we will trace the development of the "female" role(s) from adolescence through aging. Although our focus will be on the "natural" progression of women's roles through the life span, we will also consider the effects of critical events, such as divorce or widowhood, that may disrupt this progression.

Despite the existence of obvious biological differences between the sexes, there are only four behaviors that may be appropriately labeled exclusively female (menstruation, pregnancy, and lactation) or exclusively male (ejaculation). However, the behavior and experience of women and men do differ in many situations. In the final chapter we will consider the implications of our current knowledge about the nature and origins of women's experience and behavior for our understanding of human behavior.

Chapter Two

Sex as a Biological Fact

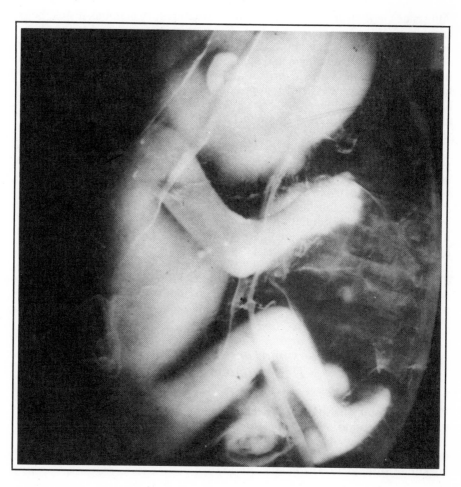

Perhaps the most dramatic differences between men and women are external and physical. Despite the popularity of long hair for men and pants for women, there are obvious differences between the two sexes. A man's hips are narrow and his shoulders broad; he has a penis. A woman's hips are rounded, and she has breasts. A woman's external genitalia are markedly different from a man's; she has a clitoris and a vaginal opening.

The external differences between men and women are paralleled by differences in their internal reproductive structures. A man has testes; he is capable of fathering a child. A woman has ovaries and a vaginal canal; she is uniquely able to bear and nurse a child. The sex hormones produced by the endocrine systems of women and men are also different. A woman produces the female sex hormones estrogen and progesterone. The levels of these hormones fluctuate cyclically, approximately every 28 days. A man produces male sex hormones called *androgens*. The primary androgen is testosterone, which is released continuously into the man's bloodstream, maintaining a stable level.

The basis of the biological differences between men and women is genetic. The pattern of sex chromosomes in every one of their respective cells is different. A man's cells contain an X chromosome plus a Y chromosome; a woman's cells contain two X chromosomes.

It is a well-established fact that genes and hormones play a critical role in the structural differentiation of males from females. Do these biological differences influence behavior? Rapidly accumulating evidence in the field of animal sexology clearly suggests that they do.

In this chapter we will review the embryological development of sex differences and outline the origins of genetic, hormonal, and structural differences between the sexes. Then we will attempt to relate these differences to behavioral differences between males and females of the same species.

Chromosomal and Early Hormonal Determinants of Sex

Elementary biology books teach us that sex is determined at the moment of conception. And this moment is certainly an important one. However, there appear to be at least three other times during the prenatal life of the human fetus when its fate as either a "male" or a "female" is open to question (Money, 1971).

Every cell of a genetically normal human being contains 46 chromosomes, 23 of which are contributed by each parent. The chromosomes are matched—one from the mother and one from the father. Twenty-two of the pairs carry genes that determine which of the cells of a developing embryo will grow into nerves or muscles or vital organs such as the heart and liver. They also determine such bodily features as height, the color of the eyes, and the length of the nose. These features are, of course, common to all humans. The 23rd pair of chromosomes determines the sex of the embryo.

The mother's contribution to the sex of her offspring is always the same, an X chromosome. Thus, at conception the sex of the fetus is determined by the presence of an X or a Y chromosome contributed by the father. If the fertilized egg contains two X chromosomes, the embryo is a genetic female (XX); if it contains an X chromosome plus a Y chromosome, the embryo is a genetic male (XY). However, the mere presence of a pair of sex chromosomes at conception does not guarantee the birth of a normal male or female infant nine months later.

The pattern of sex chromosomes represents the first stage in a four-stage sequence of sex differentiation. The presence of an XX or XY pair of chromosomes in the fertilized egg establishes a genetic blueprint for the subsequent differentiation of the gonads. The second stage in the sequence is marked by the differentiation of the gonads into either ovaries or testes. During the third stage gonadal differentiation effects the development of external genitalia into either a clitoris and vaginal opening or a penis. The fourth stage involves the differentiation of structures of the brain, specifically the hypothalamus, that will regulate the pattern of female and male hormones released into the bloodstream after birth.

At each of these four stages the developing organism is bi-potential for the next stage (Money, 1971); that is, at the beginning of each stage the course of development can take either a male or a female path resulting in both structural and behavioral changes contrary to the established genetic sex of the organism. In order to understand how such "reversals" of nature are possible, let us examine in more detail the sequence of sexual differentiation.

The genetic code established at conception results in the differentiation of the gonads into ovaries (XX) or testes (XY) sometime during the seventh week of embryological development. Before this time the structure of the gonads is undifferentiated; they are neither ovaries nor testes. Furthermore, the basic outline of both male and female internal reproductive structures is present in the form of two parallel systems of primitive genital ducts. The Müllerian duct system forms the basis of the fallopian tubes and uterus; the Wolffian duct system represents the potential development of the internal reproductive structures of the male.

Because the gonads are undifferentiated during the early weeks of embryonic life, it was originally believed that the developing organism was "neutral" or "bisexual." However, it has now been established that the basic structure of the fetus is female. In order for male differentiation to occur, "something" must be added (Money & Ehrhardt, 1972).

Genetically, that "something" is the presence of the Y chromosome. It is the Y chromosome that triggers the differentiation of the gonadal structures into testes. Once the testes have differentiated, they release a fetal hormonal substance that results in the regression of the potentially "female" Müllerian duct system. At the same time, the male hormones (androgens) produced by the fetal testes promote the elaboration of the male Wolffian duct system. If the gonads that have differentiated as testes fail to initiate the secretion of the fetal hormones, the developing embryo proceeds to differentiate as a female, regardless of its genetic sex. Therefore, the differentiation of internal female reproductive structures is not dependent on the presence of female hormones. In the absence of androgens, the Müllerian duct system elaborates into fallopian tubes and uterus and the Wolffian ducts degenerate.

A similar process regulates the differentiation of male and female external genitalia. Until the end of the third month of fetal life, the genital tubercle remains undifferentiated. Then, in the presence of the male sex hormones (androgens), it differentiates into a penis. In the absence of androgens, the external genitals proceed to develop into a vaginal opening and clitoris, even though the fetus may be genetically (XY) and gonadally male.

The effects of chromosomes and hormone levels on the masculine differentiation of internal and external reproductive structures appear direct; that is, masculine differentiation is dependent on the presence of a Y chromosome and the addition of the male hormones. Indeed, the presence of a Y chromosome in addition to two X chromosomes, as in Klinefelter's syndrome (XXY), results in the masculinization of the genitalia. Similarly, the administration of the primary androgen, testosterone, to a genetic female is powerful enough to affect masculinization of the internal reproductive structures and the appearance of the external genitalia as well. Among lower animals species-specific critical periods in the differentiation process have been identified. If testosterone is introduced during these periods, masculinization will occur. The timing and duration of these critical periods vary from species to species. At the human level the precise timing of such critical periods has not yet been specified.

Recent research suggests that the effects of androgens on the developing fetus are not limited to the masculinization of internal and external reproductive structures (Hutt, 1972; Money & Ehrhardt, 1972). There is also evidence that androgens exert an influence on the masculinization of the brain, specifically the hypothalamus. The hypothalamus is involved in the control of a variety of behaviors. It also regulates the cyclic (female) or noncyclic (male) release of sex hormones from the endocrine system at puberty.

Animal Research

Studies of lower animals, such as rats and guinea pigs, reveal that the presence of androgens during a critical period of early development abolishes the potential for the adult feminine pattern of cyclic hormone release. Even though the chromosomes, gonads, and reproductive structures of these animals are consistently feminine, the introduction of androgens during this critical period affects later reproductive behavior. As adults these "females" display mating behavior typical of male rats; they mount other females instead of presenting themselves to be mounted (Hutt, 1972). The effects of androgens are not limited to reproductive functioning. These androgenized female animals also manifest aggression, play behavior, and activity rates more characteristic of males (Goy, 1970).

Androgenized females. Perhaps the most dramatic example of the masculinizing effects of the androgens is contained in a study by Ward (1969). When she administered androgens to genetically female rats before birth and again shortly after birth, these rats differentiated as males. Not only did they possess many of the genital structures characteristic of males, but as adults they were capable of ejaculation.

Although postnatal androgenization (that is, administration of androgen after birth) occurs too late in the developmental sequence to reverse the "sex" of the genital structures, it does masculinize behavior (Sacks, Pollack, Kreiger, & Barfield, 1973; Ward, 1969). According to Barraclough and Gorski (1962), a single injection of androgen to a female rat within the first few days after birth induces sterility. As a result, ovulation is inhibited and normal female receptivity to mounting is reduced or eliminated. If these androgenized female rats are given additional androgen treatment as adults, they display mounting behavior characteristic of adult male rats. Similar results have been obtained in studies of guinea pigs (Phoenix, Goy, Gerall, & Young, 1962). The masculinizing effects of early postnatal androgenization are apparently irreversible. In several studies, attempts to "treat" androgenized adult females by giving them female sex hormones (estrogen and progesterone) did not increase their receptivity to mounting (Barraclough & Gorski, 1962; Harris & Levine, 1965; Ward & Renz, 1972).

Androgen-deprived males. As the presence of androgens masculinizes genetic females, their absence feminizes genetic males. Again, the extent of feminization depends on the time of intervention. Studies by Jost (1947; 1958) demonstrate that the castration[1] of genetically male rabbits in utero on the 19th day after conception ensures the complete feminization of the internal and external reproductive structures of the animal. Castration at this time deprives the developing organism of androgens. Prenatal castration on the 24th day occurs too late to effect a complete structural reversal, and such animals are hermaphrodites; that is, the genetic male is born with both male and female genital structures. Striking effects can also be obtained by administering antiandrogens, substances that block the effective utilization of androgens. Male rats subjected to antiandrogen treatment during critical

---

[1]Castration involves the surgical removal of the male gonads. Since the testes are the primary source of testosterone production, when castration has taken place, the androgens available to the developing organism are drastically reduced.

developmental periods are born with mammary glands and rudimentary vaginas (Nadler, 1968; Neumann, Elger, & Kramer, 1966; Ward, 1972).

The effects of androgen deprivation on genetically male animals are not limited to full or partial reversals in reproductive structure. Prenatally antiandrogenized male rats, as well as those castrated shortly after birth, exhibit impaired copulatory behavior as adults (Gerall, Hendricks, Johnson, & Bounds, 1967; Grady, Phoenix, & Young, 1965; Hendricks, 1969; Nadler, 1969). Furthermore, if prenatally antiandrogenized male rats are subsequently castrated at birth and given female-hormone therapy at puberty, they display normal female mating behavior (Neumann & Elger, 1966). Similar results have been obtained by Swanson (1970) in male hamsters. However, adult male rats castrated after the critical developmental period (on the day of birth) fail to display female copulatory patterns when administered female sex hormones.

Among lower animals the relationship between hormones and behavior appears direct. If androgens are present during critical periods of development, genetic females will display adult behaviors characteristic of genetic males. Conversely, genetic males deprived of androgens during these critical periods will display behaviors characteristic of genetic females. The fact that hormonal intervention affects behavior has been widely interpreted to suggest that hormones exert an organizing influence on the central nervous system. In the presence of androgens, the structures of the brain that control behavior are masculinized; in the absence of androgens, these structures are feminized. As we shall see, it is more difficult to assess the extent to which hormones affect the behavior patterns characteristic of human males and females.

If the effects of surgical and hormonal interventions on lower animals were limited to mating behaviors alone, they would be of little interest to us, since the reproductive behavior of lower animals is closely tied to hormonal functioning. At the human level sexual behavior is molded by experience and learning. However, a number of non-reproductive behaviors usually more characteristic of males than of females are apparently influenced by sex hormones. For example, the administration of testosterone (the primary androgen) has been found to increase the fighting and aggressive behavior of female rhesus monkeys (Goy, 1970). As we shall see in Chapter Four, sex differences in levels of physical aggression have been found consistently in studies of human males and females. These findings have led to the speculation that sex differences in human aggressive behavior may be in part biologically based (Maccoby & Jacklin, 1974).

Human Studies

Ethical considerations do not permit us to interfere with the biological mechanisms of the human fetus in order to specify critical factors in sex differentiation. But accidents of nature, both genetic and hormonal, do occur. We will consider such human cases in an attempt to determine how much of what we know about animal sex differentiation is applicable to understanding sex differences between human beings.

As we shall see, the effects of chromosomal and hormonal abnormalities on the internal and external reproductive structures of human males and females parallel those observed in studies of lower animals. However, the relationship between biology and behavior is more direct at the animal level. So much of human behavior is the result of social learning, cognition, and experience that it is difficult to assess the extent to which biological factors influence the patterns of behavior characteristic of girls and boys and of women and men.

Among humans two categories of chromosomal abnormalities are known to affect the structure and function of the reproductive system. These deviations from the normal patterns of genetic sex (XX and XY) are the result of either the absence of a sex chromosome or the addition of extra chromosomes. The pattern of sex chromosomes contains the genetic code for gonadal differentiation, which, in turn, affects the release of fetal sex hormones. As a result, chromosomal abnormalities are usually accompanied by deficits in the production of sex hormones.

A single sex chromosome. In the condition known as *Turner's syndrome*, the individual has an XO chromosome pattern instead of the normal XX or XY pattern. The single X chromosome (XO) results in the differentiation of female genitalia. Gonadal differentiation, however, is incomplete; the ovaries are represented as primitive streaks of tissue (Money & Ehrhardt, 1972). The total absence of gonadal hormones results in sterility, and the female hormone estrogen must be administered at puberty to effect breast development and the onset of menstruation. Nevertheless, the internal and external genital structures of girls with Turner's syndrome are clearly female, as are their interests and behaviors.

Money and Ehrhardt (1972) compared the interests, attitudes, and behaviors of 15 girls with Turner's syndrome ranging in age from 8 to 16 with those of 15 normal girls in the same age bracket. The experimental and control groups were matched on the basis of age, socioeconomic status, and IQ. The results of this comparison revealed that the girls with Turner's syndrome did not differ from their matched controls in tomboyish behavior, preference for male versus female playmates, or clothing preferences (slacks versus dresses); both groups were equally feminine. Furthermore, on three other measures the girls with Turner's syndrome were more feminine than their controls; as a group they displayed less interest and skill in athletics, fewer instances of childhood fighting, and a greater interest in jewelry, perfume, and hairstyling. No differences were obtained between the two groups with respect to either the display of childhood sexuality or the anticipation of romance, marriage, and motherhood. On the basis of these results, Money and Ehrhardt (1972) concluded that neither the absence of an additional X chromosome nor the female sex hormone estrogen during prenatal development precludes the differentiation of a feminine-gender identity. It is important to note that, despite the difference in their sex chromosomes, both groups of girls were reared as females exclusively.

Additional sex chromosomes. Chromosomal abnormalities involving the addition of extra sex chromosomes may take one of several forms. The presence of an additional Y chromosome (XYY) in the genetic male does not interfere with the masculine differentiation of the genitalia. As a result, little interest was shown in this genetic anomaly until the mid-1960s, when Jacobs and her colleagues (Jacobs, Brunton, & Melville, 1965) reported that males imprisoned for criminal behavior showed a higher prevalence of the XYY syndrome than that expected in the general population. This finding gave rise to the suggestion that XYY males were genetically predisposed to engage in violent and antisocial behavior (Polani, 1969).

Shah (1970), however, failed to find evidence that XYY inmates were more likely to behave aggressively than a control group of inmates with the normal male chromosome pattern.[2] Furthermore, when the criminal records of inmates with an extra Y chromosome were compared with those of inmates with an extra X chromosome (assumed to be associated with nonaggressive tendencies), no differences were obtained (Clark, Tefler, Baker, & Rosen, 1973). Money and Ehrhardt (1972) suggest that XYY males may be more impulsive and have greater difficulty in establishing long-term interpersonal relationships than normals. However, a direct relationship between the presence of an additional Y chromosome and characteristic patterns of behavior has not been established.

The presence of an extra Y chromosome is powerful enough to affect masculinization even in the presence of two X chromosomes. This occurs in *Klinefelter's syndrome* (XXY). Individuals with Klinefelter's syndrome are structurally male, although the penis is usually small and the testes underdeveloped. As a result of this condition, the individual is sterile. Because androgen production is often deficient, secondary sex characteristics may fail to develop at puberty and sex drive may be low. Although Klinefelter's syndrome is often accompanied by psychopathological problems ranging all the way from severe mental retardation to the conviction that one is trapped in the body of the "wrong" sex (transsexualism), none of these difficulties has been *consistently* associated with the syndrome (Money & Ehrhardt, 1972). Perhaps, as Money and Ehrhardt (1972) suggest, the extra X chromosome introduces an element of instability into the functioning of the central nervous system. Such instability may result in increased vulnerability to a variety of developmental deficits, including difficulty in establishing a gender identity consistent with one's anatomy.

Thus several deviations from the normal patterns of sex chromosomes result in alterations of the reproductive structures of the developing fetus. These chromosomal abnormalities are usually accompanied by deficits in the production of sex hormones.

You may recall that the pattern of sex chromosomes contains the genetic code of gonadal differentiation. If a Y chromosome is present, the gonads differentiate as testes; this results in the release of fetal hormones that exert a masculinizing influence on the developing organism. Occasionally, androgens are present during critical developmental periods in a genetic female. When this occurs, the XX fetus is masculinized.

---

[2]Although there is little evidence to suggest that XYY males behave more aggressively than XY males, they do tend to be taller than average and are more prone to acne (Shah, 1970).

Androgenized females. Two causes for the androgenization of genetic females have been identified. One is a hereditary metabolic disorder. The second was inadvertently induced during the 1950s when a synthetic female hormone (progestin) was often prescribed to prevent miscarriages. Progestin contained a testosterone derivative that resulted in the virilization of female fetuses.

The effects of androgenization are limited to the differentiation of the external reproductive structures. Mild cases of androgenization result in an enlarged clitoris. Severely androgenized genetic females may be born with a normal penis and empty scrotum (Money & Ehrhardt, 1972). The internal reproductive organs are, however, clearly female (Federman, 1967). In some cases treatment with female sex hormones is necessary to ensure the development of appropriately feminine secondary sex characteristics at puberty.

Money and Ehrhardt (1972) report several studies of androgenized human females suggesting that fetal masculinization exerts some influence on behavior (Ehrhardt, Epstein, & Money, 1968; Ehrhardt & Money, 1967). Compared to a matched group of "normal" females, those who have been fetally androgenized describe themselves as more "tomboyish"—a characterization with which both their parents and their peers agree. However, contrary to what might be expected, this tendency toward tomboyishness is not expressed in increased physical aggression. The masculinizing effects of fetal androgenization on behavior appear to be limited to interest in vigorous physical activities, often in competition against males.

As children fetally androgenized girls exhibit strong preferences for "boys' toys," such as trucks and guns. Unlike their normal female peers, they show little interest in "mothering" younger children. Although fetally androgenized girls do not reject marriage and motherhood as future goals, they tend to subordinate these interests to career concerns. Interestingly, high IQ and superior academic achievement appear to be characteristic of both males and females exposed prenatally to the influence of excessive androgens (Baker & Ehrhardt, 1974).

Androgen-insensitive males. Just as the presence of androgens in the genetic female results in structural and behavioral masculinization, the absence of androgens during critical developmental periods feminizes the genetic male.

The closest human approximation to the antiandrogenized male animal is found in the syndrome of androgen insensitivity (testicular feminization) in the genetic male. The effect of androgen insensitivity on the genetic male fetus is to suppress the masculine differentiation of the Wolffian ducts and the external genitals. Although the gonads differentiate as testes, they either fail to produce male fetal hormones, or they produce them but the fetus cannot utilize them. In either case masculine differentiation of the external reproductive structures fails to occur. As a result, the external genitalia are clearly female, although the uterus is rudimentary and the vagina shallow. Because the feminization of the external genitals is so complete at birth, such babies are labeled girls. At puberty there is breast development, and

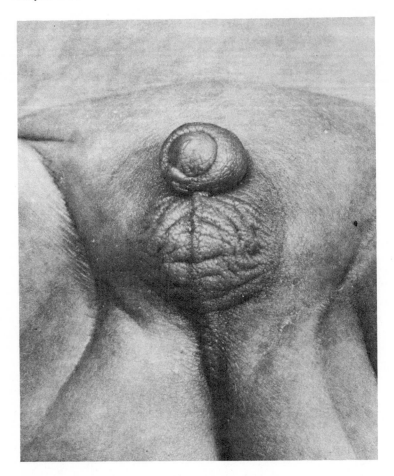

Figure 2-1. The external genitals of an androgenized genetic female (XX). (From *Man and Woman, Boy and Girl: Differentiation and Dimorphism of Gender Identity,* by J. Money and A. A. Ehrhardt, Copyright 1972 by The Johns Hopkins University Press. Reprinted by permission.)

the distribution of fat and muscle is characteristically feminine. The absence of menses is often the sole indication that the external sex of the individual is contrary to that coded in the genes. Attempts to effect masculinization at puberty through testosterone therapy are rarely successful (Money & Ehrhardt, 1972).

Among humans psychosexual differentiation usually corresponds with the sex of assignment and rearing. Pairs of hermaphrodites with the same clinical diagnosis assigned and reared as males or females, respectively,

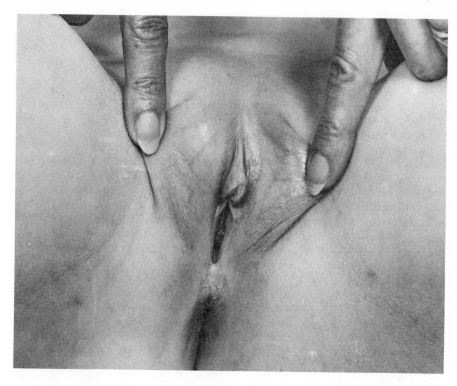

Figure 2-2. The external genitals of a genetic male (XY) with the androgen-insensitivity (testicular feminizing) syndrome. (From *Man and Woman, Boy and Girl: Differentiation and Dimorphism of Gender Identity*, by J. Money and A. A. Ehrhardt. Copyright 1972 by The Johns Hopkins University Press. Reprinted by permission.)

assume gender identities and roles appropriate to their assigned sex (Money, 1974; Money & Ehrhardt, 1972). Apparently, at the human level constitutionally based behavioral dispositions can be modified—even reversed—by social influences.

Subsequent Hormonal Events

As we have seen, sex hormones play a critical role in the structural differentiation of the sexes before birth. During childhood the effects of sex hormones on the developing organism are considerably reduced. They do not begin to play a central role again until puberty, with the onset of the reproductive cycle.

Menstruation

In females the capacity for reproductive functioning is signaled by the beginning of ovulation and menstruation (menarche). The entire cycle is regulated by female sex hormones, primarily estrogen and progesterone. The levels of these hormones fluctuate cyclically at approximately 28-day intervals. These monthly hormonal fluctuations determine the timing of ovulation and menstruation.

The process of menstruation is under the control of the pituitary, or "master," endocrine gland. This gland regulates hormone levels in the bloodstream and signals organs and tissues within the body to start (and stop) secreting their hormone products. The pituitary is itself controlled by the hypothalamus, which detects minute changes in blood chemical levels and instructs the pituitary when to send appropriate signals. These signals operate on the basis of a negative-feedback system. The pituitary signals for the production of a particular hormone. When a critical level of that hormone is reached, the hypothalamus instructs the pituitary to send out a message to stop the production of that hormone and to begin the production of another.

Menstruation is initiated by the secretion of a *f*ollicle-*s*timulating *h*ormone (FSH) by the pituitary. FSH stimulates the growth of several immature ova in preparation for ovulation and potential fertilization.[3] Follicular cells surround the maturing ovum. These cells produce the female sex hormone estrogen.

As a result of the process of egg maturation, estrogen levels within the ovary build up and estrogen is released into the bloodstream. Just before ovulation estrogen reaches a critical level and the hypothalamus signals the pituitary to stop the production of FSH and begin the secretion of *l*uteinizing *h*ormone (LH). Ovulation occurs when the level of LH exceeds that of FSH. At ovulation a single mature follicle ruptures and the ovum is released to enter the fallopian tube. This phase of the menstrual cycle is called the *proliferative phase* and lasts about 14 days in a 28-day cycle. It is during this phase that the uterine lining (endometrium) is reconstructed in preparation for the implantation of a fertilized egg.

The period after ovulation is referred to as the *secretory phase* of the menstrual cycle. During this phase of the cycle the presence of the luteinizing hormone stimulates the follicular cells that had surrounded the ripe ova before ovulation to take on a new role. These cells form a mass at the point of rupture, creating a structure called *corpus luteum*. The corpus luteum produces estrogen and progesterone. The presence of estrogen and progesterone in the endometrium aids in the implantation of the fertilized ovum and provides a temporary source of nutrition if fertilization occurs. However, the high levels of estrogen and progesterone necessary to maintain pregnancy are manufactured by the placenta.

---

[3]Since the ovaries contain approximately 400,000 immature ova at birth, it is considered unlikely that additional ova are generated during a woman's lifetime.

If conception has not occurred, the increased levels of estrogen and progesterone in the bloodstream signal the pituitary to inhibit the production of LH and simultaneously stimulate the release of FSH in preparation for subsequent ovulation. In the absence of LH, the corpus luteum is deprived of the necessary stimulant to produce estrogen or progesterone and it degenerates. As a result, the source of ovarian hormones disappears and menstruation begins.

Menstruation is the shedding of the uterine lining through the cervix and vagina. It occurs in response to the decline in estrogen level at the end of the cycle. You will recall that progesterone levels, too, decline rapidly at this time. However, they do not appear to play a role in triggering menstruation (Katchadorian & Lunde, 1975).

The cyclic release of sex hormones is a uniquely female phenomenon. During the menstrual cycle estrogen and progesterone levels fluctuate. As we can see in Figure 2-3, estrogen levels are low at the beginning of the menstrual cycle. They rise to a peak at midcycle (ovulation), dip, and then rise again at about day 22. Progesterone levels are low until after ovulation has occurred; then progesterone production steadily increases until the 21st or 22nd day of the cycle. Thus, the combined levels of estrogen and proges-

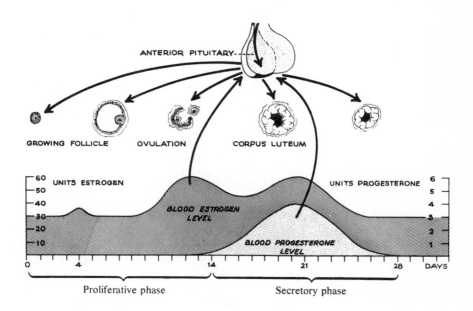

Figure 2–3. The menstrual cycle. (Adapted from *Handbook of Obstetrics and Gynecology,* 6th Edition, by R. C. Benson. Copyright 1977 by Lange Medical Publications. Reprinted by permission.)

terone peak and are maintained for a few days prior to menstruation. This peak is then followed by a rapid decline in the level of both these female sex hormones just before menstruation.

The results of a number of studies suggest that variations in the levels of female sex hormones throughout the menstrual cycle are paralleled by variations in the emotional states (Bardwick, 1971, 1974; Benedek, 1959; Coppen, 1967; Dalton, 1964; Janowsky, Gorney, & Kelley, 1966; Paige, 1971). One interpretation of these findings suggests that women's emotional responses are affected by fluctuations in estrogen and progesterone levels.

Certainly, the subjective experience of many women attests to the existence of regular, predictable cyclical changes in emotional states before the onset of menstruation. The most dramatic of these changes occur after the 22nd day of a 28-day cycle, coinciding with the rapid decline of estrogen and progesterone. This segment of the cycle has been referred to as the period of premenstrual tension (Frank, 1931) or the premenstrual syndrome (Dalton, 1964; Moos, 1969; Parlee, 1973). A variety of physical and psychological symptoms have been associated with the premenstrual syndrome. They range from water retention and pain or cramping to depression, irritability, increased levels of anxiety and hostility, and low levels of self-esteem (Coppen & Kessel, 1963; Frank, 1931; Gottschalk, Kaplan, Gleser, & Winget, 1962; Ivey & Bardwick, 1968; Moos, 1969; Paige, 1971; Schrader, Wilcoxon, & Sherif, 1975).

Negative emotional responses characteristic of the three or four days before menstruation appear distinct from the more positive responses associated with the intramenstrual, or ovulatory, phase of the cycle. In the view of some investigators, these cyclic fluctuations in emotion are caused by fluctuations in the activity of sex hormones (Bardwick, 1971, 1974; Dalton, 1966; Ivey & Bardwick, 1968). However, as we shall see, the empirical research on which this causal inference is based is far from definitive (Parlee, 1973).

Empirical studies used to support the contention that female hormones affect behavior are based on correlational data. Correlational studies can demonstrate the existence of a relationship between two factors, but correlation does not imply causation. Thus, despite the potentially dramatic implications of the results of such studies, they must be interpreted with caution. For example, Dalton (1964) reports a significant positive correlation between the premenstrual and menstrual phases of the cycle and the commission of violent crimes. Although these data suggest that women prone to committing violent crimes are more likely to do so during this phase of the menstrual cycle, they do not imply that the commission of such crimes is *caused* by premenstrual tension. Nor can they be interpreted to suggest that all women are more likely to commit violent crimes during this period (Parlee, 1973). Other variables that have been reported to be associated with the premenstrual syndrome include death by accident or suicide (Dalton, 1964), institutionalization for psychiatric illness (Dalton, 1964), alcohol abuse (Janowsky, Gorney, Castelnuovo-Tedesco, & Stone, 1969), and exaggerated maternal anxiety (Dalton, 1966).

It is interesting to note that, when causal inferences are made on the basis of correlational data, it is usually assumed that sex hormones affect behavioral states. Recently, it has been suggested that behavior exerts an influence on hormone levels. The testosterone levels of male primates low in the dominance hierarchy are characteristically lower than those of their dominant male peers; but, when such males are placed in cages with females over whom they can obtain dominance (and with whom they share sexual activity), their testosterone levels increase and remain high (Rose, Gordon, & Bernstein, 1972). Similarly, the results of a study by McClintock (1971) suggest that environmental factors may influence hormone activity among humans. She observed that the menstrual cycles of women living together tend to converge over time. It would be interesting to investigate the extent to which a woman's awareness of the cycles of those around her influences this convergence. McClintock also reported finding this same convergence among close friends living in separate residences. At any rate, the possibility that behavior influences hormones, rather than the other way around, should be examined (Weideger, 1976).

Many studies of the premenstrual syndrome have relied on subjects' reports of symptoms and mood shifts, often based on recall. For example, Moos (1969) developed an adjective checklist (the Menstrual Distress Questionnaire) to assess negative moods and physical discomfort associated with menstruation. Subjects were asked to indicate the extent to which they experienced a variety of physical and psychological symptoms on 6-point scales ranging from no experience to acute distress. Each woman made separate ratings for the menstrual, premenstrual, and intermenstrual phases of her most recent and her "worst" menstrual cycle. Cyclical changes in both physical and emotional distress were obtained, presumably coinciding with the decline of estrogen and progesterone toward the end of the cycle.

Although the results of this study do point to the existence of a premenstrual syndrome, several methodological problems should be considered. First, the subjects were aware from the outset that the study was related to menstruation, and their responses may have been more representative of menstrual stereotypes (Parlee, 1974) than of their own experience of menstrual distress. Second, subjects' responses to the Menstrual Distress Questionnaire (MDQ) were based on recollections of symptoms experienced during previous menstrual cycles. As a result, their self-reports may have been distorted or exaggerated. The MDQ does include a series of "control" symptoms characteristically associated with menopause, such as buzzing in the ears and numbness of the extremities, as a check on the tendency to "complain" of symptoms regardless of their origin. None of these "control" symptoms are consistently related to the cyclic changes in the menstrual cycle. However, most women are familiar with the particular symptoms associated with menstruation and would be unlikely to report menopausal symptoms in a study of menstrual distress.

If premenstrual and menstrual symptoms, both physical and psychological, are related to fluctuations in estrogen and progesterone levels, the reactions of women taking oral contraceptives containing these hormones should be different from those not on the pill. When Moos (1969) compared the reported symptoms of users of oral contraceptives with those of nonusers, he did find differences between these groups. There are two types of oral contraceptives—combination pills and sequential pills—both containing synthetic estrogen and progestin, which inhibit the natural secretion of these hormones. Combination pills contain both estrogenic and progestational agents in each tablet; as a result, the levels of these hormones are artificially elevated throughout the cycle. Sequential preparations, on the other hand, contain the estrogenic agent alone in the tablets for the first 15 or 16 days and a combination of estrogenic and progestational agents in the tablets for the last 5 days. This results in an exaggeration of the normal shifts in hormone production throughout the cycle.

Moos (1969) found that, in comparison to users, nonusers generally complained of greater severity of cramping, more difficulty in concentrating, greater irritability, and greater performance deficits. Comparisons between women using the two types of oral contraceptives revealed that combination-pill users reported significantly shorter and more regular menstrual periods than sequential-pill users. Also, women on the combination pill reported fewer symptoms than either sequential-pill users or nonusers. Women using sequential preparations tended to complain more and to exhibit more dramatic shifts in symptoms between the premenstrual and menstrual phases of the cycle than did women in the other two groups.

Results similar to those reported by Moos (1969) have been obtained in several studies using projective tests to assess fluctuations in emotional states during the menstrual cycle (Gottschalk et al., 1962; Ivey & Bardwick, 1968; Paige, 1971). In the Ivey and Bardwick (1968) study, subjects were asked at ovulation and two or three days before the onset of menses to detail a "memorable life experience" across two menstrual cycles. Subjects' taped responses were scored using Gottschalk's Verbal Anxiety Scale (Gottschalk et al., 1962) for themes related to death, mutilation, guilt, shame, separation, diffuse anxiety, hostility, and depression.

At ovulation, when estrogen levels are high, the responses of the subjects were characterized by low levels of negative emotions and high degrees of positive self-esteem. In the two or three days preceding menstruation, when estrogen and progesterone levels decline rapidly, the responses of these same subjects were characterized by anxiety, hostility, and depression. All subjects exhibited higher levels of anxiety premenstrually than at ovulation, and these differences were consistent across both cycles. These results paralleled those obtained in similar studies of neurotic and psychotic women (Benedek, 1952; Gottschalk et al., 1962; Shainess, 1961).

Although the method employed by Ivey and Bardwick did not rely on self-reports of symptomatology and mood, the subjects were aware that they were participating in a study on menstruation. Furthermore, when subjects were questioned about the aim of the experiment at its conclusion, most assumed that it was a study of moods. Nevertheless, Ivey and Bardwick's results do suggest that the menstrual cycle can affect the psychological behavior of women. Despite individual differences among subjects, these

symptoms is related to social factors, such as religious affiliation and social expectations. You will recall that Paige (1971) found evidence that premenstrual anxiety was related to menstrual flow. In her study, women using oral contraceptives that resulted in reduced flow were less likely to experience an increase in anxiety before the onset of menstruation. Also, these same women were less likely to abstain from intercourse during menstruation than those who experienced normal heavy flow.[4]

Interestingly, the observance of the menstrual sex taboo was also associated with the religious preferences expressed by the women in Paige's study. Most Jews and Catholics but only half of the Protestants reported adhering to the menstrual sex taboo. Differences in menstrual anxiety were also related to religious affiliation. Jews maintained high levels of anxiety throughout their cycles, while Catholics showed a dramatic increase in anxiety premenstrually. Protestants' anxiety levels were comparatively low and relatively constant across the cycle.

In order to explore these preliminary findings more thoroughly, Paige (1973) conducted a survey of unmarried college women. Included in her sample were 181 Protestants, 54 Jews, and 63 Catholics. The incidence of reported menstrual symptomatology was relatively equal among the three groups of women. However, the social factors related to reported distress differed across groups. Among Jewish women adherence to the menstrual sex taboo was most closely related to the experience of menstrual symptoms. Since traditional Judaism regards menstruation as taboo and unclean and most of the women in this group were actively religious, it appears reasonable to suggest that the meaning attributed to menstrual symptoms among these women was largely determined by cultural values.

Catholic women, on the other hand, were more likely to attribute menstrual distress to the traditional role of femininity. The belief that a woman should devote full time to her family was related to reported menstrual distress in this group. Unfortunately, the Protestant sample was too heterogeneous to establish clear relationships between distress and social factors for this group. However, Paige's findings do suggest that social factors play a role in determining menstrual distress.

Further support for the hypothesis that cultural expectations regarding menstruation influence the expression (or experience) of menstrual distress has been obtained in a series of studies by Koeske. She found that college women report a generally consistent set of beliefs about menstruation and the symptoms associated with it (Koeske, 1973). In order to examine the tendency to associate a woman's expression of negative moods (for exam-

---

[4]The results of a recent study by Weideger (1976) suggest that whether or not a woman abstains from intercourse during menstruation is less influenced by the type of contraceptive she uses (although the methods do affect the amount of flow and pain) than by her partner's response to the amount of "mess" associated with the method of contraception. In her study, the partners of women using the IUD (which tends to increase flow) were most likely to object to having sex during menstruation (51%). In contrast, only 40% of the partners of women who used the diaphragm (which can be used to keep the lower portion of the vagina free of blood) objected.

ple, depression and irritability) with her biology, Koeske and Koeske (1975) provided male and female subjects with information about a hypothetical female and asked them to assess the extent to which "Miss A's" behavior was a function of mood or of environmental factors. Stories were varied according to menstrual-cycle phase (pre- versus postmenstrual), environment (pleasant versus unpleasant), and mood (positive versus negative). As predicted, subjects linked the expression of negative mood to the premenstrual phase of the cycle rather than to environmental factors. These results clearly suggest that the tendency to attribute premenstrual mood shifts to biological factors may play a role in causing premenstrual distress.

In a similar study, Koeske (Koeske & Koeske, 1975) asked male and female subjects to rate the mood, personality, and behavior of one of the three targets (a premenstrual female, a postmenstrual female, or a male) reacting to either a hostile or a pleasant situation. The approach of menstruation was used by the subjects to explain hostile behavior on the part of the female target. Furthermore, the hostility of the premenstrual female was judged to be less sex-role appropriate, more unreasonable, and more indicative of a changeable personality than identical hostility displayed by either a postmenstrual female or a male. These data suggest that the tendency to attribute a woman's negative behavior to biology does not reflect the actual incidence of positive and negative behaviors displayed before menstruation but, rather, the cultural belief that women's negative behavior is biologically determined.

Interestingly, neither Paige (1973) nor Fisher (1973) found any evidence to suggest that women's own reactions to menstruation are related to either sex education or individual physiological factors such as length of cycle or age at onset of menses. It would seem that individual experience is a less potent predictor of menstrual reactions than the widely shared expectation that women are unpredictable prior to menstruation.

As we have seen, decreases in levels of estrogen and progesterone have been correlated with the negative emotional states characteristic of the premenstrual syndrome.[5] A similar and even more dramatic decline in the levels of these hormones follows childbirth.

Hormonal Changes following Childbirth

Following conception, a woman's estrogen and progesterone levels increase rapidly and are maintained at high levels throughout pregnancy.[6] Shortly before delivery, during the second stage of labor, progesterone de-

---

[5]Although cyclic fluctuations in sex-hormone levels have generally been considered to represent a uniquely female phenomenon, recent research suggests that men may also experience cyclic fluctuations in endocrine production (Bardwick, 1974; Doering, Brodie, Kraemer, Becker, & Hamburg, 1974; Ramey, 1972). Whether these shifts in levels of male hormones are associated with mood changes has not been determined.

[6]Estrogen increases rapidly after the first missed menstrual period. The greatest rise occurs between the 6th and 20th weeks following conception. By the onset of labor the estrogenic content of the urine has increased at least 100 times (Brown, 1956). Increases in

clines rapidly (Hamburg, 1966; Hamburg, Moos, & Yalom, 1968). Immediately after childbirth estrogen levels decrease, returning to normal in 5 to 25 days (Brown, 1956). Given the parallel between hormonal activity before menstruation and hormonal activity following delivery, it is hardly surprising that declines in estrogen and progesterone have been implicated in postpartum depression (Bardwick, 1971, 1974; Hamilton, 1962; Treadway, Kane, Jarrahi-Zadeh, & Lipton, 1969).

Estimates of the number of women experiencing some form of emotional disturbance following childbirth range from 20 to 45% (Gordon & Gordon, 1959; Pleshette, Asch, & Chase, 1965; Treadway et al., 1969). The symptoms associated with postpartum depression range from lack of energy and episodic crying to depressive psychoses.

Several investigators (Robin, 1962; Yalom, Lunde, Moos, & Hamburg, 1968) have found evidence of increased emotionality and short-term depression among 45 to 75% of postpartum women. Interestingly, Yalom and his colleagues point out that episodic crying may represent increased sensitivity rather than depression. Short-term depressive reactions have been correlated with length and difficulty of labor (Hamburg et al., 1968).

The extent to which negative emotional responses, including feeling let down after delivery, represent a biological rather than a psychological fact has not been determined. My own experience following delivery suggests that any postpartum state would be viewed as a "low" when compared to the "high" associated with birth. The anticipation and occurrence of birth is certainly arousing, if not exhilarating. It also involves a considerable expenditure of energy. In some cases the "letdown" may be analogous to that experienced after the successful completion of an exam for which you prepared long into the night. Although I was depressed after the birth of my son, the feeling was similar to the depression I experienced after defending my dissertation. However, individual reactions to childbirth vary greatly, and I do not regard my personal experience as normative.

Because giving birth to a child causes biochemical changes as well as changes in a woman's social situation, it is difficult to assess the relative contribution of these factors to the occurrence of postpartum depression (Protheroe, 1969; Shainess, 1961; Treadway et al., 1969). However, it is interesting to note that the administration of estrogen has been found effective in the treatment of some cases of postpartum depression (Kane, Lipton, & Ewing, 1969). The results of studies that suggest a connection between biochemical changes and postpartum depression are correlational and must be interpreted with caution (Wallach & Garcia, 1968). The occurrence of severe mental disturbance following childbirth is relatively rare and appears

---

progesterone are of similar magnitude (Hamburg, 1966). Despite the number of studies investigating the effects of sex hormones on women's moods during the menstrual cycle, there are no studies currently available on the effects of increased levels of estrogen and progesterone on women's psychological state during pregnancy. This is particularly surprising, since the production of estrogen and progesterone during the nine months of pregnancy differs so dramatically from that characteristic of any other period in a woman's life.

to be limited to individuals with histories of mental illness prior to pregnancy (Keeler, Kane, & Daly, 1964; Idestrom, 1966).

Climacterium

The *climacterium* (critical period) is a term used to refer to the entire period during which ovarian functioning declines. This gradual decline during middle age parallels the increase in the production of female sex hormones following puberty. During the climacterium menstruation ceases (menopause) and the reproductive organs atrophy.

Menopause commonly occurs sometime between the ages of 45 and 55. The cessation of menses is accompanied by a decline in the production of estrogen and progesterone. Estrogen levels in the postmenopausal woman are as low as or lower than those of a menstruating woman in the last days of her menstrual period (Brown & Matthew, 1962).

Although menopause is, of course, a uniquely female phenomenon, the climacterium occurs in both sexes. However, the decline in the production of male sex hormones is comparatively slight from 30 to 90 years of age. Among women the symptoms associated with the climacterium include hot flashes, chills, headaches, dizziness, heart palpitations, and pains in the joints. While almost all women are affected to some degree by such symptoms, only about 15% report severe difficulties. Psychological responses include irritability, depression, and confusion (Neugarten & Kraines, 1967).

Greenblatt (1955) and Wilson (1966) have hypothesized that the symptoms experienced during this period are associated with estrogen deficiency, and a number of investigators report positive results from estrogen administered to menopausal women (Goldberg, 1959; Kantor, Michael, Boulas, Shore, & Ludvigson, 1966; Klaiber et al., 1971; Wilson, 1966). Estrogen treatment appears to be particularly effective in alleviating depression associated with menopause.[7]

The literature on menopause is not extensive. However, the normal decline of estrogen and progesterone during the climacterium is accompanied by many potentially depressing changes in a woman's life.

The extent to which depression is related to the normal decline of estrogen and progesterone during menopause has not been established (Rosenthal, 1968; Winokur, 1973). As a matter of fact, depressions that do occur during this time may be more related to such psychological factors as the departure of children from the home (Deykin, Jacobson, Klerman, & Solomon, 1966) or anxiety over the prospect of losing one's husband through death (Neugarten & Associates, 1964) or fears about aging (Sontag, 1972) than to hormone changes. We will consider the psychological impact associated with the changing roles of older women in Chapter Nine.

---

[7]Although estrogen-replacement therapy has been used successfully to treat a variety of psychological and physical symptoms associated with menopause, the potential side effects of this therapy are not well understood. Consequently, caution should be exercised in its administration (Weideger, 1976).

Summary

The anatomical differences between males and females are biologically determined. Although the genetic sex of the fetus is established at conception, this is only the first step in a four-stage sequence of sex differentiation. The basic structure of the fetus is female. Male differentiation requires the presence of both a Y chromosome and androgens. Androgens influence the masculinization of the internal and external genitalia and the development of the central nervous system as well. Critical developmental periods for sex differentiation have been determined for lower animals. The timing of such periods in humans has not yet been specified.

Research with animals indicates that androgens (or their absence) during critical periods may result in structural and behavioral changes contrary to genetically determined sex. Similar, although less dramatic, effects have been observed among humans with chromosomal and hormonal abnormalities.

However, while biology appears to exert a direct influence on the characteristic behavior patterns of male and female rats and guinea pigs, psychosexual differentiation in humans is more dependent on learning. At the human level biologically based behavioral dispositions may be modified by social factors.

Sex hormones play a minor role in human development from birth until the onset of the reproductive cycle at puberty. Even then the influence of hormonal fluctuations on behavior appears to be more significant among females than among males. Fluctuations in estrogen and progesterone levels during the menstrual cycle seem to be related to shifts in the emotional states of women. However, behavioral and emotional changes associated with the premenstrual syndrome have been found to be affected by cultural factors such as religious upbringing.

The dramatic reduction in levels of female sex hormones following childbirth has been implicated in postpartum depression. There is evidence suggesting that estrogen therapy is effective in alleviating the depression that some women experience after giving birth. It should be kept in mind, however, that motherhood involves significant changes in a woman's social role, which may contribute to shifts in her emotional state.

The climacterium is accompanied by a gradual decline in the production of sex hormones. The extent to which declining levels of estrogen and progesterone influence the psychological symptoms associated with menopause has not been determined. Middle adulthood is another period in which a woman's social situation may change substantially, particularly if she loses her spouse.

Chapter Three

Sex-Role Development

The delivery room is filled with anticipation as the expectant mother and all in attendance await the verdict "It's a girl" or "It's a boy." These three words exert a powerful influence on an individual's social behavior. The label "girl" or "boy" is assigned on the basis of external genitalia, and, as Money and Ehrhardt (1972) have observed, "the penis is the final arbiter." If the infant possesses even a rudimentary penis, a male-sex assignment is usually made; if not, the child is declared female.

Girl babies leave the hospital nursery delicately swathed in pink; boy babies sport blue. Once sex has been assigned, anatomy may indeed become destiny, for the child is then exposed to the different cultural experiences that are related to the rearing of male or female children (Gagnon & Simon, 1973). The culture dictates that everyone must develop a gender identity (Money, 1974). Even in cases in which the genital structures are ambiguous, assignment is made into one of two categories—male or female.

Imagine receiving a birth announcement heralding the arrival of X, gender unknown because the parents are waiting to see (Grady, 1975). When X is 1 month old, you may decide that a green or yellow blanket is an appropriate gift, but what about a gift for X's second birthday? Furthermore, and perhaps more importantly, how will X "itself" know how to respond to your choice?

People's reactions to an individual are partially determined by that individual's gender. Also, when the child has identified his or her own sex organs as either male or female, he or she can begin to make comparisons between himself or herself and others of the same sex that culminate in gender identity. Gender identity is characterized by "the sameness, unity, and persistence of one's individual identity as either male, female, or ambivalent, . . . especially as it is experienced in self-awareness and behavior" (Money & Ehrhardt, 1972, p. 4). The public or private expression of ambivalent gender identity is, of course, relatively rare. On the basis of their work with ambiguous or contradictory cases of sex assignment, Money and Ehrhardt (1972) and Hampson and Hampson (1961) have concluded that gender role is primarily the result of a learning process that is quite independent of chromosomal, gonadal, or hormonal sex.

One dramatic illustration of the predominance of learned gender identity and role over contradictory endocrine functioning is presented by Money (1974). It is based on a case history involving an androgenized genetic female. At birth the child's external genitals appeared male (a penis and a fused but empty scrotum), and she was reared as a boy until the age of

12, when the existence of her uterus, ovaries, and fallopian tubes was discovered. On the assumption that "biology is destiny," female hormones were administered to induce menstruation and feminization of body contours. But, since the child had thought of herself as a boy for 12 years, her masculine-gender identity was firmly established. She did not want to be a girl; she hated her developing breasts and wanted to be rid of them. Imagine how you would react today if someone told you that your "sex" had been incorrectly assigned. The acquisition of gender identity is influenced by social learning and experience. Once established, it does not automatically reverse to coincide with physiological changes in endocrine functioning.

As we saw in Chapter Two, the effects of prenatal hormone levels on subsequent gender identity have not yet been established. However, the evidence cited by Money and his colleagues (Money & Ehrhardt, 1972) clearly indicates that the primary differentiation of gender identity occurs after birth. Matched pairs of hermaphrodites (chromosomally, hormonally, and diagnostically similar) reared differentially as male and female display gender-role behavior appropriate to their assigned sex. Similar behavior patterns characterize biologically congruent "normals" who, because of accidents, have undergone surgical sex reassignment.

Money and Ehrhardt (1972) report one such case, involving the sex reassignment of a genetic male infant whose penis was destroyed as the result of an accident during circumcision. The child was reassigned female at the age of 17 months and is now 10 years old. To date all the follow-up information on this case indicates that the sex-typed behavior of this child is quite "gender different" from that of her identical twin brother. Money (1974) reports that, according to the child's mother, the girl is feminine in her concern with cleanliness and clothes. Described by her mother as the dominant twin from birth, the girl asserts her dominance over her brother in a traditionally feminine fashion by playing "mother hen" (Money, 1974).

In Chapter Two we examined the evidence relevant to the biological bases of sex differences and concluded that, among humans, there is little evidence to suggest that genetic and hormonal differences between the sexes determine later behavioral differences directly. While the acquisition of certain sex-typed behaviors such as aggression may be a result of sex-linked biological predispositions, it is generally agreed that socialization plays a critical role in the development of patterns of behavior considered more characteristic of one sex or the other. The specific mechanisms through which these behaviors are acquired is, however, a matter of some controversy. In this chapter we will consider three general approaches that have been used to explain the development of sex roles. The *psychoanalytic approach* relies on the Freudian concept of identification; *social-learning theories* focus on the role of reinforcement in establishing gender-appropriate behaviors; and *theories of cognitive development* stress the importance of defining oneself as either female or male. Since the psychoanalytic explanation is perhaps the best known of the three, let us begin by outlining this approach.

The Psychoanalytic Theory of Identification

According to Freud (1950a, 1950b), psychological differentiation between the sexes begins during the phallic stage of psychosexual development. It is during this period (sometime between the ages of 3 and 5) that identification with the same-sex parent occurs, resulting in the formation of the superego. The superego is comprised of the conscience and the ego ideal, which includes idealized standards of behavior. According to Freud, the differential development of masculine and feminine ideal standards results in the characteristic behavioral differences between the sexes.

Infants of both sexes are helpless and dependent on others for survival. As a result, both boys and girls form strong emotional attachments to their mothers (or caretakers). In Freud's view, as the boy grows older, his attachment to his mother takes on sexual overtones. During this time he becomes increasingly aware that he must compete with his father for his mother's attentions. Viewing father as a rival gives rise to the boy's aggressive impulses. However, the child fears that his powerful father may retaliate by castrating him. Freud referred to this phenomenon as the Oedipal conflict.

For boys the process of identification with the same-sex parent hinges upon the resolution of this conflict. The child's castration anxiety forces him to repress both his desire for mother and his hostility toward father. Instead, he identifies with his father (the aggressor) in an attempt to become like him and to ensure his mother's affection. In the process of identifying with the same-sex parent, the child internalizes the social standards for behavior exemplified by that parent.

Freud viewed the process of identification as somewhat more complex for females than for males. Like the boy, the girl forms an early attachment to her mother. As she grows older, however, her increasing disappointment with her mother prompts her to turn away. According to Freud, the primary cause for the girl's disappointment is the discovery that she lacks a penis—a discovery that results in penis envy. On the assumption that her mother has castrated her, the girl turns toward her father in an attempt to secure a penis. Over time the girl's desire for a penis is replaced by a fantasied desire for the father's child. Once the girl has transferred her primary attachment to the father, she develops an Oedipal complex analogous to that of the boy (Fenichel, 1945).

Because the girl already perceives herself as castrated, castration anxiety is not the primary motive for same-sex identification among females. Rather, her identification is motivated by the fear of losing her mother's love (anaclitic identification). Because Freud felt that the underlying motivation for resolving the Oedipal conflict is stronger for boys than for girls, he hypothesized that females never fully resolve this conflict. Consequently, he viewed the female superego as weaker than that of the male and believed that women never fully internalize the values of society (Freud, 1950a).

In her excellent review of the research relevant to Freud's theory of female identification, Sherman (1971) concludes that attempts to provide empirical support for Freud's notions have met with limited success at best. For example, if, as Freud suggested, penis envy is central to the development of the Oedipal conflict in females, it should be possible to obtain evidence for its existence among girls and women. But 3- to 5-year-old girls are no more likely than boys to express castration concerns (Conn, 1940; Hattendorf, 1932; Kreitler & Kreitler, 1966). And when Hattendorf (1932) interviewed mothers of preschoolers regarding their children's questions about sex, she found that only 3 out of 865 questions were indicative of castration anxiety and that these three questions were asked by boys. There was no evidence to suggest that girls suffered from penis envy. Similarly, Kreitler and Kreitler (1966) failed to obtain evidence of castration concern among 4- and 5-year-olds of either sex.

Two attempts to assess the incidence of behavior indicative of penis envy in everyday life have been reported (Johnson, 1966; Landy, 1967). Although the Freudian hypothesis received support in both studies, it is not clear that the behaviors assumed to reflect penis envy really do. Landy (1967) investigated the expression of sublimated penis envy, which he operationally defined[1] as the manner in which female subjects extract the first cigarette from an unopened pack. According to this formulation, penis envy would be expressed by gently pushing the bottom of the pack to create a cavity and expell the cigarette (penis object). Thus he hypothesized that females would be more likely than males to open cigarette packs in this way. The results of the study did confirm Landy's hypothesis. However, nonsmokers also opened cigarette packs in this fashion more often than smokers, who tended to pull or force cigarettes out of the pack by hitting the bottom against something hard. Johnson (1966) hypothesized that, in contrast to men, women students would evidence penis envy by failing to return special pencils to the instructor after completing a final exam. As predicted, significantly more women than men had to be reminded to return their pencils. But, since women are less likely to smoke and more likely to carry pencils in their pocketbooks than men, it is difficult to assess the validity of the Freudian interpretation of these results.

The results of several investigations that have analyzed the content of male and female dreams for evidence of penis envy and castration anxiety tend to support the contention that penis envy is more likely to be expressed in the dreams of college women (Hall & Van de Castle, 1965, 1966). However, females' dreams reflecting a wish for a penis were obtained in less than 5% of the dreams analyzed. Thus, evidence supporting Freud's contention that penis envy is a critical factor in the development of the Oedipal complex is tentative at best. As Bardwick (1971) observes, it is difficult to imagine that the development of feminine identification depends on the arousal of envy toward something totally alien to the realm of female experience.

---

[1]Operational definitions assign meaning to constructs (such as penis envy) by specifying the way in which the construct is to be measured.

Although the Freudian concept of penis envy has proved difficult to substantiate, the literature relevant to sex-role preference does suggest that adults of both sexes believe that it is preferable to be male. For example, women are more likely than men to report having experienced the desire to be members of the opposite sex (Chesser, 1956; Landis, Landis, & Bolles, 1940; Roper, 1946; Terman, 1938). The preferential status of men in contemporary society is also reflected in parental preferences for male offspring (Pohlman, 1969; Williamson, 1976). Parental preferences for male firstborn and only children are particularly strong (Williamson, 1976). For example, when Hammer (1970) asked unmarried college students to imagine themselves as prospective parents of an only child, 90% of the males and 78% of the females indicated that they would prefer a male child. Comparable results were obtained among noncollege adult males. However, only 30% of the noncollege women expressed a preference for a son. Hammer interprets these findings as a reflection of differences in social class. In his view, less-educated women may be more likely than their middle-class peers to view daughters as a source of help and companionship in a male-dominated world (Sherman, 1971).

One need not postulate the existence of anatomically based "penis envy," as Freud did, to come up with a variety of reasons why women might envy men. The fact that males are afforded positions of power and prestige is a social reality. If women express more often than men the desire to be members of the opposite sex, it may be because they see men as the more advantaged sex. In this regard it is logical for a girl to want to be a boy, and the reverse would be peculiar.

It is not surprising that studies of sex-role preference among children suggest that, as age increases, girls learn to value themselves less and boys learn to value themselves more (Mendelsohn & Dobie, 1970; Prather, 1971; Smith, 1939) and that boys prefer the male role more than girls prefer the female role (Hetherington & Parke, 1975). It is, of course, possible to interpret these data as evidence for the existence of penis envy. But, as we shall see, a more plausible explanation for these findings has been suggested by social-learning theorists, who maintain that greater cultural value is attributed to the male role.

You will recall that, in Freud's view, penis envy represents the pivotal point in the development of the Oedipal complex among females. Researchers, however, have failed to obtain any evidence for the existence of the Oedipal complex among preschool-age girls (Sherman, 1971, 1975). Neither Anderson (1936) nor Simpson (1935) obtained support for the Freudian hypothesis that girls prefer father to mother, particularly during the Oedipal period (ages 3 to 6). More recently, Kohlberg and Zigler (1967) and Piskin (1960) failed to obtain differences in the parent preferences of 3- to 5-year-old male and female children. As a matter of fact, in Piskin's study children of both sexes expressed preferences for the mother.

There is also little empirical evidence to support Freud's contention that the female superego is weaker than that of the male (Baltes & Nesselroade, 1972; Sherman, 1971, 1975). In comparison to males, females display greater concern over moral issues, protest more vehemently when they perceive injustices, and adhere more closely to social mores and codes of social conduct (Eisenman, 1967; Hutt, 1972; Johnson & Gormley, 1972; Oetzel, 1966). Females are no less likely than males to cheat in academic situations (Hetherington & Parke, 1975), although they are less likely to admit that they have cheated (Krebs, 1968). Contrary to Freud's theory, castration anxiety does not appear to promote the development of the superego. If it did, girls, who presumably do not experience castration anxiety, should be less concerned about social ethics and moral behavior than boys. They are not. Thus, despite the popularity of Freud's conceptualization of the identification process, it seems reasonable to conclude, as Sherman (1971, 1975) did, that his views regarding identification and superego development are incorrect.

Social-Learning Theories of the Acquisition of Gender-Appropriate Behaviors

An alternative explanation for the development of sex roles focuses on the role of social learning in the acquisition of sex-typed behaviors. Social-learning theorists such as Bandura (1969), Gewirtz (1969), and Mischel (1970) argue that the acquisition of gender-appropriate behaviors may be explained as a result of reinforcement and imitation or modeling. In this view, social agents (particularly parents) shape the child's performance by articulating expectancies regarding gender-appropriate behavior, positively reinforcing desired behaviors, punishing those that are deemed unacceptable, and providing models for the child to emulate.

Parents of girl babies appear to view and label the behavior of their newborns somewhat differently than parents of boys (Rubin, Provenzano, & Luria, 1974; Krieger, 1976). For example, Rubin et al. asked 30 pairs of parents of firstborns (the parents of 15 girls and of 15 boys) to describe their infants on an adjective checklist before leaving the hospital. Compared to parents of boys, parents of girls rated their infants as significantly softer, finer-featured, smaller, and less attentive. This was true despite the fact that there were no significant sex differences in weight, length, or physical condition among the babies at birth. Interestingly, both mothers and fathers agreed on the direction of the differences, although fathers' sex-typed ratings of both daughters and sons were more extreme than mothers'. There was also an interaction between the gender of the parent and that of the child; thus, mothers of boys rated their babies as more "cuddly." The reverse was true of fathers, who rated their daughters as more "cuddly" than their sons.

To the extent that parents' perceptions of their newborn infants are differentially influenced by gender, it seems reasonable to hypothesize that they will treat them differently as well (Krieger, 1976). However, attempts to provide empirical support for this hypothesis have produced inconsistent results. For example, mothers of boys may view their infants as "more cuddly" than do mothers of girls (Rubin et al., 1974), but in six of the nine observational studies of mother-infant interaction reviewed by Maccoby and Jacklin (1974) mothers of children under 2 were no more likely to hold, touch, or show affection to sons than to daughters. Nor have consistent differences been reported in recent studies of mothers' verbal interactions with daughters versus sons (Maccoby & Jacklin, 1974).

On the other hand, parents do seem to be more inclined to treat little girls as though they were more fragile than little boys. Both mothers and fathers appear to value strength and gross motor skills in sons more than in daughters and encourage these activities through rough-and-tumble play (Kagan, 1971; Lewis & Freedle, 1973). Parents, particularly fathers, also display somewhat more concern about the health and physical safety of daughters than of sons (Minton, Kagan, & Levine, 1971; Pederson & Robson, 1969).

Once the children are past infancy, parents continue to view certain behaviors as more characteristic of one gender or of the other (Ainsworth, 1973; Kagan, 1971; Lambert, Yakley, & Hein, 1971). However, there is little evidence to suggest that parents use direct positive reinforcement as a means of differently shaping the behavior of their children to conform to their expectations. Despite the commonly held stereotype that boys and men are (or should be) more independent and aggressive than girls and women, parents do not seem to be more likely to reinforce displays of independence or aggression on the part of boys than on the part of girls (Baumrind, 1971; Maccoby & Jacklin, 1974; Newson & Newson, 1968). Nor are parents more likely to encourage girls to be dependent (Maccoby & Jacklin, 1974).

Indeed, when parents do use reinforcement to encourage sex typing (the definition of oneself as male or female) directly, such reinforcement usually takes the form of punishment against boys for behaving in a manner that is inappropriate for their sex role. For example, Fling and Manosevitz (1972) and Lansky (1967) report that cross-sex behavior evokes greater parental concern when it is displayed by a boy than when it is displayed by a girl. Parents of both sexes are more likely to discourage sex-inappropriate interests on the part of sons than on the part of daughters. No differences were obtained in parents' attitudes toward the expression of sex-appropriate behavior. These results are consistent with Hartley's (1959) suggestion that the male role is shaped through the differential application of negative reinforcement.

The results of a number of studies suggest that young boys are more likely than girls to avoid the display of behavior inappropriate for their sex role. Hartup, Moore, and Sager (1963) reported that nursery-school boys were more likely to select an unattractive neutral toy than an attractive "feminine" one, particularly if the experimenter was present. In contrast, little girls preferred the attractive "masculine" toy, and their choices were not influenced by the presence of the experimenter. Ross (1971) observed children playing store and found that boys were more concerned than girls when the "customer" chose a toy inappropriate for his or her sex role. Similarly, Barkley, Ullman, Otto, and Brecht (1976) reported that girls were more likely than boys to imitate a model who behaved sex-inappropriately.

In general children appear to prefer sex-appropriate activities to sex-inappropriate ones. However, this finding is consistently stronger among boys than among girls (Nadelman, 1974; Ward, 1968).

These results suggest that the role of the male child is more rigidly defined than that of the female. Thus, parents (and other adults) are more likely to impose restrictions on the behavior of boys than on the behavior of girls (Fagot, 1973, 1974; Maccoby & Jacklin, 1974; Stayton, Hogan, & Ainsworth, 1971). On the other hand, neither parents (Maccoby & Jacklin, 1974) nor nursery school teachers (Etaugh, Collins, & Gerson, 1975) appear to rely on direct positive reinforcement as a means of differentially shaping the behavior of children of either sex.[2]

Of course, the use of direct positive reinforcement for sex-role-appropriate behavior is only one means of conveying sex-typed expectations for behavior. Parents do select clothes, hairstyles, and toys for their children on the basis of gender; they seldom compliment their "pretty" sons or buy their daughters baseball mitts. Strangers attempting to establish some basis of rapport with a child are likely to do so within the context of the child's gender. If the child is female, the adult is likely to focus on her appearance—"What beautiful blue eyes you have." In contrast, the boy is met with "I bet you keep your mother busy."

In a recent study, Seavey, Katz, and Zalk (1975) asked female and male nonparent volunteers to participate in a study of infants' responses to strangers. The adult subjects were observed interacting with a 3-month-old infant under three conditions: the child being introduced as a boy, the child being introduced as a girl, and no gender information given. When the child was introduced as a girl, subjects of both sexes were more likely to offer "her" a doll than a football or a teething ring. Male and female subjects responded to the "genderless" child quite differently. Men tended to offer the infant a neutral toy and handled "it" least. Women, on the other hand, offered the child either the football or the doll and interacted with "it" most. All of the subjects in the "genderless" condition attempted to guess the gender of the child (who was a female), and the majority guessed incorrectly. Interestingly, each subject supported his or her gender guess by alluding to cues such as strength and lack of hair (boy) and softness and fragility (girl). Thus, this study indicates that the interactions of nonparent adults with an infant are influenced by the presence (or absence) of information regarding the child's gender.

Strangers are responsive to displays of gender-inappropriate behaviors even when parents are not. When my son Sean was 2, he wanted a pocket-book like Mommy's. I gave him one of my old shoulder bags. On our next

---

[2]The fact that researchers have found it difficult to substantiate the differential-reinforcement hypothesis of sex-role learning does not mean that it does not occur. Most studies of nursery school children are conducted in university communities where both parents and teachers may be more sensitive to the aversive consequences of rigid sex typing. Furthermore, the results of these studies are based on short-term observations; differential reinforcement may occur relatively infrequently and only in critical situations or settings. It is also possible that the impact of differential reinforcement is not dependent on a single incidence but, rather, is reflected in subtle patterns of reinforcement across time and situations.

trip to the grocery store, Sean, who was dressed in jeans and a numbered T-shirt, carried his purse. Within the course of 45 minutes three different customers expressed surprise at seeing a little boy with a pocketbook. I was interested to observe that, although Sean continued to take the purse in the car for several weeks, he never again appeared with it in public.

By the time most children are 4 years old, they have a relatively clear idea of the activities and behaviors considered appropriate for members of their own (and the opposite) gender. This knowledge is often reflected in their behavior (Emmerick, 1974; Nadelman, 1974; Sears, Rau, & Alpert, 1965). Boys prefer playing with blocks, trucks, and carpenter's tools, while girls prefer playing house and dress up. Yet, the preferences of children for activities and behaviors considered more appropriate for boys or for girls do not appear to be contingent on the differential application of direct reinforcement (positive or negative) alone. Other, less direct, social-learning processes have been suggested to account for the sex typing of behavior.

Observational Learning

Social-learning explanations for the acquisition of gender-appropriate behavior rely heavily on the concept of observational, or imitative, learning. The behavioral repertoire of an individual can be expanded merely by observing the actions of others. Indeed, research has clearly demonstrated that new responses can be acquired and existing responses modified through imitation (Bandura, 1969).

Because observational learning takes place in the absence of direct reinforcement, a number of mechanisms have been proposed to account for its occurrence. Perhaps the most important of these is identification. You will recall that Freud viewed identification with the same-sex parent as the result of the successful resolution of the Oedipal conflict. Social-learning theorists use the term *identification* to refer to the process through which observers learn and adopt the attributes, attitudes, and behaviors of others (Mischel, 1970). Certain attributes of the model, such as nurturance, power, and his or her perceived similarity to the observer, may facilitate the process of identification and result in imitation (Bandura & Huston, 1961; Bandura, Ross, & Ross, 1963; Hetherington, 1965; Hetherington & Frankie, 1967). In this view, one means of acquiring sex-typed behavior patterns is through the selective identification with and imitation of same-sex models (particularly parents).

Same-Sex Identification

The selective-imitation hypothesis has a great deal of intuitive appeal. It seems reasonable to suggest that children perceive similarity between themselves and the parent of the same sex (mother-daughter, father-son) and match their behavior accordingly. However, there is little empirical evidence to support the hypothesis that children are more likely to reproduce the behaviors of same-sex models than those of opposite-sex ones.

Maccoby and Jacklin (1974) cite over 20 studies in which children were exposed to models of both sexes and their tendencies to imitate same-sex versus opposite-sex models were compared. At neither preschool nor grade-school ages did children exhibit consistent preferences for same-sex models. Similarly, when Hetherington (1965) compared children's preference for parental models, she failed to find evidence for the predicted match between child and same-sex parent.

Of course, measurement of the overt reproduction of a same-sex model's behavior is only one means of assessing identification. A number of studies have measured sex-role identification by comparing the responses of adult children and their parents on paper-and-pencil personality inventories (Roff, 1950; Rosenberg & Sutton-Smith, 1968; Troll, Neugarten, & Kraines, 1969). In none of these studies were the correlations between the responses of the children and those of their same-sex parents consistently higher than those between the responses of the children and those of their opposite-sex parents.

Attempts to demonstrate similarities between young children and same-sex parent have not been any more successful. In one study, Mussen and Rutherford (1963) used a projective technique (the "It" test) to measure the preferences of first-grade children for sex-typed activities. "It" is a neuter cut-out paper doll. The child is asked to select activities for "It" from a variety of sex-typed alternatives. The extent to which the children perceived their parents' behavior as sex-typed was also assessed in a play situation using "mother" and "father" dolls. Finally, the Gough Femininity Scale was administered to both parents (Gough, 1957), and the children's mothers were interviewed to determine their interests and the extent to which they encouraged their children to behave according to the role appropriate for their sex. Although the girls' femininity scores (derived from their "It" activity preferences) were related to their perceptions of "mother" as warm and nurturant in the doll-play situation, there was no relationship between the femininity scores of mothers and daughters. Nor were the daughters' femininity scores related to the extent to which their mothers encouraged them to engage in feminine activities. Similar results were obtained in a more recent study by Fling and Manosevitz (1972).

Selective imitation and modeling may play a role in acquisition of sex-typed behavior. However, empirical support for the selective-imitation hypothesis is weak. You may recall that children tend to imitate dominant and nurturant models. As Maccoby and Jacklin (1974) have recently pointed out, in the typical two-parent family the mother is more nurturant and the father more powerful. Thus, children of both sexes should, for different reasons, emulate the behavior and attitudes of both parents.[3]

Of course, same-sex parents are not the only role models to whom children are exposed. One obvious source of models for sex-appropriate

---

[3]Of course, the acquisition of sex-typed behaviors through observational learning depends upon the availability of an appropriate model. For example, the range of "masculine" behaviors to which a child of either sex is exposed may be restricted in a father-absent home.

behavior is children's books and television programs. Males are portrayed as the central characters in stories and programs more than twice as often as females (Child, Potter, & Levine, 1946; Gerbner, 1972). Also, male and female roles are clearly differentiated along sex-stereotypic lines. Boys are pictured as active and aggressive; they make plans and build things while girls watch. Girls are generally portrayed as kind, timid, and inactive; when they are portrayed as active, they are likely to be punished for their behavior (Sternglanz & Serbin, 1974). Male characters manipulate and control their environment by doing; when female characters manipulate and control their environment, they are usually creatures who possess magical powers, such as fairies and witches (Sternglanz & Serbin, 1974).

Through observation children may acquire the complex patterns of behavior considered appropriate for both the female and male roles. Whether they actually perform these behaviors depends on a variety of factors (Mischel, 1970). For example, a woman may have learned through observation how to change a flat tire, but whether she ever engages in the learned behavior will depend on situational factors. If every time she has a flat tire an alternative means of repair (a male companion) is available, she may never have reason to demonstrate her skill. Furthermore, as Maccoby and Jacklin (1974) suggest, the knowledge that a given behavior is inappropriate may reduce the probability that it will be displayed. Most 3-year-olds know how to light matches. The fact that they do not may reflect the knowledge that such behavior is inappropriate for a child and may lead to negative consequences. Similarly, girls may learn that overt displays of aggression are behaviors traditionally reserved for boys, who are less likely than girls to be punished for behaving aggressively—at least on TV.

The recognition that certain behaviors are sex-typed may direct a child's attention toward (or away from) voluntarily exposing himself or herself to specific activities. Just after his second birthday my son entered the "what's that" stage and insisted that I identify each unfamiliar object he saw. As a result, I became very aware of a number of things for which I had no specific label. For example, he wanted to know the proper name for each of the many varieties of heavy machinery he observed at highway-construction sites. My global response "tractor" did not satisfy him. Of course I could see the physical differences between a backhoe and a trenching machine, but I could not provide a name for each. Yet, at some time I must have been exposed to the information Sean requested; for example, my younger brother must have asked my father similar questions. Presumably I ignored my father's answers because I regarded such information as inconsequential or irrelevant to my role. My brother, on the other hand, would be hard pressed to distinguish between percale and broadcloth.

The prediction that the acquisition of sex-typed behavior is contingent upon identification with same-sex adult models has proved difficult to substantiate. However, the results of several studies suggest that it is not the sex of the model per se but, rather, the sex-typed attributes of the model that facilitate the adoption of gender roles (Barkley, Ullman, Otto, & Brecht, 1976). Thus, mothers who are warm, nurturant, and protective foster "femininity" in their daughters (Kagan & Moss, 1962; Sears et al., 1965; Wright & Taska, 1966), whereas mothers who are cold and rejecting do not (Stein & Bailey, 1973).

Cross-Sex Identification

An alternative explanation for the acquisition of sex-typed behavior through identification focuses on the role of the opposite-sex parent. Fathers appear to be particularly influential in fostering femininity in their daughters.

The results of several studies suggest that fathers behave differently toward daughters than toward sons (Block, 1973; Lambert et al., 1971; Rothbart & Maccoby, 1966). For example, fathers of infant daughters talk more to their offspring (Rebelsky & Hanks, 1971) and are more "apprehensive over their well-being" (Pederson & Robson, 1969) than fathers of infant sons. At least one study suggests that fathers are very aware of their daughters' femininity even when the girls are only 2 or 3 and that they are more concerned than mothers that their little girls acquire feminine attributes such as long hair (Goodenough, 1957).

Several theorists have proposed explanations for sex-role identification that focus on the father's role (Johnson, 1963; Kohlberg, 1966; Lynn, 1969; Mowrer, 1950). Johnson (1963) suggests that the father plays the crucial role in determining the sex-role development of both boys and girls. Using the distinction between predominantly expressive (social-emotional) and predominantly instrumental (task) orientations to interpersonal interactions (Parsons & Bales, 1955), Johnson views the mother's responses to both her male and female children as consistently expressive (warm and permissive). In contrast, fathers vary their style according to the sex of the child with whom they interact. Fathers behave expressively toward their daughters, while their orientation toward their sons tends to be instrumental; they are critical of boys' performances and demand competence and task mastery from them. Consequently, Johnson reports, daughters view their fathers as more expressive than do sons. The fact that fathers respond differently to male and female children suggests that they may also reinforce them for displaying different behaviors. By reacting expressively toward a female child, the father may encourage her to behave in an expressive (feminine) manner and thereby facilitate her adoption of the female role.

Mussen and Rutherford (1963) obtained positive correlation between girls' femininity scores and their fathers' expectations for their feminine behavior. Thus, girls whose fathers expected (and perhaps reinforced) ladylike behavior on their part had higher femininity scores than girls whose fathers did not. Furthermore, daughters' femininity was positively related to fathers' masculinity. Perhaps fathers who are highly sex-typed themselves are more concerned about the sex typing of their female children than fathers who are less likely to describe themselves in stereotypically masculine terms.

If daughters learn the feminine role through their interactions with the opposite-sex parent (reciprocal learning), we would expect girls who spend a fair amount of time with their fathers to be more feminine than those who do not. Indeed, Fish (1969, reported by Fisher, 1973) obtained a positive correlation between the amount of time fathers spend with their children and daughters' femininity.

In an extensive examination of parent identification and sex-role behavior, Heilbrun (1970) found that the psychological adjustment of adolescent males was facilitated by identification with a masculine father. In contrast, girls who identified with feminine mothers were less well-adjusted than girls who did not (Heilbrun & Fromme, 1965). Heilbrun (1970) also found that among girls effective psychological adjustment was associated with identification with a masculine father.

In each of these studies the degree and type of parent identification were assessed independently. First, subjects were asked to rate themselves on a number of personality traits, such as deference and achievement. Then they indicated the extent to which descriptions of behaviors associated with these traits were more characteristic of their mothers or their fathers. The subjects' primary identification with the parent of the same or of the opposite sex was then determined on the basis of perceived similarity between parent and child. Finally, sex-role model scores were obtained by comparing the behaviors rated as characteristic of either parent with the sex-typed criteria for these behaviors. Such a procedure yields the sex of the primary model as well as the sex-typed attributes of that model. Subjects' own masculinity and femininity scores were assessed on a scale comprised of adjectives that have been found to distinguish between adolescent males who identify with masculine fathers and adolescent females who identify with feminine mothers (Cosentino & Heilbrun, 1964).

According to Heilbrun (1973), identification with a masculine father is a critical determinant of adolescent males' masculinity. In contrast, adolescent females may achieve a feminine identity through identification with either a masculine father or a feminine mother.

When Heilbrun (1968) compared the behavior of father-identified and mother-identified females, he found that girls who identified with a masculine father were more instrumentally oriented. There were no differences in expressiveness between the groups. These results suggest that among females identification with a biological and psychological male enhances instrumentality (presumably a masculine characteristic) but does not affect expressiveness. Recall that masculine-father identification has been found to be related to effective psychological adjustment among adolescent females. Perhaps girls who identify exclusively with feminine mothers adhere to a sex-role definition that is primarily expressive. Such a narrow definition of the female role may prove less adaptive than a broader-based identity incorporating both instrumental and expressive orientations (Williams, 1973). As we shall see in Chapter Six, Bem (1975, 1976) reports some rather compelling evidence in support of this suggestion. For girls the availability of an opposite-sex model appears to exert an influence in the development of a broader sex-role identity.

Father absence has been found to disrupt the development of the male role (Hetherington & Deur, 1971; Biller, 1973). Little boys who have been separated from their fathers before the age of 5 are less aggressive and more dependent than boys from intact families. These boys also have more "feminine" self-concepts and exhibit more feminine patterns of play and social interaction (Hetherington & Parke, 1975).

The effect of father absence on girls does not become apparent until adolescence, when it may result in difficulties in establishing relationships with males. For example, Hetherington (1972) found that daughters of widows and divorcées reported more anxiety over relating to males than did girls from intact homes. It is interesting to note that the two father-absent groups used different methods to cope with this anxiety. Daughters of divorcées tended to be openly flirtatious and assertive in the presence of male peers and adults. In contrast, daughters of widows were shy and retiring in the presence of males. Interviews with the mothers of the girls failed to reveal any differences in their attitudes or child-rearing practices. Nor were any differences obtained in either mothers' femininity or their attitudes toward men in general. Divorced mothers did, however, have less-positive attitudes about themselves and their marriages than did widows. These maternal attitudes were reflected in the attitudes of the daughters toward their fathers; daughters of divorcées were critical of their fathers, while daughters of widows held their fathers in high esteem.

In the recently reported results from a follow-up study of these girls, only 11 of the 24 daughters of widows were reported as married, compared with 21 of the 24 daughters of divorcées and 16 of the 24 daughters from intact families (Hetherington & Parke, 1975). Consistent with the results of the original study were the findings that the daughters of divorcées married younger and several were already separated or divorced.

The married daughters of divorcées and widows also perceived a greater similarity between their fathers and husbands than did the girls from intact families. Hetherington and Parke interpret these results to suggest that girls from father-absent homes may not have had adequate opportunity to work through their relationships with their fathers. As a result, they maintain their childhood images of their fathers and seek similar relationships with their spouses. Girls whose paternal relationships have not been interrupted by death or divorce do not attempt to replicate their relationships with their fathers in their choices of spouses. Their attitudes toward husbands and "most men" are balanced compared to the unrealistically favorable attitudes held by the daughters of widows toward husband and father and the negative attitudes toward men expressed by daughters of divorcées.

Grayson (1967, reported by Fisher, 1973) compared the effects of the death of same- and opposite-sex parents on the sex-role development of college women. Although few significant differences were obtained in the amount of psychosexual conflict exhibited by those women who come from families in which the mother or the father was absent, on one projective measure girls whose fathers were dead did express more sex-role conflict.

The results of neither of these studies may be regarded as definitive. However, they do point to the importance of the opposite-sex parent in facilitating the acquisition of the feminine role.

Cognitive Theories of Sex Typing

As we have seen, social-learning explanations for the acquisition of gender-appropriate behavior emphasize the importance of reinforcement and modeling. A more cognitive explanation for gender-role acquisition has been proposed by Kohlberg (1966; Kohlberg & Ullman, 1974). In Kohlberg's view, a child's ability to differentiate between gender roles and to categorize himself or herself as either male or female precedes, rather than follows, identification. On the basis of physical evidence (the external genitals) and sex differences in clothing, hairstyle, and characteristic activities, the child develops a conception of his or her sexual identity. Once this categorical determination has been made, it becomes reinforcing to behave in a manner appropriate for one's sex role and to imitate same-sex models. Thus, the girl says "I am a girl since I am more like my mother and other girls than boys; therefore I want to dress like a girl, play girl games, and feel and think like a girl" (Hetherington & Parke, 1975, p. 365).

Kolhberg assumes the existence of a strong tendency to maintain consistency between one's self-categorization as either male or female and the adoption of the corresponding gender-appropriate role. In his view, sex-role identity cannot be established until a child's level of cognitive development permits him or her to group objects according to their common characteristics (that is, all balls are round, all mothers are women, and so on).

Consistently with Kolhberg's formulation, brighter children tend to be more same-sex oriented in their sex-typed preferences than children of average intelligence (Kohlberg & Zigler, 1967). However, if, as Kohlberg suggests, the acquisition of gender identity is contingent upon mental maturity, we would expect young children who engage in sex-typed behavior to have more knowledge about sex-role stereotypes than those who do not. The results of a recent study by Vroegh (1975) failed to provide support for this hypothesis.

Furthermore, as Maccoby and Jacklin (1974) point out, the assumption that categorizing oneself as either male or female leads to the acquisition of values and behaviors consistent with one's gender does not explain how particular sets of sex-typed behaviors are adopted. There are a variety of characteristic attitudes and behaviors regarded as appropriate for girls and boys and for women and men. As a result, it is necessary to postulate other mechanisms, such as differential reinforcement and modeling, in order to account for individual differences in the acquisition of gender-appropriate behavior.

Recently, Block (1973) has proposed a more integrated cognitive model for the development of sex roles, which takes all of these factors into account. In Block's view, sex-role definition represents a synthesis of biological and cultural forces. This combination of biological and cultural forces is modified by the individual's level of cognitive and ego development. Extrapolating from Loevinger's (1966) and Loevinger and Wessler's (1970) hierarchical model of ego development, Block traces sex-role identity from the presocial period of infancy to the integrated, or highest, level of ego functioning (see Table 3-1).

During the presocial period the primary cognitive task of the infant is to distinguish self from other objects. At this stage the concept of gender is too sophisticated to be relevant. However, at the impulse-ridden level the infant begins to develop primitive notions about gender and to apply the label "girl" or "boy" differentially. During the third (self-protective) stage the child's primary concern is with self-assertion and self-extension.

It is not until the fourth (conformity) stage that sex-role stereotypes are established and the characteristic patterns of culturally approved male and female behaviors are adopted. During this period the socialization pressures exerted on boys and girls are markedly different. Boys are encouraged to control the expression of emotion, and girls to control the expression of aggression.

The fifth (conscientious) level of ego development requires a higher level of cognitive functioning. Societal norms and values are internalized, and the ability to introspect and evaluate oneself against an abstract standard is developed. For the first time the individual may become aware of the two opposing forces of human existence: agency and communion (Bakan, 1966). Agency is manifested in separation, mastery, and self-assertion; communion is manifested in fusion, intimacy, and acceptance. Thus, agency may be conceived as masculine and communion as feminine (Carlson, 1972).

At the sixth (autonomous) level of ego development the individual becomes increasingly aware of the potential conflict between these two tendencies and attempts to move toward a resolution of the conflict. In order to reach the highest level of ego development (integration), a balance between agency and communion must be achieved. In sex-role terms this requires the integration of the masculine and feminine aspects of self.

According to Block (1973), in our society the integration of agency and communion is a more difficult task for women than for men. In her view, during the conformity level of ego development both sexes develop a set of sex-role stereotypes that conform to the culturally approved definitions of male and female roles. The female stereotype focuses almost exclusively on communion, or interpersonal concern, whereas the male stereotype emphasizes agency, or self-assertion. It is during this developmental period that sex typing, or the definition of oneself as male or female, is established. However, socialization—or the more general process involving the internalization of social values and norms—does not occur until the conscientious stage, when the individual's own values are weighted against those set forth by society.

The socialization process appears to have differential effects on the personality development of males and females. For males socialization tends to enhance the perception of personal options; the "masculine" emphasis on competence and self-assertion is joined to a concern with "feminine" inter-

Table 3-1. Loevinger's Milestones of Ego Development and Extrapolations to Sex-Role Development

| Stage | Loevinger's milestones of ego development | | | Sex-role development extrapolated |
	Impulse control	Interpersonal style	Conscious concerns	Conceptions of sex role
Presocial/symbiotic Impulse-ridden	Impulse-ridden, fear of retaliation	Autistic, symbiotic Exploitive, dependent	Self versus nonself Sexual and aggressive bodily feelings	Development of gender identity, self-assertion, self-expression, self-interest
Self-protective (formerly opportunistic)	Expedient, fear of being caught	Exploitive, manipulative, wary	Advantage, control, protection of self	Extension of self, self-extension, self-enhancement
Conformity	Conformity to external rule	Reciprocal, superficial	Things, appearance, reputation, self-acceptance	Conformity to external role, development of sex-role stereotypes, bifurcation of sex roles
Conscientious	Internalized rules, guilt	Intensive, responsive	Differentiated inner feelings, motives, self-respect	Examination of self as sex-role exemplar vis-a-vis internalized values
Autonomous	Coping with conflict, toleration of differences	Intensive concern for autonomy	Differentiated inner feelings, role concepts, self-fulfillment	Differentiation of sex role, coping with conflicting masculine-feminine aspects of self
Integrated	Reconciling inner conflicts, renunciation of unattainable	Cherishing of individuality	All of the above plus identity	Achievement of individually defined sex role, integration of both masculine and feminine aspects of self, androgynous sex-role definition

From "Conceptions of Sex Role: Some Cross-Cultural and Longitudinal Perspectives," by J. H. Block, *American Psychologist*, 1973, 28 (6), 512-526. Copyright 1973 by The American Psychological Association. Reprinted by permission.

dependence (Block, Van der Lippe, & Block, 1973). Highly socialized women, on the other hand, adhere to a rigid, stereotypic definition of the female role that emphasizes nurturance, submission, and conservation (Block et al., 1973). Thus, the attainment of higher levels of ego functioning for women involves conflict with the prevailing cultural norms.

As we have seen, societal sanctions regarding sex-inappropriate behaviors are more clearly articulated for boys than for girls. Given the greater emphasis placed on adherence to the male role during the conformity stage, boys may experience less ambiguity regarding their role definition than girls. Later, during the conscientious stage, boys may be better able than girls to evaluate their sex-role identity against the socially proscribed norms. Furthermore, the rigid prohibitions that restrict the gender-inappropriate behavior of boys relax over time. The reverse is true for girls. "Tomboyish" behavior is tolerated up to puberty, and it is not until early adolescence that girls are subjected to pressures to conform to the feminine stereotype. If during the conformity stage the female role is relatively ambiguous, the task of evaluating that role in light of internalized values may be more difficult. To the extent that girls begin to internalize societal values before attaining a clear conception of the female role, they may be unable to distinguish their self-definitions from the feminine stereotype.

When Block et al. (1973) examined the personality structures and early experiences of males and females representing different patterns of sex-role typing and socialization, they found evidence that sex roles are acquired through identification, modeling, reinforcement, and reciprocal-role learning. Both high-masculine/high-socialized men and high-feminine/high-socialized women came from homes in which the sex-role behaviors and attitudes of the parents were clearly differentiated along traditional stereotypic lines. These individuals appeared to have internalized parental values through the process of identification with the same-sex parent.

In contrast, the sex-inappropriate/high-socialized men and women (low-masculine/high-socialized and low-feminine/high-socialized) were from homes in which both parents provided models for their children that crosscut traditional sex-role stereotypes. These individuals may be regarded as having identified androgynously; that is, they internalized the positive characteristics of both their male and female parents.

The third group of individuals identified by Block et al. (1973) comprised high-masculine/low-socialized men and high-feminine/low-socialized women. These individuals had not achieved their sex-role definitions through identification with same-sex parent but, rather, through the reactions of the opposite-sex parent. This process is termed *reactivity* and may take two forms. In the first, the opposite-sex parent behaves in a gender-appropriate fashion, thereby providing the child with the opportunity to respond in terms of her or his own gender role (reciprocal-role learning). The second form involves differential reinforcement of the child's gender-appropriate behavior by the opposite-sex parent.

Finally, low-masculine/low-socialized men and low-feminine/low-socialized women appear to have established their gender identity by emulating the parent of the opposite sex. The same-sex parents of these individuals were distant and emotionally uninvolved with both their children and their spouses. As a result, the opposite-sex parent assumed a central role in the child's acquisition of gender identity.

Thus, an individual may become appropriately sex-typed in one of two ways—either through identification with or modeling of the same-sex parent or through interactions with the opposite-sex parent. Culturally deviant sex typing may result from identification with both parents (androgynous identification) or from emulating the behavior of the opposite-sex parent.

The results of the analysis presented by Block and her colleagues (Block, 1973; Block et al., 1973) clearly suggest that sex-role typing, socialization, and identification are different processes. One can be sex-typed without having identified, and one can identify without being socialized (Block et al., 1973). The processes underlying the acquisition of gender role most likely involve some combination of all of the mechanisms we have examined—identification, modeling, reinforcement, and reciprocal-role learning, mediated by the child's level of cognitive development (Maccoby & Jacklin, 1974). The relative contribution of each of these mechanisms to what is obviously a complex learning process is difficult to specify. Because the process is so complex, it is not surprising that attempts to explain the development of sex roles on the basis of a single mechanism, such as identification or reciprocal-role learning, have proved difficult to substantiate empirically.

Although the core of an individual's gender identity as either masculine or feminine may be established in early childhood, there is little reason to believe that it is inalterably "fixed" at that time. As children enter school, they begin to rely less on their parents and more on their peers as models for appropriate behavior and as sources of positive reinforcement. Their conceptions of themselves and of their sex roles continue to develop through adolescence into adulthood. The significance of one's gender identity as expressed in behavior is subject to modification across time and situations.

As we shall see in the next chapter, the evidence for sex similarities on a number of psychological dimensions is much stronger than the evidence for sex differences. Most behavioral differences between girls and boys and between women and men appear to be the result of social learning and experience. The expression of sex-role-appropriate behavior on the part of both females and males appears to be more dependent on their expectations that such behavior will be reinforced (either positively or negatively) in a given situation than on fixed conceptions of masculinity and femininity established in early childhood.

Summary

The culture dictates that everyone must develop a gender identity. Even in cases in which the genital structures are ambiguous, assignment is made into one of two categories: male or female. Once sex has been assigned, gender identity and gender role develop through a process that appears quite independent of chromosomal, gonadal, or hormonal sex.

Some traits may reflect a biologically based predisposition. However, it is generally agreed that among humans socialization plays a critical role in the acquisition of behaviors considered characteristic of one sex or the other. In this chapter we have considered three general approaches that have been used to explain the development of sex roles: the psychoanalytic approach, social learning theories, and theories of cognitive development.

In Freud's view, the acquisition of sex roles was dependent on the resolution of the Oedipal conflict through identification with the same-sex parent. Freud believed the motivation for resolving the Oedipal conflict is stronger in boys (fear of castration) than in girls (fear of loss of love). Thus, he hypothesized that girls never fully resolve the conflict and have weaker superegos than males. Freud's notions regarding penis envy, castration anxiety, and even the existence of the Oedipal conflict have proved difficult to substantiate.

The literature on sex-role preference does indicate that adults of both sexes believe that it is more desirable to be a male and that prospective parents generally prefer male to female offspring. One need not postulate the existence of anatomically based "penis envy," as Freud did, to come up with a variety of reasons why women might envy men, since in our society males are afforded greater power and prestige than females.

An alternative explanation for the development of sex roles focuses on the role of social learning in the acquisition of sex-typed behaviors. Parents seem to perceive certain behaviors as more typical of children of one sex or of the other. However, parents do not appear to rely on direct positive reinforcement as a means of shaping their children's behavior to conform to their expectations. When direct reinforcement is used, it is usually negative reinforcement directed toward boys for behaving in a fashion that is inappropriate for their sex role. Of course, direct reinforcement is only one means of differentially shaping behavior. Parents' selections of clothes and toys for their children are generally based on gender; stories and TV programs portray males and females differently; and strangers often react to children along sex-role stereotypic lines. But the differential application of direct reinforcement alone (either positive or negative) does not appear to provide an adequate explanation for sex-typed behavior.

In the social-learning view, sex roles are acquired through imitation, or modeling, based on identification. There is, however, little empirical support for the contention that children are more likely to imitate the behavior of the same-sex than of the opposite-sex parent. Furthermore, correlational studies fail to reveal consistent similarities between child and same-sex parent. It has been suggested that it is the sex-typed attributes of the model, not the model's sex per se, that facilitates the adoption of gender role.

There is some evidence to suggest that the opposite-sex parent plays a critical role in the development of sex-typed behavior through reciprocal-role learning. Johnson has suggested that the father exerts the major influence on gender identity and roles among both boys and girls. While boys are affected by the absence of their father when they are very young, girls from father-absent families do not display difficulties in psychosexual adjustment until adolescence.

A cognitive developmental explanation for gender-role acquisition has been proposed by Kolhberg. He views the child's ability to differentiate between gender roles and to categorize himself or herself as either male or female as preceding, rather than following, identification. Once the concept of gender is established, it is reinforcing to behave in a manner appropriate for one's sex role and to imitate same-sex models. However, Kolhberg's theory does not account for how particular sets of sex-typed behaviors are adopted. There are a variety of characteristic attitudes and behavior regarded as appropriate for girls and boys and for women and men.

Block offers a more integrated cognitive model that defines sex-role adoption as a synthesis of biological and cultural forces mediated by cognitive and ego functions. She suggests that the attainment of the highest level of ego development is dependent in part on the integration of the masculine (agency) and feminine (communion) aspects of self.

According to Block, in our society the integration of agency and communion is a more difficult task for women than for men. The socialization process appears to enhance the perception of personal options for men. Highly socialized women, on the other hand, adhere to a rigid stereotypic definition of the female role, which emphasizes nurturance and interdependence. Distinguishing between socialization and sex typing, Block maintains that sex roles may be acquired through all of the mechanisms we have examined—identification, modeling, reinforcement, and reciprocal-role learning. Furthermore, sex-role development is mediated by the individual's level of cognitive development and may be modified through adolescence into adulthood.

The learning processes underlying the acquisition of gender identity and role are complex. Girls and boys, women and men do behave differently. However, sex differences in behavior appear to be more dependent on expectations that a given behavior will be reinforced in a given situation than on a "fixed" conception of gender identity established in early childhood.

Chapter Four

Psychological Differences between Females and Males

At a recent parent-teacher conference, my son's nursery school teacher began our interview with the observation "Sean is a very active child; I mean, he's all boy." She went on to say that he enjoys playing with cars and blocks and prefers to be outdoors. He shows little interest in group dancing, has not yet learned to count to ten, and cannot distinguish red crayons from blue ones. She concluded by characterizing Sean as "bright, well liked, well adjusted, and cooperative." Would she have reached the same conclusion if my child's name had been Shannon rather than Sean? Probably not.

Some of the teacher's comments about my 3-year-old son are consistent with the empirical studies of sex differences. For example, the results of several studies suggest that little girls count higher and make fewer errors than little boys (Buckingham & MacLatchy, 1930; Gesell, Halverson, Thompson, Ilg, Castner, Ames, & Amatruda, 1940). Most of the observations of my son's teacher, however, reflect popularly held beliefs about the nature of psychological differences between the sexes. If we had been discussing Shannon rather than Sean, the teacher might have characterized "her" as overactive or aggressive and uncooperative. She might have been concerned about Shannon's lack of interest in dancing or her preference for trucks and blocks.

Until recently it was widely assumed that the obvious and universal biological differences between females and males were paralleled by clearly delineated psychological differences. A number of comprehensive reviews of the literature on sex differences published in the 1960s (Garai & Scheinfeld, 1968; Maccoby, 1966; Tyler, 1965) pointed to the existence of such differences in many areas of psychological functioning. These areas included intellectual ability, cognitive styles, self-esteem, dependency, passivity, sensation, and perception. In many cases the reported findings appeared to favor males; others, to favor females. However, under closer scrutiny (Maccoby & Jacklin, 1974), a number of the postulated differences between males and females have been identified as representing social myths rather than verifiable facts. Some have been supported; others remain untested assumptions.

In this chapter we will begin by reviewing the research in four areas in which sex differences have been fairly well established. These areas are verbal ability, visual-spatial ability, mathematical ability, and aggression. Then we will turn to an examination of several areas (for example, passivity, dependence, and compliance) in which sex differences have been postulated but empirical support has been equivocal at best. Finally, we will briefly examine several areas (for example, concern with social stimuli, suggestibility, and self-esteem) in which postulated sex differences have not withstood the test of time and additional study. Because the sex-difference literature is vast and because our focus is primarily on women, the topics covered in this chapter are not exhaustive. The reader is referred to Maccoby and Jacklin (1974) for an extensive review of the recent literature on sex differences.

Before we begin, it should be noted again that, with the exception of menstruation, pregnancy, and lactation in women and ejaculation in men (Money, 1974), there are no other behaviors that are exclusively male or exclusively female. Rather, some behaviors appear to be more or less characteristic of one sex or the other. For example, the fact that boys and men are generally more aggressive than girls and women does not mean that females never behave aggressively. Similarly, although girls have been found to excel in tasks involving verbal ability, individual boys may do just as well or better than the average girl on these tasks.

Intellectual Performance

Historically, one popular but unfounded explanation for women's inferior social status was that women were less intelligent than men (Shields, 1975). Perhaps the most frequently cited evidence in support of this position was the observation that females were underrepresented in the ranks of recognized geniuses. It is true that Einstein's name was Albert and not Alberta, but, as a number of writers have recently suggested, society's failure to recognize women's genius is more a reflection of cultural values than of inherent ability (Sherman, 1971; Shields, 1975). Indeed, in the past some of the (few) women who did attain recognition for their intellectual ability, such as Aurore Dudevant and Mary Ann Evans, did so under assumed male names.[1]

During the early part of the 20th century, social-psychological explanations (Hollingsworth, 1914; Thompson, 1903) for the virtual absence of women from lists of eminent persons were largely ignored. Instead, sex differences in intellectual functioning were explained on the basis of what has come to be called the *variability hypothesis* (Heim, 1970; Thorndike, 1910; Tyler, 1965). The variability hypothesis refers to the observation that on a number of psychological dimensions the scores of males are distributed more widely around the mean than those of females. For example, although the mean IQ scores of males and females are the same, a greater number of men than women obtain extreme scores (both high and low). Thus, it was argued that one could reasonably expect to find more male geniuses and more male mental defectives in any large sample of women and men. The variability hypothesis has not been disproven (Tyler, 1965); in fact, some investigators view it as a plausible explanation for sex differences (Heim,

---

[1]Aurore Dudevant wrote under the pen name George Sand. Mary Ann Evans was better known as George Eliot.

1970; Hutt, 1972). However, on most psychometric measures the variation of scores around the mean within each sex is much greater than the variation in the dispersion of scores between the sexes. Even on measures in which significant differences in the mean scores of females and males are obtained, the distribution of male and female scores overlap considerably. A definitive test of the variability hypothesis would be to test the difference in variance between the two sexes on some psychological measure. Unfortunately, if such tests have been conducted, the results have not been reported, and in their absence the value of the variability hypothesis as an explanation for sex differences cannot be accurately assessed (Maccoby & Jacklin, 1974; Shields, 1975).

Although there is no evidence to suggest that males and females differ in average intelligence, relatively consistent sex differences have been obtained in comparative studies of verbal, mathematical, and visual-spatial abilities (Maccoby & Jacklin, 1974; Unger & Denmark, 1975). Females excel in tests of verbal ability; males outperform females on measures of visual-spatial and mathematical ability.

Verbal, Visual-Spatial, and Mathematical Ability

The results of early studies of sex differences in verbal ability indicated that preschool age girls talk earlier, use sentences with greater facility, and articulate more clearly than boys. For example, McCarthy (1943) found that, among 2-year-olds, 78% of the girls' speech was comprehensible as compared to only 49% of the boys'. Boys do, of course, catch up, usually by the age of 4 (Sherman, 1971).

One popular explanation for the greater verbal precocity of preschool girls is that mothers of girls provide a richer language environment for their young offspring than do mothers of boys (Cherry & Lewis, 1976). The results of several studies suggest that mothers vocalize more to infant daughters than to infant sons (Goldberg & Lewis, 1969; Lewis & Freedle, 1973; Moss, 1967). Also, infant girls have been found to be more responsive to their mothers' vocalizations than infant sons (Lewis & Freedle, 1973). In a recent study of the verbal interactions between mothers and their 2-year-old children, Cherry and Lewis (1976) found that, compared to mothers of boys, mothers of girls talked more, asked more questions, repeated their children's utterances more often, and used longer utterances. Although there was a tendency for girls in Cherry and Lewis's study to talk more than boys, significant differences were observed only in the mothers' verbal behavior, not in that of their children. Furthermore, several recent studies have failed to obtain differences in language abilities between female and male preschoolers (Dickie, 1968; Koenigsknecht & Friedman, 1976; Mehrabian, 1970).[2]

---

[2]Interestingly, Maccoby and Jacklin (1974) cite two recent studies of disadvantaged children in which girls were ahead of boys in language development.

Consistent sex differences in tests of verbal ability do not emerge until late childhood (Maccoby & Jacklin, 1974). By the fifth or sixth grade, girls have begun to outperform boys on tests of language usage involving spelling, grammar, and punctuation (Droege, 1967; Svensson, 1974; Tyler, 1965). Girls continue to outperform boys on measures of verbal ability through high school and college (Maccoby & Jacklin, 1974).

Alternatives to the environmental explanation for females' superior verbal skills focus on biological differences between the sexes. It is generally agreed that females attain physical maturity at an earlier age than males (Tanner, 1962). Maturational differences between males and females in functional brain asymmetry have been postulated as one explanation for females' verbal superiority. As the human brain matures, the left hemisphere, which is the major site of language function, becomes increasingly dominant over the right hemisphere. If, as Buffery and Gray (1972) suggest, girls are developmentally ahead of boys in attaining left hemispheric dominance (and therefore show greater brain laterality), they may have greater facility for language development at a younger age. Males, who generally mature less rapidly, may never become as lateralized for speech as females.

Although the suggestion that women are more lateralized for verbal functioning than men is an interesting one, the results of two studies that examined the effects of left hemisphere damage (or removal) on the verbal functioning of adult females and males have failed to support this hypothesis (Landsell, 1976; McGlone, 1976). For example, McGlone did not obtain evidence of greater verbal deficits among women with left, as compared to right, temporal lesions resulting from tumors or from vascular accidents such as strokes. Men with left hemisphere lesions did show impaired verbal functioning in comparison to men with right hemisphere lesions and to women with lesions on either the right or the left side of the brain. McGlone's findings imply a more asymmetrical, left-hemisphere control of verbal abilities in men than in women. Waber (1976) has recently suggested that rate of physical maturation at puberty is a more potent predictor of brain lateralization than biological sex, although, as we shall see, the relationship between physical maturity and cognitive functioning is much clearer in the case of spatial abilities (in which males excel) than in the case of verbal abilities.

An alternative biologically based explanation for sex differences in verbal skills is based on the assumption that the female sex hormone, estrogen, facilitates the neural transmission involved in verbal tasks that require the demonstration of simple, overlearned perceptual motor skills (Broverman, Klaiber, Kobayashi, & Vogel, 1968; Hutt, 1972). However, there is no evidence that females' superior verbal ability is restricted to the performance of tasks that require a minimum of mediation by higher cognitive processes (Broverman et al., 1968). As Parlee (1972) so aptly observes, females surpass males on almost all measures of language performance, including reading comprehension and verbal creativity (Droege, 1967; Backman, 1972). It is difficult to accept the categorization of either of these measures as reflecting a facility for the performance of simple overlearned tasks.[3]

Whereas females outperform males on tests of verbal ability, males excel on measures of visual-spatial and mathematical ability. Visual-spatial skills involve the ability to organize and relate visual inputs in a spatial context without the aid of verbal mediation (Petersen, 1976). Tests specifically designed to measure visual-spatial ability require some form of mental manipulation of objects or figures in space, although high scores on more general tests of analytic ability often depend on the manifestation of this skill (Sherman, 1967). Tasks such as aiming at a target, arranging objects in two-dimensional space, and map reading involve visual-spatial ability. Males have been found to score consistently higher than females on a variety of tasks that involve space perception (Anastasi, 1958; Hutt, 1972; Maccoby & Jacklin, 1974; Tyler, 1965). It should be noted, however, that males' superiority reflects a small average group difference, not individual achievement.

Perhaps the most compelling evidence for sex differences in visual-spatial perception comes from studies of the ability to maintain accurate spatial orientation and to detect spatial relationships within complex configurations, an ability commonly referred to as *field independence* (Witkin, Dyk, Faterson, Goodenough, & Karp, 1962). The two tests most often used to evaluate field independence are the Rod and Frame Test and the Embedded Figures Test. In the Rod and Frame Test the subject is asked to determine the verticality of a rod in relationship to a frame that may be tilted at various angles. The task is performed in a darkened room, in order to eliminate the influence of environmental cues (verticle doors, walls, and so on), and the rod and frame are both luminous. The Embedded Figures Test requires the subject to extract a simple figure embedded in a more complex one. On both of these tests males are less distracted than females by misleading contextual cues. Females tend to perceive the rod as vertical when it is parallel to the frame, despite the fact that both are tilted. Females are also less proficient than males at picking out "hidden figures" embedded in a complex, geometric design. Early investigations in this area equated field independence with overall analytic ability. As a result, males were assumed to be more analytic than females. However, the results of recent research indicate that the sexes do not differ on tests of analytic cognitive style, unless the task specifically requires visual-spatial skills (Maccoby & Jacklin, 1974; Sherman, 1967). Even then, the sex-role appropriateness of the context in which visual-spatial tasks are presented has recently been found to affect the performance of females and males. For example, Naditch (1976) assigned an equal number of males and females to a standard Rod and Frame

[3]Broverman and his colleagues (1968) hypothesize that females' superior performance on simple repetitive tasks is a result of the effects of females' high levels of estrogen, which activate the central nervous system and reduce the capacity to inhibit responses required for tasks that involve cognitive restructuring (on which males excel). However, as Parlee (1972) points out, the relationship between cognitive function and the activity of the autonomic nervous system in humans has yet to be demonstrated empirically.

Test and to a modified version substituting the figure of a person for the rod. Subjects in the standard condition were told that the test measured perceptual abilities related to spatial aspects of intelligence, while those in the modified condition were told that the test measured empathy. In the standard condition males scored higher than females in field independence. However, the findings were reversed in the person condition, in which females scored higher in field independence than males. Similar reversals have been noted by Coates (1974) among preschool-age children in studies using measures of field independence that may be more person-oriented than the adult versions (Naditch, 1976).

A variety of explanations, both social-psychological and biological, have been proposed to account for the superior performance of males on visual-spatial tasks. For example, Witkin and his colleagues hypothesized that field independence was related to cultural factors, such as permissive child-rearing practices (Witkin, 1964, 1969; Witkin, Lewis, Herzman, Machover, Meissner, & Wapner, 1954). The results of several cross-cultural investigations lend support to this hypothesis. Dawson (1967) compared the visual-spatial performance scores of adult males from two African cultures. The males who had been reared in a culture that encouraged children to behave autonomously scored higher than those reared in a more restrictive environment. Sex differences in visual-spatial ability are most pronounced in cultures in which males exercise strong dominance over females (Berry, 1966). Studies of Eskimos, who grant children of both sexes considerable independence, have failed to obtain sex differences in visual-spatial ability (Berry, 1966; MacArthur, 1967).[4]

The results of a number of studies suggest that visual-spatial ability is learned (Gibson, 1953; Santos & Murphy, 1960) and that performance, particularly women's performance, may be improved through practice (Brinkman, 1966; Elliot & McMichael, 1963; Goldstein & Chance, 1965; Chance & Goldstein, 1971; Sherman, 1974). Sherman (1967, 1974) has suggested that sex differences in visual-spatial ability may be based, at least in part, on differential practice on sex-typed tasks that require spatial visualization.

As Sherman (1967) aptly observes, boys are more likely than girls to spend time constructing models and tinkering with car motors. They are also more likely to become involved with activities that require map reading and that develop a sense of direction (sailing, hunting, camping, and so on). In high school, males are more likely than females to enroll in courses in mechanical drawing and analytic geometry. The fact that consistent sex differences in visual-spatial abilities favoring males are generally not ob-

---

[4]In a comparative study of the primary mental abilities of Black and White children reported by Baughman (1971), no sex differences in visual-spatial ability were obtained in the Black sample. Historically, the genetic pools of Blacks and Eskimos have been more restricted than those of Whites. This suggests that visual-spatial ability may have a genetic base. However, the fact that the differences in visual-spatial ability scores of Blacks and Whites were much greater than the differences between the sexes within each race suggests that cultural influences are more important determinants of visual-spatial ability than heritability.

tained until midadolescence (Maccoby & Jacklin, 1974; Witkin et al., 1954)—an age when cultural demands for sex-role differentiation are particularly strong—has been interpreted by Sherman (1967) as reflecting the differential learning that results from the sex typing of activities at this time. The results of a recent study by Nash (1975), who found that superior visual-spatial performance among 14-year-old girls was related to their expressed preference to be boys (and, by implication, preference for "masculine" activities), lend support to this view.

Although the emergence of clear-cut differences in visual-spatial performance may be influenced by learning and cultural expectations, there is also some evidence indicating that it may be influenced by biological factors. For example, it has been suggested that visual-spatial ability is influenced by a recessive gene carried by the X chromosome (Bock & Kolakowski, 1973; Stafford, 1961). According to this hypothesis, males would be more likely to manifest this recessive X-linked trait because they receive only one X chromosome. In order for a female to manifest this trait, she would have to have received two recessive genes. The probability of this occurrence is relatively low.

The visual-spatial performance scores of individuals with Turner's syndrome (XO) and of those who are androgen insensitive have been found to be typically feminine (Bock & Kolakowski, 1973; Garron, 1970). These results suggest that the expression of the hypothesized X-linked trait for visual-spatial ability may be contingent on the presence of testosterone.

An alternative hypothesis implicating sex hormones in the development of visual-spatial ability has been suggested by both Waber (1976) and Petersen (1976). Waber (1976) found that, regardless of sex, late-maturing adolescents performed better on tests of spatial ability than on tests of verbal ability. Waber also found that late maturers showed greater hemisphere lateralization for speech than early maturers. Petersen (1976) obtained similar results for late-maturing adolescent males. The relationship between the timing of physical maturity at puberty and brain lateralization is not yet understood. There is, however, some evidence to suggest that, as adults, males show greater right temporal lateralization for spatial functioning than females (McGlone, 1976; Sherman, 1974).

While these findings indicate that males' superiority in spatial visualization may be in part physiologically based (Wittig, 1976), it should be kept in mind that the effects of this sex difference may be enhanced by the sex typing of activities that promote the acquisition of this skill. Furthermore, girls' early verbal advantage over boys may encourage them to adopt a more verbal (less visual-spatial) strategy for problem solving (Sherman, 1967).

Consistent sex differences in quantitative ability are not obtained until adolescence (Maccoby & Jacklin, 1974). By high school, however, boys generally score higher than girls on tests of mathematical ability (Droege, 1967; Flanagan, Dailey, Shaycoft, Gorham, Orr, Goldberg, & Neyman, 1961; Keating & Stanley, 1972). The most popular explanation for males' superiority in quantitative ability focuses on the greater interest males display in acquiring these skills. There is no doubt that males are more likely than females to select math courses as electives, but the reasons for this preference are not clear. Do males "like" mathematics more than girls? Or do they see the acquisition of mathematical skills as more central to their career plans than do females?

According to a recent study, there are no significant differences between girls and boys in achievement and grades in math at the end of the first year in high school (Fennema & Sherman, reported by Berman, 1975). However, the number of girls enrolled in math courses declines sharply after the second year. Among the reasons girls gave for dropping math were fear it might hamper their relationships with boys or make them feel masculine and the belief that math was less useful to girls than to boys. These results suggest that females' inferior mathematical performance may be due, at least in part, to differential practice. On the other hand, mathematical ability may be related to visual-spatial skills (Maccoby & Jacklin, 1974); as you may recall, males outperform females on tests of both skills.

Although males and females differ somewhat in specific areas of intellectual ability, the distribution of male and female scores on all measures of specific abilities overlap considerably. Most differences are small average differences. Some of them may indeed be biologically based. But none are of sufficient magnitude to place serious constraints on the kinds of intellectual (or social) roles males *and* females are capable of fulfilling (Kagan, 1975).

Aggression

Perhaps the most consistent evidence for behavioral differences between the sexes has been obtained in studies of aggression. Whether aggression is defined as committing violent crimes, administering shocks, imitating a model hitting a doll, or playing rough and tumble in nursery school, males appear to be the more aggressive sex.

Are males more aggressive than females because they can better endure physical punishment when (and if) they do fight? Certainly the fact that males are taller, heavier, and stronger than females gives them a clear advantage in hand-to-hand combat. For example, although my brother is three years my junior, by the time he was 5, his physical advantage over me was apparent. I quickly learned to contain my attacks to verbal insults, delivered from a safe distance. Are males more aggressive than females because social norms dictate that they should be? Arm wrestling, boxing, and football are a part of the early experience of males in this society. Little boys are expected to participate in culturally approved displays of physical violence and are rewarded for excelling. Or do the observed differences in aggression between males and females reflect some more basic biochemical difference between the sexes? Each of these alternatives has been proposed to account for the greater tendency on the part of males to behave aggressively, and, as we shall see, there is some empirical support for each of these explanations.

Observational studies of the spontaneous play behavior of nursery school children indicate that boys are more likely to engage in displays of physical aggression than girls. Although the incidence of actual physical assault is low, little boys do engage in more mock fighting (rough-and-tumble play) than little girls (Hutt, 1972; McIntyre, 1972; Sears, Rau, & Alpert, 1965). Two popular explanations for the greater incidence of rough-and-tumble play among boys are based on the assumptions that (1) boys are generally more active than girls and (2) boys are more likely to be encouraged to "behave like boys." With regard to the first explanation, there is little evidence supporting sex differences in general activity rate before 1 year of age (Maccoby & Jacklin, 1974). After the first year, when sex differences are obtained, they generally favor boys, but the specific situations that evoke higher activity among boys have not been determined. Loo and Wenar (1971) found no differences in the activity rates of 4- and 5-year-olds as measured by "actometers" that recorded the amount of gross motor movement in which children engaged. Teachers, however, reported that boys were more active than girls. Recently, Maccoby and Jacklin (1971) have suggested that boys are more likely to display greater activity rates in play with other boys. This is interesting because the incidence of rough-and-tumble play among boys is specific to sex of playmate. Boys do aggress more than girls, but only against other boys (Hutt, 1972).

Despite the intuitive appeal of the hypothesis that mothers of boys are more likely to encourage aggressive displays on the part of their children than mothers of girls (Sears, Maccoby, & Levin, 1957), there is little evidence to suggest that parents differentially encourage aggressive behavior in their children according to their sex (Newson & Newson, 1968; Sears et al., 1965). However, it does appear that boys are more likely than girls to be punished for behaving aggressively (Lambert, Yakley, & Hein, 1971; Minton, Kagan, & Levine, 1971)—a topic to which we shall return later in our discussion.

It is important to note that adults do not always agree on the specific behaviors that constitute "aggression" and that, as Bardwick (1971) suggests, girls may express aggression in a different way than boys; boys hit, and girls withdraw support or express their aggression through insult or hostility. Consistent with this view are Feshbach's (1970) findings that first-grade girls are more likely to exclude, ignore, and reject a newcomer from their group than are boys, regardless of the sex of the "new" child. Although exclusion and rejection do not constitute direct displays of aggression, they may be interpreted as such. Boys, on the other hand, are somewhat more likely to aggress directly against the newcomer if the child is a male. To the extent that boys are more likely than girls to express their aggression directly, parents may be likely to label boys' behavior as aggressive.

Several studies suggest that girls are no more likely than boys to engage in indirect forms of aggression, such as verbal hostility (Bandura, Ross, & Ross, 1961; McIntyre, 1972). In fact, when sex differences in verbal hostility are obtained, males generally score higher than females (Hatfield, Ferguson, & Alpert, 1967; Sears et al., 1965; Whiting & Edwards, 1973).

It has also been suggested that females are less likely to behave aggressively than males because they have less opportunity to acquire appropriate aggressive responses. In order to test the validity of this hypothesis, Bandura (1965) exposed children to a film of a model who behaved aggressively. The consequences of the model's behavior were varied in one of three ways. In one condition the children observed the model being rewarded for his behavior; in another the model was punished; and in the third the model experienced no consequences for his actions. After exposure to the model, boys engaged in more spontaneous displays of aggression than did girls—a result consistent with those of a number of studies on aggression (Bandura, 1973). The sex differences were most pronounced when the children observed a model who was punished. Following the performance test, the children in each of the three groups were offered a reward for each modeled response they could reproduce accurately. Under these conditions the sex differences were eliminated. On the basis of these findings, Bandura (1973) concluded that the failure of females to imitate the aggressive behavior of a model was not due to differential learning but, rather, to differential inhibition.

The results of several other studies provide support for Bandura's interpretation (Dubanoski & Parton, 1971; Madsen, 1968). Apparently, females acquire aggressive responses just as boys do, but they also learn that aggressive behavior is not appropriate for their sex role and hesitate to display such behavior unless they are assured that it is "acceptable." It has been noted that, when angry male subjects are given the opportunity to attack a punitive opponent, they show a decrease in physiological arousal. The opportunity to aggress does not result in a corresponding reduction in females' arousal levels. However, when female subjects are given a chance to respond to their aggressor in a friendly fashion, they exhibit a decrease in physiological arousal similar to that of males. This would indicate that overt aggression leads to tension reduction only if it has been learned as an "appropriate" means of resolving conflict (Hokanson & Edelman, 1966).

In American society aggression is presented as an exclusively male-appropriate behavior. This message is conveyed in a variety of ways. For example, when Child, Potter, and Levine (1946) analyzed the content of children's books, they found that females were most often portrayed as submissive and inactive and that males were characterized as both active and aggressive. Gerbner (1972) found that female characters in children's television shows rarely behaved aggressively and, when they did, they were less likely than males to avoid punishment for their actions. Thus, it appears that children learn at an early age that aggressive behavior is appropriate for males but not for females.

Consistent with this view is the fact that females are more anxious than males about displaying aggression. Kagan and Moss (1962) found that a male who behaved aggressively as a boy was more likely to become an aggressive adult but that there was no corresponding relationship between the aggressiveness of girls and women. Kagan and Moss interpret these findings to suggest that socialization pressures may have an equally strong inhibitory impact on all females. Females do experience (or at least report) more anxiety over the display of aggression than boys (Sears, 1961). This is surprising, since boys are more likely than girls to be physically punished for behaving aggressively (Bardwick, 1971). Because boys have more experience with adverse consequences of aggression, we might expect males (not females) to exhibit higher levels of aggression-related anxiety.

It has been suggested that girls are as able as boys to respond aggressively but refrain from doing so because they fear the consequences. If this is the case, girls should be more likely to express aggression in covert ways, such as acting out (mock fighting) or engaging in aggressive or hostile fantasies. Yet, boys engage more frequently in attenuated forms of aggression (contact sports) and are more prone to aggressive fantasies (Maccoby & Jacklin, 1974).

Not only are females less likely than males to engage in acts of physical aggression, but they are also less likely to be the victims of aggression, at least in laboratory settings.[5] In studies of aggression among college students, subjects were asked to administer shocks to "learners" (Buss, 1966; Taylor & Epstein, 1967; Youssef, 1968). The sex of the learner (victim) was systematically varied. Subjects of both sexes administered fewer and less intensive shocks to female "learners." Similarly, when 11-year-olds were asked to "punish" another child by administering a loud noise, girls were "punished" less frequently than boys (Shortell & Biller, 1970).

Even as young as nursery-school age, girls are less likely to be the targets of aggression than boys. This suggests that in our society it is considered inappropriate to aggress against girls. Recent support for this hypothesis was obtained in a study by Sandidge and Friedland (1973). Children (aged 9 to 10) were shown cartoons of a child (either a boy or a girl) speaking aggressively to another child of either the same or the opposite sex. The subjects were asked to respond as they thought the "victim" would. Both male and female children gave more aggressive responses when the aggressor was a boy and responded more aggressively when they were answering for a girl. Apparently, girls should not be attacked, but if they are, they are seen justified in retaliating strongly.

The cultural prohibition against aggressive displays on the part of females seems to affect researchers who study aggression. In a recent analysis of sex bias in experimental design, McKenna and Kessler (1974) report a disproportionate number of male-only experiments on the topic of aggression. Also, when female subjects are used in studies of aggression, the independent variable rarely involves the active treatment or arousal of the subject and the dependent measure is likely to be a paper-and-pencil rating of aggressive feelings rather than an overt behavior such as administering shock.

---

[5]As Unger (in press) has recently observed, care must be exercised in generalizing the observation that females are less likely to be victims of aggression to situations outside the experimental laboratory. Women are frequently the victims of rape.

The fact that sex differences in aggression (1) have been observed across cultures, (2) appear at an early age, (3) are found among higher primates, and (4) are subject to the influence of sex hormones has given rise to the contention that they are biologically based (Maccoby & Jacklin, 1974). Evidence that males are more aggressive than females has been obtained in several cross-cultural studies (Omark, Omark, & Edelman, 1974; Whiting & Edwards, 1973). Furthermore, sex differences in aggression are found as early as the age of 2, presumably before the time when socialization pressures should have a differential impact on males and females.

The observed sex differences in human aggression are paralleled among higher animals. Male monkeys and apes are more aggressive than females; they aggress against each other and rarely against females. As we noted in Chapter Two, testosterone treatment of fetal or newborn animals masculinizes them and increases their aggression. Edwards (1969) found that the administration of testosterone to newborn female rodents increased their fighting in adulthood. Rose, Holaday, and Bernstein (1971) report that more-aggressive male monkeys tend to have higher levels of testosterone than their less-aggressive male cagemates, suggesting that hormone levels affect behavior. However, in a subsequent study, Rose, Gordon, and Bernstein (1972) found that placing a low dominant male monkey in a cage with females over whom he could dominate and with whom he engaged in sexual activity resulted in an increase in testosterone level. These results suggest that behavior may affect hormones. It has been found that, after an animal is defeated in a fight, his testosterone level decreases. Similarly, repeated defeats have been shown to reduce the fighting behavior of strains of laboratory animals bred to be aggressive, whereas submissive animals can be made somewhat more aggressive through combat victories (Ginzberg & Allee, 1942; Lagerspitz, 1964, 1969). Unfortunately, measures of testosterone levels were not obtained in these latter studies.

Several recent correlational studies have looked at the relationship between aggression and hostility and level and production of testosterone among men. Persky, Smith, and Basu (1971) found a correlation between testosterone production and measures of aggression and hostility among human males. However, their findings held only for young men, who produce more testosterone than older men. When Kreuz and Rose (1972) measured the plasma testosterone of prison inmates, they failed to obtain a correlation between verbal aggression and fighting in prison, although the men with higher testosterone levels had committed more violent and aggressive crimes during adolescence.

The administration of female sex hormones decreases aggressive behavior among male animals but not among females (Bronson & Dejardins, 1968; Levine & Mullins, 1964). In one study, Work and Rogers (1972) administered estrogen to male rats who were dominant over their cagemates. Following treatment, the previously dominant males lost their position in the social hierarchy. However, they did regain it after the treatment was terminated.

Aggression among animals appears to be influenced by sex hormones. Whether sex differences in human aggression are biologically based is difficult to determine. Biological factors may indeed predispose the human male to respond aggressively, as Maccoby and Jacklin suggest. However, human behavior is influenced to a great extent by learning; whether aggression will be displayed depends on social circumstances and cultural values (Bandura, 1973).

Passivity, Dependency, and Compliance

Many of the empirical attempts to specify behavioral differences between girls and boys reflect commonly held stereotypic beliefs about women and men. According to the stereotype, women are (or should be) more passive, dependent, and compliant than men. It was assumed that the origins of sex differences in adult behavior reflect biological predispositions or differences in the early socialization experiences of girls and boys. Although early studies of sex differences in children appeared to confirm hypotheses based on these stereotypes (Kagan, 1964; Oetzel, 1966; Tyler, 1965), the results of recent studies have not consistently supported the view that females are more passive, dependent, or compliant than males.

Passivity

Psychoanalytic theories of personality development have tended to view femininity and passivity as synonymous. According to Freud (1933), the origins of passivity in women were the natural result of the receptive (and masochistic) nature of female sexuality. Helene Deutsch (1944, 1945) expanded the Freudian analysis of feminine development. Her views were presented in a two-volume work entitled *The Psychology of Women,* published over 30 years ago. These volumes represent the first comprehensive attempt to address the topic of women from a psychological perspective.

Deutsch saw the transition from an active, masculine sexual orientation to a feminine, passive one as essential to the development of mature female sexuality. She believed, as did Freud (1933), that the clitoris was the primary focus of sexual gratification for girls in the early stages of psychosexual development but that sexual maturity involved shifting this focus from the active (male) clitoris to the passive (female) vagina. To achieve sexual maturity a woman had to accept the passive sexual role dictated by her "inferior" anatomy. As we shall see in Chapter Eight, recent evidence suggests that the sexual passivity of females, assumed by psychoanalytic theorists to be biologically based, is the result of cultural conditioning.

If, as psychoanalytic theory suggests, "anatomy is destiny" and female passivity is biologically based, it is reasonable to expect some evidence of sex differences in the activity rates of infants. The results of several studies have been interpreted to suggest that boys are more motorically active than girls (Bell, 1960; Knof, 1946; Lewis, Myers, Kagan, & Grossberg, 1963). However, as Maccoby (1972) has pointed out, in two of these investigations (Knof, 1946; Lewis et al., 1963) sex differences in motoric activity did not reach statistical significance, and in the third (Bell, 1960) the suggestion that girls might be less active than boys was speculative, since only male infants were studied. The results of recent attempts to document sex differences in infant activity rates have been inconclusive (Bell, Weller, & Waldrop, 1971; Korner, 1969; Krieger, 1976; Moss, 1967; Moss & Robson, 1970).

The majority of studies of preschool children have failed to obtain consistent differences in the activity levels of boys and girls (Maccoby & Jacklin, 1974), although it is true that, when sex differences in activity rates are reported, they tend to favor boys. The most consistent evidence for sex differences in activity rates comes from studies of older children that rely on teacher ratings rather than on direct behavioral observations and the results of which may have been influenced by the teachers' stereotypic expectations. When passivity is operationally defined in terms of the motoric activity of children, consistent sex differences are not obtained. Attempts to demonstrate sex differences in passivity by other measures, such as timidity or the tendency to withdraw under conditions of stress, have been no more successful (Maccoby & Jacklin, 1974).

Of course, motoric activity and timidity are not the only ways to measure passivity. As we have seen, the origins of passivity in females cannot be traced to sex differences in the activity rates of children. However, if passivity is defined as the lack of assertiveness, the results of a number of studies of adult behavior do provide evidence that women are less likely than men to assert themselves, particularly in the presence of males. For example, in mixed-sex group situations women are less likely than men of comparable ability to influence group processes (Wahram & Pugh, 1974). Like low-status males in single-sex groups, women in mixed-sex groups talk less (Alkire, Collum, Kaswan, & Love, 1968), neither initiating nor receiving as much interaction as men (Aries, 1974). Since the frequency of initiation and reception of group interaction is related to the assumption of leadership, men are more likely than women to emerge as group leaders (Strodtbeck, James, & Hawkins, 1957).

Megargee (1969) found that women were reluctant to assume leadership positions, particularly when their subordinates were male. When women with a high need for dominance were paired with other women low in dominance, they assumed the leadership role. However, high-dominance women deferred to males, even to those males who were low in dominance. These results indicate that females are not necessarily more passive (or submissive) than males but that their behavior is more likely to be influenced by the sex of the people with whom they interact. As Bardwick (1971) suggests, passivity may be defined in a variety of ways. It may be used to refer to sexual receptivity during intercourse, in which case it may be accurate to characterize females as relatively more passive than males, in the sense that they are the recipients of penile penetration. Passivity has also been used to refer to the desire to be dominated by others and as a manipulative tactic used to force others to act (passive aggression).

Bardwick (1971) offers a more positive and psychodynamic definition of female passivity. In her view, "passivity, in the sense of indrawing, of elaborating a rich, empathetic, intuitive, inner life—in contrast with activity directed outward—may be a necessary part of the personality equipment of healthy women" (Bardwick, 1971, p. 125). Her suggestion is provocative but remains speculative in the absence of empirical research. Viewing passivity as a valued female attribute is consistent with the widely held stereotype of womanhood. It is also consistent with the definition of female mental health endorsed by many therapists (Kirsch, 1974). However, displays of extreme passivity among either women or men are usually indicative of pathology.

If, as psychoanalytic theory suggests, passivity is a feminine trait, it is difficult to explain why females fail to display this trait in the presence of other females. And, if passivity is indicative of mental health, it is difficult to explain why it is sex specific.

Passivity has been defined and measured in a variety of ways. However, the contention that females are consistently more passive than males has proved difficult to substantiate even within studies that have used the same definition and similar measures.

Dependency

Dependency is another attribute commonly assumed to differentiate between the sexes. When a child is born, he or she is dependent on others for survival. However, as commonly used in the psychological literature, the term *dependency* refers to "a class of behavior that maintains contact between a child and one or more other individuals and elicits reciprocal attentive and nurturant behavior from these individuals (Maccoby & Masters, 1970). Given this definition, dependency can be measured in a variety of ways, including clinging, touching, proximity seeking, and social responsiveness in relation to either parents and other adults or peers (Maccoby & Jacklin, 1974).

Several comprehensive reviews of the literature published in the 1960s supported the commonly held assumption that females are more dependent than males (Garai & Scheinfeld, 1968; Kagan, 1964; Oetzel, 1966; Tyler, 1965). For example, Oetzel (1966) concluded that, after the age of 6, girls consistently exhibit greater dependency than boys. However, most of the studies on which this conclusion was based relied on general measures of dependency that were derived by combining a variety of performance scores into a single "dependency" measure.

Perhaps the most frequently cited finding in support of the contention that females are more dependent than males is contained in the results of a longitudinal study by Kagan and Moss (1962). Of all the measures taken during the course of their 25-year study, female scores on dependency were the most stable; that is, girls who were dependent in childhood grew up to become dependent women. Parallel correlations were not obtained for boys, who tend to become more independent as they grow older. You may recall from our discussion in Chapter Three that young boys are more likely than young girls to be discouraged for displaying behavior considered to be sex-inappropriate, and dependency is not an appropriate masculine characteristic.

It has been suggested that the origins of female dependency lie in the close contact girls have with their mothers (Garai & Scheinfeld, 1968). Under the age of 3, however, little girls do not appear to be any more likely than little boys to cling to their mothers or to remain close to them (Maccoby & Jacklin, 1974). As a matter of fact, in several studies of young children's resistance to separation, boys were found to exhibit more distress than girls (Corter, Rheingold, & Eckerman, 1972; Maccoby & Jacklin, 1974). Young children of both sexes often seek close contact with parents or other adults in unfamiliar situations; the need to seek reassurance in the face of uncertainty is not sex-specific. Although little girls are no more likely than boys to be positively reinforced for displays of dependency, parents may encourage boys to confront uncertain situations directly.

Since it has been suggested that the tendency of girls to maintain close ties with their families is indicative of their greater dependency, it should be pointed out that boys form close ties with same-sex peers (Hollander & Marcia, 1970) and therefore that it is inaccurate to characterize girls as more dependent on others than boys.

Like passivity, dependency may be expressed in a variety of ways. Bardwick (1971) distinguishes among three types: instrumental, emotional, and aggressive. Instrumental dependency is manifested in objective attempts to seek help. Reviewing the literature on sex differences in achievement motivation among children, Stein and Bailey (1973) cite several studies in which girls were more likely than boys to seek help and approval from adults. However, in one study of nursery school children, Serbin, O'Leary, Kent, & Tonick (1973) found no differences in the frequency with which boys and girls sought attention, but they found that the teachers were more likely to respond to boys' than to girls' requests for attention. This finding may be interpreted as an attempt on the part of the teacher to exert more control over the behavior of boys than over the behavior of girls (Cherry, 1975). In a recent study of maternal help giving, Rothbart and Rothbart (1976) found no differences in mothers' spontaneous offers of help to their daughters and to their sons. However, mothers were more likely to respond to their daughters' requests for help than to their sons'. This may indicate that mothers are more concerned about fostering the independence of boys than about fostering the independence of girls.

The results of several studies indicate that adults (particularly men) are more likely to offer aid at the request of a woman than at the request of a man (Gruder & Cook, 1971; Hendricks, Cook, & Crano, 1973; Pomazal & Clore, 1973); overall, however, adults tend to be more responsive to requests for help from members of the opposite sex (Deaux, 1976).

According to Bardwick (1971), emotional dependence is manifested when the goal of the individual is to obtain comfort, affection, and support.

In her view, girls are more likely than boys to be emotionally dependent on others (particularly men). There is some evidence to suggest that girls are more concerned about social approval than boys (Hoffman, 1972), and the results of several studies indicate that in comparison to boys girls are more likely to display emotional dependence (McCandless, Bilous, & Bennett, 1962; Sears, Maccoby, & Levin, 1957).

Although parents do not encourage children of either sex to be dependent, they tend to be more tolerant of dependent behavior on the part of their daughters than on the part of their sons (Hoffman, 1972). Girls and women are expected to be more dependent than boys and men; so much so, that women who deviate from this expectation may be labeled emotionally disturbed (Chesler, 1972; Feinblatt & Gold, 1976). In a recent study, Costrich and her colleagues found that passive-dependent women were perceived as significantly better adjusted than aggressive-assertive women and that the reverse was true of men (Costrich, Feinstein, Kidder, Marecek, & Pascale, 1975).

To the extent that females are expected to be more dependent than males, they may feel freer to express their emotional dependence directly by crying or asking for help. Indeed, they may have to be direct in order to obtain a response; males, on the other hand, often receive support (particularly from females) without asking. Women are supposed to be more sensitive to and aware of the needs of others than men. Many wives pride themselves in their ability to detect and respond appropriately to subtle variations in their husbands' moods.[6]

The fact that women are able to recognize and articulate their needs for emotional support may be beneficial to their psychological adjustment. In Bardwick's view, healthy interdependence has its origins in "the ability to trust and the confidence that allows one to permit another to come close, to be dependent, to love, and even to reject" (Bardwick, 1971, p. 115). On the other hand, extreme dependence on others results in an unhealthy sense of vulnerability.

Some women may behave dependently in an attempt to protect themselves from feeling vulnerable. Bardwick (1971) refers to this type of behavior as aggressive dependence, or the "tyranny of the weak." As such, it may represent a learned tactic to exert influence over others. The request that one's husband take out the garbage because "it's too heavy" may be interpreted as evidence for dependency, although it is also a socially acceptable excuse for avoiding a relatively unpleasant task. Female roommates do not find this kind of excuse acceptable, nor do women use tears on one another in order to get their way. The display of "dependent" behaviors in the presence of males may be rewarding, but for many females the use of such tactics appears to be situationally determined.

According to the traditional stereotype, women are supposed to be

[6]People do need people. However, it is not considered sex-role appropriate for men to acknowledge their needs for comfort and support. The fact that single men are more likely than married men to experience emotional difficulties suggests that the availability of a concerned other is as important (if not more important) to men as to women.

more passive and dependent than men. Even therapists define mature, healthy women as less active and independent than men (Broverman, Broverman, Clarkson, Rosenkrantz, & Vogel, 1970). Of course, extreme dependency is not a valued attribute in either women or men (Cohen, 1966). The results of several recent studies by Bem (1975, 1976) suggest that the behavior of women whose sex descriptions reflect the traditional feminine stereotypes is restricted. Spence, Helmreich, and Stapp (1975) found that the self-esteem scores of such women are low.

The distinction Bardwick draws among the ways in which psychological dependence may be expressed is interesting, but empirical research is necessary to assess the validity of her observations. As we have seen, the hypothesis that females are consistently more dependent than males has proved difficult to substantiate although, when women do behave dependently, they may be less likely to be punished than men (Costrich et al., 1975).

Compliance

To the extent that females are more dependent than males, it appears reasonable to anticipate that they are also more likely to comply with the demands of others. The results of several studies of preschool-age children do suggest that girls are more responsive to parental requests than boys (Minton, Kagan, & Levine, 1971; Serbin, et al., 1973; Whiting & Edwards, 1973).

For example, Minton and his colleagues found that girls responded more quickly than boys when admonished by their mothers. In two studies (Stouwie, 1971, 1972), girls were more likely than boys to comply with the request of an adult experimenter not to play with toys. On the other hand, no consistent differences have been obtained in studies investigating the tendency of girls and boys to comply with the wishes of other children (Maccoby & Jacklin, 1974).

Comparative data on the willingness of college students to participate in psychological research reveal that generally females are more likely to volunteer than males (Rosenthal & Rosnow, 1975). It should be kept in mind, though, that both the type of study (stressful versus nonstressful) and the incentives offered (pay versus "love of science") for participating in the research affect sex differences in volunteer rates. Women are less likely than men to volunteer for studies involving physical or emotional stress but more likely than men to agree to participate for pay. In other words, the tendency of adult females to comply with the requests of others is influenced by the nature of the request and the reinforcements offered. Women do not comply automatically.

Nor are they consistently more likely than men to behave cooperatively (Davis, Laughlin, & Komorita, 1976; Maccoby & Jacklin, 1974). In two laboratory studies comparing the play behavior of same-sex and mixed-sex pairs, females playing against females were found to be more competitive than males playing against males (Komorita, 1965; Rapaport & Chammah, 1965). In a more recent study, Hottes and Kahn (1974) found that male pairs were more likely to play opportunistically (that is, cooperate whenever that would maximize their rewards) whereas female pairs tended to play defensively (that is, minimize their opponents' rewards even at a loss to themselves). In mixed-sex pairs, the play behavior of females was influenced by the attractiveness of their partners (they were more cooperative when playing against a male they viewed as attractive). The attractiveness of their partners did not influence men's behavior.

Peplau (1976) found that, when traditionally oriented females were asked to "play" against their boyfriends on an anagram task, they performed less well than when they joined their boyfriends in an attempt to "beat" another couple. In contrast, the sex of the competitor had little effect on the competitive behavior of either males or nontraditionally oriented females. As we shall see in the next chapter, for females the decision to compete depends in part on their definition of the female role.

Social Orientation, Suggestibility, and Self-Esteem

As we have seen, the evidence for psychological sex differences in passivity, dependence, and compliance is not compelling. Attempts to demonstrate differences in these areas are subject to numerous definitional and methodological criticisms. There are many other areas in which postulated differences between the sexes have not been confirmed. We will briefly mention three: social orientation, suggestibility, and self-esteem.

Social Orientation

Females are generally believed to be more socially oriented than males. Thus, the report that female infants spent more time looking at social stimuli (faces) than male infants (Lewis, Kagan, & Kalafat, 1966) was readily accepted and led to the suggestion that the origin of adult females' sociability lay in their early interest in people, as opposed to objects (Garai & Scheinfeld, 1968). The hypothesis that early perceptual differences between the sexes account for their later behavioral orientation is interesting.

However, the results of recent research fail to support the contention that female infants are more visually responsive to social stimuli than males (Maccoby & Jacklin, 1974; Shepard & Peterson, 1973; Krieger, 1976). In a recent review of the literature on neonatal sex differences, Krieger (1976) tabulated the results of studies that had appeared in five major developmental journals between the years 1970 and 1974. Of 16 studies comparing the visual orientation of girls and boys only 2 obtained significant results (favoring girls). In 7 of the 26 studies in which sex differences in response to nonsocial stimuli were compared, male infants were more responsive than females. However, no sex differences were obtained in 16 of the studies. Thus, the hypothesis that female neonates are more socially oriented than males has proved difficult to substantiate. Nor is there any evidence that as infants males are more oriented toward visual stimuli and females toward auditory stimuli (Maccoby & Jacklin, 1974).

Suggestibility

As we have seen, although little girls are more likely than boys to comply with the requests of parents and other adults, in adulthood sex differences in compliance appear to be situation-specific. Moreover, the suggestion that females are more easily influenced than males has not been substantiated empirically.

The topic of attitude change has been of interest to social psychologists for many years. In 1959 Janis and Field concluded that, after a persuasive communication, the attitudes of females were less resistant to change than those of males. The fact that the results of several conformity studies indicated that females were more likely than males to yield to group opinion (even when it was objectively incorrect)[7] appeared to provide additional support for the contention that females were more suggestible. However, the situations used to demonstrate conformity either relied on visual-spatial skills, in which males excel (for example, the Asch situation described in Footnote 7), or were extremely ambiguous (as in the autokinetic effect also described in Footnote 7). In both situations males may have been more confident of their opinion and thus better able to withstand group pressure to conform.

Confidence in one's own judgment does affect susceptibility to social influence. As we shall see in Chapter Five, females are generally less confident in their ability than males. However, when the issue is clearly female-appropriate, women are less likely to conform than men, and when it is neutral, no sex differences are obtained (Sistrunk & McDavid, 1971). Thus, females appear to be more easily influenced than males only under specific conditions.

When spontaneous imitation of others (modeling) is used as a measure of suggestibility, no sex differences are obtained. Boys and girls are equally likely (or unlikely) to imitate models, depending on the model's characteristics (see Chapter Three).

Self-Esteem

As we shall see in Chapter Six, both males and females assign greater value to stereotypically masculine traits (independence, competence, and assertiveness) than to stereotypically feminine ones (warmth, expressiveness, and concern for others). This finding, in conjunction with the observation that the ascribed status of women is lower than that of men, has led a number of researchers to suggest that women have lower self-esteem than men. However, there is little evidence to suggest that females score lower

[7]In the Asch conformity paradigm, subjects are asked to indicate which of two lines is longer. Confederates of the experimenter consistently select the shorter line as "correct," and conformity is measured in terms of the naive subject's tendency to yield (publicly) to group pressure in the face of an objective fact. The autokinetic effect (Sherif, 1935) is another, more ambiguous situation used to study conformity. The autokinetic effect refers to the illusion that a stationary "pinprick" of light is moving in an otherwise dark room. In this situation, opinion or preference for one's estimate of movement has no basis in objective fact.

than males on general measures of self-esteem (Maccoby & Jacklin, 1974), although the basis of positive self-esteem among women may be different from that among men.

Despite the fact that women are not consistently more dependent and passive than men, they do seem to rely more heavily on their ability to maintain good social relationships as a primary means of determining their self-worth (Carlson, 1965, 1971). In contrast, males tend to measure their value in terms of their objective accomplishments. Thus, on measures of self-esteem that tap both interpersonal skills and mastery over the environment, female and male subjects score higher on those items most central to their ego concerns. As a result, no significant differences in self-esteem scores between the sexes are obtained.

The fact that females are more likely than males to obtain high self-esteem scores on the basis of social rather than personal orientations does not imply that males are not affected by the reactions of others. Kipnis (1974) has recently argued that males, who rely on the approval of their same-sex peers as a means of evaluating their performance, are more other-directed than females. Interestingly, in one study of sex differences in social self-esteem, Lundgren and Schaub (1974) found that, when adults of both sexes evaluated their self-worth, they were influenced by their perceptions of how they were viewed by others (particularly their families). However, the status (prestige) of those others was more important to males, whereas intimacy was more important to females.

The results of empirical research that support the null hypothesis (that is, the hypothesis that there are no significant differences between the sexes) are rarely published. As a result, the literature on sex differences is much more extensive than the literature on sex similarities. Traditionally, reports of psychological sex differences were readily accepted if they conformed to stereotypically defined expectations. And yet, as we have seen, the evidence for sex similarities in infants and young children on a number of psychological dimensions is much stronger than the evidence for differences. Furthermore, in two (verbal ability and mathematical ability) of the four areas in which sex differences appear to be relatively well established in childhood and early adolescence, there is little evidence to suggest that these differences are biologically based. Most behavioral differences between women and men and between girls and boys appear to be the result of the socialization experiences to which the individuals are subjected and are determined to a large extent by situational factors.

Summary

Until recently it was widely assumed that the obvious and universal biological differences between females and males were paralleled by clearly delineated psychological differences. However, under closer scrutiny a number of the postulated differences between males and females have been identified as social myths rather than verifiable facts. Others remain untested assumptions. In their extensive review of the literature on psychological sex differences, Maccoby and Jacklin (1974) conclude that there are only four areas of study in which the performance of females and males differ consistently: verbal ability, visual-spatial ability, mathematical ability, and aggression. It is, however, important to note that few behaviors are exclusively male or exclusively female.

While recent studies have failed to obtain sex differences in the language abilities of preschool and early-school boys and girls, researchers have generally reported that, by the fifth or sixth grade, girls outperform boys. Boys, on the other hand, have been found to surpass girls in performance of tasks measuring visual-spatial ability. Consistent sex differences are not obtained until midadolescence. The evidence bearing on the visual-spatial superiority of males appears to suggest that visual-spatial performance is both physiologically and culturally determined; that is, the expression of the X-linked trait for visual-spatial ability may be both contingent on the presence of testosterone and enhanced by the sex typing of activities that promote the acquisition of this skill. Similar explanations have been proposed to account for the finding that males are more aggressive than females. For example, a link between testosterone production in men and the expression of aggression has been postulated. However, the complex social and cultural influences on human behavior play a large role in determining where, when, and if aggressive behavior will be displayed.

Researchers have found evidence suggesting sex differences in verbal abilities, visual-spatial abilities, and aggression, although the sources of these differences have not been defined. On the other hand, recent studies have not consistently supported the stereotypic assumption that females are more passive, dependent, and compliant than males. Similarly, hypothesized sex differences in social orientation, suggestibility, and self-esteem have not been persuasively demonstrated. Most researchers have not been able to support the stereotypic expectation of pervasive sex differences, nor has the contention that psychological sex differences are biologically based received much support.

Chapter Five

Female Achievement

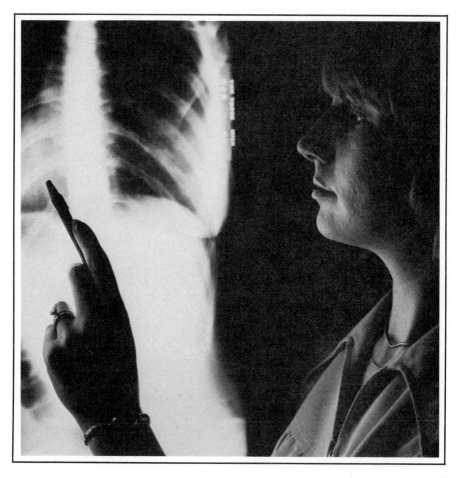

As we grow older, one of the recurring questions most of us seek to answer is "What shall I do with my life?" This quest begins when we are very young. Adults are fond of asking children "What do you want to be when you grow up?" What they really want to know is "What will you achieve?" When boys express the desire to be doctors or lawyers or astronauts, it is assumed that setting such goals and attempting to move toward them reflect a concern with achievement and success in the economic marketplace. Girls also set goals, but their goals are usually more "modest"; they want to be nurses or teachers or mommies. Because success as a teacher or nurse is not regarded as comparable to success as a doctor or attorney, it has been easy to conclude that girls and women are not as interested in achieving as boys and men.

American society emphasizes striving, accomplishment, and success. Women constitute over 50% of the population. Why have they failed to pursue occupational goals that require intellectual competence and leadership potential, which are the earmarks of American success?

Until recently it was generally agreed that discriminatory hiring practices were responsible for the underrepresentation of women in positions of power and prestige. But times are changing. The federal Pay Act of 1963 and Title VII of the federal Civil Rights Act of 1964 have provided women with increased opportunities for occupational advancement. Yet, this increase in opportunity has been accompanied by a decline in the proportion of women seeking every level of higher education (Horner, 1972).

In 1940 45% of the technical and professional positions in this country were held by women; by 1968 the proportion of women in technical and professional occupations had declined to 35%. Even among those women who do hold professional-level jobs, most are employed in fields traditionally considered appropriate for the female sex role. For example, 97% of all registered nurses, 92% of all dieticians, 85% of all elementary school teachers, and 70% of all health technicians are women. In contrast, only 2% of the engineers, 5% of the attorneys, and 9% of the physicians in this country are women (U. S. Department of Commerce, 1973).

A variety of explanations have been proposed to account for women's failure to set and strive for those goals that are inherent in the American dream of individual success. In this chapter we will consider three general approaches to understanding why women are less likely to achieve than men: *expectancy-value theory*, which emphasizes sex differences in achievement motivation; *attribution theory*, which focuses on the role of cognition in determining performance; and explanations stressing *sex differ-*

ences in socialization, which focus on the conflict between achievement and affiliation. Since the majority of research in this area has been based on the expectancy-value theory, let us begin by outlining this theory.

Expectancy-Value Theory

The most widely known theory of achievement motivation was originally proposed by McClelland, Atkinson, Clark, and Lowell in 1953. The theory assumes that there are three primary determinants of achievement behavior: the tendency to achieve success, the tendency to avoid failure, and extrinsic motivation. The interaction of these three variables determines the direction, magnitude, and persistence of goal-oriented performance.

The *tendency to achieve success* (T_s) is itself comprised of three factors. The first of these, the motive to achieve success (M_s), is regarded as a relatively general (situation-free), stable, and enduring personality characteristic. It is acquired early in life and can be aroused in situations in which the person expects that performance will be evaluated against some standard of excellence. Thus, individuals who are high in the motive to achieve success may be expected to set high goals for their own performance in many situations. Such people are concerned not only about graduating cum laude but about winning a varsity letter and throwing the best party of the year as well.

The motive to achieve is modified by two situational factors: P_s (the expectancy, or probability, of success on a given task) and I_s (the incentive value associated with that success). According to the expectancy-value theory, the tendency to achieve success is the product of the motive to achieve times the expectancy of success times the incentive value associated with success $(T_s = M_s \times P_s \times I_s)$.

It is an everyday experience that goals that are difficult to achieve are valued more than those that are easily attained. For example, getting an A in an easy course is less satisfying than getting an A in a difficult one. It has been postulated that the strength of the incentive value associated with a given goal is directly related to the difficulty of the task. Because it is assumed that achieving success on a difficult task is more attractive to most people than achieving success on an easy one, expectancy for success and the incentive value associated with success are defined reciprocally: $I_s = 1 - P_s$; that is, the incentive value of success on a given task increases as the probability of success on that task decreases. As a result, the tendency to achieve success is greatest when the task is of intermediate difficulty— that is, when the values of both P_s and I_s are near .5 and the product of these two factors is of maximum numerical value.

As the theory predicts, when individuals high in the motive to achieve are asked to select a task from among several activities of varying difficulty, they prefer tasks that are moderately difficult (Atkinson & Litwin, 1960; Litwin, 1958; McClelland, 1958). Confronted with extremely difficult tasks, these same individuals perceive the probability of success as low; as a result, their tendency to achieve such tasks decreases. In sum, the individual who is motivated to achieve may be characterized as one who has developed an internal standard of excellence, is independent and persistent, and sets realistic goals.

Like the tendency to achieve success, the *tendency to avoid failure* (T_{-f}) is the product of the motive to avoid failure (M_{af}) times the expectancy of failure (P_f) times the negative incentive value associated with the consequences of failing (I_f): $T_{-f} = M_{af} \times P_f \times I_f$. The motive to avoid failure predisposes the individual to avoid achievement-related situations in which her or his performance is likely to be evaluated.

According to Atkinson (1966), "The implications concerning the arousal of the tendency to avoid failure are just the same as those . . . for the tendency to approach success, but the behavioral implications are just the opposite" (p. 246). In other words, a strong tendency to avoid failure inhibits action; a strong tendency to achieve success stimulates activity. Because the effects of these two tendencies $(T_s$ and $T_{-f})$ are diametrically opposed, the tendency to avoid failure may suppress the tendency to achieve success.

The third determinant of achievement behavior is *extrinsic motivation* (T_{ext}). Extrinsic motivation refers to the individual's expectations that goals not related to achievement in a particular situation, such as power or money or social approval, will be satisfied by attaining a given goal.

In summary, the expectancy-value theory of achievement motivation defines achievement-oriented behavior (T_a) as the sum of the tendency to approach success (T_s), the tendency to avoid failure (T_{-f}), and extrinsic motivation (T_{ext}). The equation may be written as $T_a = T_s + T_{-f} + T_{ext}$. The sum of these three factors will determine whether an individual will strive for success in a situation in which his or her performance will be evaluated and the results of that evaluation made available.

Sex Differences in Achievement Motivation and Performance

Although the situational determinants of achievement behavior (expectancy of success and incentive value of success) are considered to be of theoretical importance, most of the research based on this theory has focused on the motivational component of the equation. The emphasis on the motivational explanation for differences in achievement is based on the assumption that individual differences in performance reflect differences in stable personality dispositions.

Assessing the motive to achieve. The strength of the achievement motive is measured by asking people to write stories about a series of pictures. Subjects are shown a picture and given four minutes to write a story in answer to the questions: What is happening? Who are the persons? What led up to this situation? What is being thought? What will happen? How will it end? (Atkinson, 1958, Appendix III). The stories are scored for the number of achievement-related ideas or themes (called *achievement imagery*) that they contain. Usually each subject is shown three or four different pictures to ensure an adequate sample of fantasy responses. Because the pictures provide a minimum of structure to the situations portrayed, it is assumed that the subjects' responses represent the projection of their own needs and motives.

The use of projective measures to assess individual differences in motivation is based on Freud's suggestion that those personal dispositions of which people are not aware may be more readily expressed in ambiguous contexts. On the assumption that projection is facilitated when the individual can identify with the major character, pictures in which the central figure is of the same sex as the subject are generally used. Also, the activities portrayed in different pictures are varied in order to increase the chances that the subject will find some of them personally meaningful. As we shall see, both the sex of the character and the context depicted in the cues used to elicit achievement motivation affect subjects' responses.

A number of studies have compared achievement-motivation scores obtained under instructions stressing competence and mastery with those obtained under neutral or relaxed conditions. When men are exposed before the test to instructions aimed at arousing their achievement concerns, their achievement-motivation scores increase. Under relaxed conditions, women's achievement-need scores are higher than men's, but under arousal conditions women's scores do not increase (Veroff, Wilcox, & Atkinson, 1953). The fact that instructions intended to arouse the motive to achieve do not work for female subjects has been interpreted as evidence that women are not as motivated to achieve as men.

The one exception to this finding was obtained by Angelini (1958) in a sample of Brazilian college women. Because this finding was consistent with other attempts to increase women's achievement-motivation scores by emphasizing the importance of "intellectual and leadership" ability, it was suggested that the women in Angelini's sample were not representative of the female population (Atkinson, 1958). Few women in Brazil are given the opportunity to go to college, and those who do must place special emphasis on intellectual accomplishment.

Intrigued by the suggestion that only highly competitive women respond to attempts to arouse achievement motivation (Angelini, 1958; Field, 1953), Lesser, Krawitz, and Packard (1963) undertook a study of achievement motivation among a select group of high school students. They drew their sample from Hunter High School for girls in New York City. The atmosphere of the school is intensely competitive, and a great deal of emphasis is placed on academic achievement. But even at Hunter the overall effect of the attempt to arouse females' achievement motivation was not successful. One explanation for the results was that the arousal instructions used in the study stressed intelligence and leadership ability—two characteristics that are regarded as stereotypically masculine and that females do not find personally meaningful or arousing.

Some support for this interpretation has been obtained in several studies that employed arousal instructions emphasizing social acceptance and interpersonal skills. For example, Field (1953) found that college women's achievement-motivation scores increased when they were provided with feedback indicating that their performance was socially appropriate. Similarly, French and Lesser (1964) found that arousal instructions stressing the importance of success in traditionally feminine areas, such as family management and social skills, increased the achievement-motivation scores and task performance of college women. However, Friedrich's (1976) recent attempt to increase the achievement-motivation scores of female undergraduates at Cornell University by using (feminine) value-appropriate arousal instructions was unsuccessful.

The achievement-motivation scores of females are affected not only by the content of arousal instructions but also by the sex of the central character depicted in the cue. In the Hunter High School study, Lesser and his colleagues (Lesser et al., 1963) used pictures of both male and female characters to elicit achievement imagery. On the basis of the girls' grades, they divided their sample into underachievers and achievers. They found that the achievers' motivation scores had increased under arousal instructions, but only in response to female cues. On the other hand, the scores of girls classified as underachievers had increased in response to the male cues under instructions stressing competence and mastery.

One interpretation for these findings suggests that, unlike men, who respond uniformly with achievement-related imagery to cues depicting male figures, females' scores are more dependent on the women's definitions of the female role. Achievers, who were presumably disposed to strive for excellence, identified with the female figures and projected their own motives onto the cue. Underachievers, who did not see achievement as relevant to the female role, failed to respond by increasing their achievement-imagery scores to pictures of females but did respond to male cues with increased imagery. Presumably, underachievers saw competitive success as compatible with the male role but did not find it personally meaningful.

A number of studies indicate that women attach higher value to performing well at tasks that are appropriate for the female role than at tasks requiring skills that are appropriate for the male role. Children from the 2nd through the 12th grade characterize verbal and artistic skills as feminine and athletic, mechanical, and spatial skills as masculine. Math is also considered masculine by adolescents, although not by younger children (Stein, 1971; Stein & Smithells, 1969). Consistently with the sex typing of certain skills, schoolgirls have higher standards for their own performance in English, verbal skills, social skills, and artistic competence than for their performance in natural sciences, athletics, and mechanical skills. The value attached to a given task is a good predictor of both achievement motivation and performance (Battle, 1965; Crandall, Katkovsky, & Preston, 1962; Stein, Pohly, & Mueller, 1971).

Early studies of achievement behavior showed that male subjects who obtained high scores on the projective measure of achievement motivation performed better on tasks such as anagram solutions and addition problems than subjects who scored low. Thus, it appeared that achievement behavior could be predicted accurately by knowing the level of an individual's motive to achieve.[1] However, subsequent work using female subjects failed to demonstrate the predicted relationship between achievement motivation and performance. We have already examined the evidence indicating that females' responses to the cues used to assess the achievement motive may vary as a result of the sex of character depicted in the cue and the conditions under which the motive is measured.

The sex-role appropriateness of the task used to measure behavior also affects females' actual performances. Milton (1958) conducted a series of experiments in which he varied the sex-role appropriateness of the context in which he presented a mathematical problem. Half the subjects were asked to divide a circle, the other half to divide a cake. Two samples of female college students scored higher on the feminine-context test; the reverse was true for males. When females are asked to achieve in traditionally masculine contexts, they may neither aspire to nor expect success.

You will recall that the expectancy, or subjective probability, of success is one situational determinant of the expectancy-value theory. Atkinson (1966) defined expectancy as the probability of reaching a given goal in a given situation at a given time. It has been demonstrated that expectations of success (or failure) affect people's behavior in achievement situations. Several studies show that people with high expectations of success actually perform better on tasks in which their success is evaluated by others (Battle, 1965; Feather, 1966). Research on sex differences in expectations of success indicates that, even when task difficulty is held constant, girls and women generally have lower expectations than boys and men. For example, Crandall (1969) reported that elementary school girls had lower initial expectancies of success than boys on tasks that involved estimating the number of blocks in constructions, solving jigsaw puzzles, and brain teasers. She obtained similar results for eighth graders on a digit-substitution task that was presented as a test of intellectual competence. These findings have been replicated numerous times using a variety of tasks and age groups (Montanelli & Hill, 1969; McMahan, 1971; Small, Nakamura, & Ruble, 1973).

Two studies compared the expectations of college men and women regarding final grades in a course. The initial expectancies reported by women were lower than those reported by men, despite the fact that women actually received higher grades than men (Crandall, 1969; Vaughter, Gubernick, Matassian, & Haslett, 1974). When independent measures of actual ability were taken into account, males tended to overestimate their future success in relation to their level of ability. In contrast, women tended to underestimate their performance, although overall women's expectancies were more accurate.

Many of the studies that have found sex differences in expectancies favoring males have used tasks that are novel (the subject has little or no previous experience with the task) or sex typed, so that success on the task

---

[1]Despite the fact that males' scores on fantasy-based measures of achievement motivation have been found to be related to performance, the magnitude of the correlations is generally low (.30 to .40) (Entwistle, 1972).

may be regarded as appropriate for the male sex role (Frieze, Fisher, McHugh, & Valle, 1975). When presumably neutral tasks, such as anagrams, are introduced as sex-linked, female subjects' expectancies of success are affected. For example, Deaux and Farris (1974) found that female college students expected to solve fewer anagrams than males when they were told that males typically do better on the task than females. No sex differences were obtained in expectancies of success on tasks characterized as feminine.

Apparently, women's estimates of the probability that they will be successful on a given task are affected not only by the difficulty of the task, as Atkinson (1966) maintained, but also by whether they see it as compatible with the culturally defined female role. It is difficult to determine whether women's tendency to express lower expectancies of success reflects an internalized belief that "girls are not as good as boys" or merely the endorsement of a culturally determined stereotype.

In a recent study, Stake (1976) found that both female and male subjects set higher goals for their own performance on a task when they were told that members of their own sex typically outperformed those of the opposite sex. However, when the performance goals of males and females were examined independently of the subjects' beliefs about sex-performance norms, no significant sex differences were obtained. Stake suggests that sex differences in goal setting (or expectancies) may reflect the cultural norm that calls for higher achievement among males than among females. Providing women with information that contradicts this norm may be an effective means to raise the level of the goals to which they aspire.

Assessing the tendency to avoid failure. Up to this point our discussion has focused on research related to sex differences in the expression of the tendency to achieve success. There is also some evidence to suggest that males and females differ in the tendency to avoid failure—a tendency that conflicts with and may inhibit achievement striving. According to Atkinson (1966), people are motivated to avoid failure because they are worried about the negative consequences associated with it. Presumably, individuals whose disposition to avoid failure is high feel that it is safer to avoid a task than to risk the shame of not succeeding.

Because fear of failure is based on concern about the consequences of failing, paper-and-pencil measures of test anxiety are usually used to assess the strength of the motive to avoid failure. The most popular measure is the Mandler-Sarason Test Anxiety Questionnaire, which asks subjects to indicate their feelings and attitudes toward examinations—for example, "How confident do you feel before you take a course examination?" (Mandler & Sarason, 1952). A high score on the scale is used as an indicator of high fear of failure, which would be expressed behaviorally by avoiding a task.

Females generally score higher than males on measures of test anxiety (Feld & Lewis, 1969; Hill & Sarason, 1966; Sarason, Lighthall, Davidson, Waite, & Ruebush, 1960; Wallach & Kogan, 1965). The difference in reported anxiety between females and males increases with age. One explanation for this difference is based on the observation that females are more willing to express emotions than are males. Thus, when asked about their reaction to tests, females are more willing to admit that they are anxious. A different interpretation has been proposed by Stein and Bailey (1973), who have suggested that the same cultural norm that permits females to express anxiety more readily may also lead them to experience it more intensely. As a result, females may never learn to cope with their anxiety as effectively as do males.

Whether the arena is the business world or the baseball diamond, men and boys are expected to rise to the challenge and play to win. When one competes, the possibility of failure is difficult to ignore. In this society males may be forced to develop appropriate methods to deal with failure-related anxiety. Females, who are not expected to compete successfully, may lack such crucial training. Consistent with this suggestion are the findings of Kagan and Moss (1962), who found that girls who in childhood were anxious about failing remained fearful into adulthood. No relationship was found between males' anxiety scores in childhood and a tendency to fear failure as adults. Perhaps the acquisition of coping mechanisms to deal with failure is responsible for the decreased anxiety scores of adult males.

Support for the suggestion that females protect themselves less well from failure than men can be found in several studies that compared the reactions of females and males who had experienced failure. Males tended to attribute the cause of their failure to some external source. Females, on the other hand, assumed personal responsibility for their lack of success. Using a scale to measure the extent to which a person accepts personal responsibility for academic achievement, Crandall, Katkovsky, and Crandall (1965) found that 11- to 17-year-old girls were more likely than boys of the same age to blame themselves for failing.

Mead (1949) has suggested that during childhood boys learn to anticipate the shame and emasculation of defeat. As a result, males may be more concerned than females with protecting themselves from public humiliation. One way to defend oneself from the negative reactions of others is to attribute failure or defeat to something or someone else—for example, blaming the "stupid" professor for not knowing a good paper when she or he sees one. Whereas males may be socialized to defend against assuming personal responsibility for failure, females are apparently socialized to not only accept it but also feel guilty about failing.

In many areas of interpersonal relationships in which women play a role, they are expected to assume the responsibility (and guilt) for failure even though they do not have complete control over the outcome. For example, society tolerates the young man who "sows wild oats"; however, if pregnancy results, "she" should have stopped or at least been more careful. Similarly, marriages fail because "wives let themselves go." Women's magazines abound with articles advising their readers how to keep their men alive longer by properly feeding and caring for them. The implicit suggestion that "his heart attack may be her fault" may indeed evoke feelings of guilt. On the other hand, rarely are a man's health and happiness attributed to his wife's "successful" care.

To the extent that females are more likely than males to be anxious about failing and to blame themselves and feel guilty when they do fail, they may hesitate to strive for success. One effective means of avoiding failure and the anxiety associated with it is to withdraw from situations in which the outcome (either success or failure) is uncertain. The results of several studies using male subjects suggest that individuals who have a high fear of failure seldom select career goals suited to their abilities (Mahone, 1960) and have lower levels of aspiration than individuals with low fear of failure (Burnstein, 1963; Littig, 1963; Rim, 1963). Unfortunately, there have been no studies comparing the extent to which males and females exhibit the tendency to avoid failure. Such research is necessary in order to test the validity of the hypothesis that women are more vulnerable than men to fear of failure. In the absence of comparative data, the suggestion that fear of failure may tend to inhibit women's achievement strivings must remain speculative.

The Tendency to Avoid Success

In the original formulation of the expectancy-value theory of achievement motivation, the motive to avoid failure was regarded as the primary source of achievement inhibition. However, nearly a decade ago Matina Horner acknowledged the possibility that negative consequences might be associated with success as well as with failure. Thus, she introduced an additional factor into the equation, a factor she called "the tendency to avoid success" (Horner, 1968).

The tendency to avoid success is a tendency that inhibits achievement-directed behavior and that stems from concerns about the negative consequences of succeeding. As in the case of the other achievement-related tendencies, the strength of the tendency to avoid success is a result of the interaction of the motive to avoid success (M_{-s}), the incentive value associated with success (I_{-s}), and the expectancy of success (P_{-s}). Thus, Horner (1968) extended the original expectancy-value equation to include the tendency to avoid success, so that $T_a = (T_s - T_{-f}) - T_{-s} + T_{ext}$.

In Horner's view, the motive to avoid success is aroused only in situations in which the individual feels anxious about competitiveness and its aggressive overtones. Under such conditions, the negative value of the inhibitory tendency is high and will act against the positive tendency to achieve; the result is performance inhibition. Although fear of success was not postulated as a female-specific motive, Horner suggested that women are more likely than men to associate negative consequences with success; that is, a woman whose achievement motivation is high may refrain from expressing her motivation by striving for success if she perceives the negative consequences associated with success as outweighing the positive ones.

For example, a bright young woman who aspires to be an attorney may settle for a career as a legal secretary because she fears that success as an attorney will reduce her chances to be seen as a desirable woman and wife.

According to Horner, "Many achievement-oriented women, especially those high in the motive to avoid success, when faced with the conflict between their feminine image and developing their abilities and interests, compromise by disguising their ability and abdicating from competition in the outside world" (Horner, 1968, p. 64). It is assumed that the strength of the negative incentive associated with success will be strongest for women in achievement situations in which the emphasis is on competitive success, particularly if the competition is against males.

In her initial study, Horner (1968) used a projective test to measure the motive to avoid success. Subjects' written responses to the verbal cue "After first-term finals, Anne finds herself at the top of her medical school class" were analyzed for the presence or absence of fear-of-success imagery. Female college students were labeled high in fear of success if their responses to the cue associated some negative consequence or feeling with the success, stressed goal-directed activity away from the success, or denied the reality of Anne's achievement. The following are excerpts of fear-of-success responses cited by Horner (1970; pp. 60 to 62; Horner, cited in Bardwick, 1971, p. 182).

> No one will marry her. She has lots of friends but no dates.

> Unfortunately, Anne suddenly no longer feels so certain that she really wants to be a doctor. She wonders if perhaps it isn't normal.

> Anne is a code name for a nonexistent person created by a group of med students.

> She starts proclaiming her surprise and joy. Her fellow classmates are so disgusted with her behavior that they jump on her body and beat her. She is maimed for life.

Male college students wrote responses to the same cue, but for them the central character in the verbal lead was named John instead of Anne. The difference between the responses of males and those of females to the success cue was dramatic. Less than 10% of the male responses contained fear-of-success images. In contrast, 65% of the female subjects wrote stories reflecting fear of success. Although the incidence of fear-of-success imagery varies from study to study (Tresemer, 1973), numerous replications of Horner's work indicate that some women associate competitively derived success with negative consequences. But so do some men.

In fact, several recent investigations have found the incidence of fear-of-success imagery of males to be as high as or higher than that of females (Garske, 1975; Hoffman, 1974a). Horner (1972) herself reported an increase in the fear-of-success images expressed by men in response to cues depicting successful males. In 1972 Hoffman replicated Horner's original study and found that the frequency of fear-of-success imagery expressed by males was higher than that expressed by females—77% to 65%. Both Horner and Hoffman explain these findings as indicative of a growing tendency on the part of college males in contemporary society to devalue competitive success.[2]

You will recall that the scoring system used to categorize story themes into fear-present versus fear-absent responses is a simple one. Any imagery that reflects either anxiety over or denial of achievement is scored as reflecting the motive to avoid success. Thus, the themes of male subjects that reflect a general disillusionment with the American achievement ethic and concern for finding "nonmaterialistic happiness and satisfaction in life" (Horner, 1972, p. 163) receive the same score as female subjects' images reflecting concern over loss of popularity as a consequence of success. Clearly, there is a conceptual difference between devaluing a cultural norm and expressing anxiety over the conflict between femininity and competitive achievement.

It is difficult to resolve the question of whether the presence of fear-of-success imagery in response to projective measures reflects the existence of an internal disposition to avoid success or simply an accurate characterization of the prevailing cultural norms dictating sex-role-appropriate achievement. For example, Monahan, Kuhn, and Shaver (1974) extended Horner's original study so that half of their sample responded to Anne's success in medical school and half to John's. They found that many male and female subjects wrote stories about Anne's achievement that contained fear-of-success themes. In contrast, few subjects of either sex responded to John's success with fear-of-success imagery. Monahan and her colleagues interpreted these results to suggest that the fantasy-based measure used to assess the motive to avoid success does not arouse a personal disposition. Rather, it measures an awareness on the part of subjects of both sexes that a woman who achieves in a predominantly masculine field is behaving in a manner regarded as inappropriate for the female sex role.

When cues depicting females succeeding in traditionally feminine contexts are used to measure the motive to avoid success, the proportion of female responses containing negative images decreases dramatically. For example, Katz (1973) found a significant decrease in the frequency of fear-of-success themes generated by college women to the Anne-in-medical-school cue when subjects were presented with additional information suggesting that Anne's success was not sex-role inappropriate; that is, subjects were told that the distribution of men and women in Anne's medical school class was approximately equal. Similarly, Alper (1973) obtained

---

[2]Douvan (1976) has suggested a different explanation for the sex differences in negative imagery obtained in early studies of fear of success. In her view, males have been socialized to deny the awareness of inner conflicts of any kind. As a result, they have traditionally responded to fantasy-based measures with bland, conventional stories. Only recently have men been encouraged to recognize the value of keeping in touch with their feelings. As men have begun to accept the legitimacy of their own inner awareness, their responses to projective measures of fear of success have become richer and more varied and reflect more conflict.

fewer fear-of-success responses to Anne's academic achievement when the medical reference was dropped.

As Horner hypothesized, women do not fear success per se. The motive to avoid success is aroused only in situations that stress the possibility of conflict between femininity and competitively derived achievement. Furthermore, not all women fear success. In Horner's original sample 35% of the women subjects responded favorably to Anne's success.

Women may define the feminine role in a number of ways. Some may see any form of competitive striving as unfeminine, and others may regard competitive success in a masculine field as perfectly consistent with their views of the female role. O'Leary (1974a) attempted to specify the type of competitive success that achievement-oriented women deem inappropriate. She asked 169 women who had achieved academic honors at a Midwestern university to give written responses to four cues depicting successful females. The cues represented (1) success in a traditionally masculine competitive context, (2) success in a traditionally feminine competitive context, (3) social-domestic competitive success, and (4) success achieved vicariously through the accomplishment of a husband. Each subject responded to all four cues.

The lowest percentage of fear-of-success imagery (32.5%) was obtained in response to the masculine competitive-success cue "Mary's boss has recently been transferred to the California branch of the company she works for. The board of directors has chosen Mary above many other junior executives to take over his highly valued position." Horner (1971) used this same cue and obtained fear-of-success imagery from 85% of a sample of secretarial personnel. The highest percentages of fear-of-success responses were obtained to the traditionally feminine competitive cue "Barbara has been appointed head of nursing in a large metropolitan hospital" (50.3%) and to the vicarious-success cue "Evelyn's husband, Tom, has just been promoted vice president of his company" (53.9%). These findings are consistent with Horner's suggestion that fear of success is aroused only in achievement contexts regarded by the subjects as sex-role inappropriate. In this sample of achieving young women, cues that depicted feminine success in a traditionally feminine competitive context and as success achieved vicariously aroused more negative imagery than success in a traditionally masculine context. The social-domestic competitive-success cue "Lisa, the wife of a prominent lawyer, has been named hostess of the year by the newspaper in the large city in which she resides" was not seen by these women as threatening enough to arouse the motive to avoid success. Similarly, Alper (1973) reported obtaining fewer fear-of-success themes in response to a pictorial cue depicting a female figure painting a child's portrait in a kitchen than in response to a cue showing two women working in a scientific laboratory.

Thus, a woman's definition of her role appears to be an important determinant of her tendency to fear success. Her role definition may be expected to affect her perception of both the appropriateness of success on a given task and the probable consequences of such success.

Alper (1973) hypothesized that women whose role orientation is traditional are less likely to be achievement-(career-) oriented than women whose role orientation is nontraditional. After selecting cues to elicit achievement imagery, Alper divided the responses of college women to these cues into success- and avoidance-of-success-theme categories and found that theme category and role orientation were related. Nontraditionally oriented women were more likely than traditionally oriented ones to write success stories in response to achievement cues.

In a similar study, O'Leary and Hammack (1975) used the Wellesley Role Orientation Scale (Alper, 1973) to divide female high school students on the basis of role orientation (traditional versus nontraditional). The 72 subjects, all of whom had high grade-point averages (3.0 or above) responded to four verbal cues depicting a female succeeding in a variety of achievement contexts. As predicted, nontraditionally oriented subjects wrote fewer fear-of-success stories to any of the cues than traditionally oriented subjects. It is interesting to note that only the responses of nontraditionally oriented females differed according to the achievement context in which success was presented. Among these subjects, female success in both traditionally masculine and traditionally feminine competitive contexts evoked a high percentage of fear-of-success imagery. However, despite the fact that the subjects' responses to both these cues reflected negative imagery and were thus scored for fear of success, the stories themselves revealed different types of concern. In response to the masculine competitive-success cue, the negative themes reflected concern with social rejection. But examination of the negative imageries contained in the responses to "Susan's success in nursing school" suggested that nontraditionally oriented subjects focused primarily on Susan's failure to "compete like a man" rather than on concerns about loss of femininity or popularity. For example, one story written in response to the traditionally feminine competitive-success cue by a nontraditionally oriented subject was:

> Susan wanted to be a doctor but due to public opinion and stiff competition in doctor's school she decided to become a nurse. She had the brains and drive it takes, but people tend to look down on female doctors. Besides, she did want to get married some day, and everyone knows you can't hold a job and a household together at the same time. Right??! [O'Leary & Hammack. 1975, p. 232.]*

Apparently, the nontraditionally oriented girls viewed Susan's success as a "copout." For these subjects competitive success in a traditionally feminine context may have been devalued because it represented the acceptance of the prevailing cultural stereotype. Thus, the arousal of the motive to avoid success appears to be dependent on the context within which a woman's success is presented and the individual's conception of appropriate feminine

*From "Sex-Role Orientation and Achievement Context as Determinants of the Motive to Avoid Success," by V. E. O'Leary and B. Hammack, *Sex Roles*, 1975, *1*(3), 225-234. Reprinted by permission of Plenum Publishing Corporation.

behavior. The results of the recent research on fear of success do not support the contention that women are less predisposed to achieve than men; rather, they indicate that certain achievement contexts appear more attractive to some women than others.

Despite the assumption that the motive to avoid success is a relatively stable personality disposition acquired by females early in their lives, the results of several studies suggest that the arousal of the motive may be influenced by a woman's life situation. For example, Schwenn (1970) found that college women who obtained high fear-of-success scores were more likely than their low-scoring peers to change their career aspirations toward traditionally feminine occupations during their college years. Furthermore, the young women who shifted their aspirations in the direction of the traditional feminine stereotype either were dating men who disapproved of nontraditionally oriented women or were not dating at all. These findings substantiate Horner's (1968) emphasis on fear of social rejection as a key factor in arousing the tendency to avoid success. On the other hand, those women in Schwenn's study who maintained their nontraditional career aspirations throughout their college careers were either engaged to or seriously dating men who were not opposed to or threatened by successful women. Similarly, Hawley (1972) found that the adoption of a stereotypically masculine-role definition does not necessarily result in fear of social rejection among professional women. In her sample, career-oriented women reported that the men in their lives had a model of femininity much like their own. Since these women viewed their significant men as endorsing their life-styles, it is doubtful that they saw achievement as incompatible with femininity. Apparently, when an achievement-oriented woman finds environmental support for the view that the consequences of success are positive, she has little reason to fear success. Further research is necessary to determine whether the presence of social support for competitive success diminishes the influence of a stable disposition to avoid success or merely reduces the impact of culturally defined stereotypes.

Up to now we have focused on the conditions under which women are likely to respond to achievement cues with fear-of-success imagery. However, demonstrating that many women associate negative consequences with competitively derived success is not very meaningful unless fear-of-success scores can be used to predict behavior in achievement situations.

Horner (1968) found evidence to suggest that fear of success can inhibit a woman's performance. In her initial study, she found that women who feared success performed less well when they were asked to compete against men than when they worked alone. Conversely, women who did not fear success performed better when they were competing against men. Subsequent attempts to verify Horner's prediction that opposite-sex competition results in performance inhibition among women have not been completely successful (Mednick & Weissman, 1975). Performance inhibition among women in competitive contexts has been reported by Makosky (1972), Pappo (1973), and Grozsko and Morgenstern (1972). Makosky's (1972) results not only supported Horner's finding that women who fear success perform better alone than in mixed-sex competition but indicated that these women perform best when they are competing with other women and the task is described as one at which females are expected to excel. In the same study, women who did not fear success performed best on a task characterized as "masculine" when competing with men. Presumably, each group performed in a manner consistent with the achievement goals they deemed appropriate for their role. Furthermore, those women who did not fear success did not perceive their behavior to be in conflict with their feminine image; in fact, they rated themselves as more feminine than the women who feared success. These results suggest that both the sex of the competitor and the sex-role appropriateness of the task influence women's behavior in achievement situations.

However, in one recent study, Sorrentino and Short (1974) found that women performed better on a task characterized as masculine (drafting ability) than on one characterized as feminine (domestic ability). These results were stronger for women who obtained high fear-of-success scores. Similarly, Garske (1975) found that college women performed better on a task requiring analytic ability (masculine) when competing with a male. These results are clearly contrary to Horner's theory. Although female subjects were not directly engaged in competition against males in Sorrentino and Short's study, they were in Garske's. Since 76% of the women in Garske's study responded to Anne's success in medical school with fear-of-success imagery, it seems apparent that Horner's cue is measuring more than the motive to avoid success. As Feather and Raphelson (1974) and Monahan et al. (1974) have suggested, the medical-school cue readily evokes stereotypic notions of appropriate role behavior for women. Moreover, the cue is neither subtle nor ambiguous (Morgan & Mausner, 1973). Thus, the measure itself makes it difficult to separate stereotypic reactions from the presence of a motive to avoid success (Garske, 1975). When Horner analyzed the responses of a group of female law students to the Anne-in-medical-school cue, she found a high proportion (86.6%) of imagery reflecting fear of success (Horner & Walsh, 1974). Yet these same women were actively involved in academic competition in a field dominated by men. Spence (1974) has recently suggested that the variety of responses scored as fear of success include not only personality dispositions but values and attitudes as well as realistic estimates of the risks associated with success in certain situations. Not all of these factors can be considered as enduring psychological characteristics reflecting the existence of a motive.

Despite the fact that further research is necessary to assess the validity and reliability of the fear-of-success construct (Tresemer, 1976; Zuckerman & Wheeler, 1975), this theory has generated an "energetic new look" (Mednick & Weissman, 1975) at the dynamics of achievement motivation among women. The question of whether women's reluctance to strive for success in occupations traditionally reserved for men is the result of a personality disposition or a learned response to social pressure is of considerable theoretical importance. The resolution of this question will depend on the results of further empirical work. But we may conclude, as Horner did, that women are not less motivated to achieve than men.

Attributions for Success and Failure

People who engage in a task have ideas and beliefs about what they are doing; for example, they have an expectation about the likelihood that they will be successful. They also make judgments about why particular events occur. Attribution theory deals with the way in which people assign causes for both their own behavior and that of others. It has been demonstrated that the causal attributions an individual makes for his or her success or failure on a task influence the feelings, future expectancies, and subsequent achievement strivings of that individual (Frieze et al., 1975).

As we noted earlier in this chapter, boys and men have higher expectations of success than girls and women. These expectations affect behavior in achievement situations. The results of a number of recent studies suggest that men and women attribute the cause of their success or failure to different factors. Four causes for performance outcomes have been studied extensively: ability, effort, luck, and task difficulty (Weiner et al., 1971). A person may succeed on a task because of his or her ability, hard work, good luck, and/or easiness of the task. Failure, on the other hand, may result from low ability, lack of effort, bad luck, and/or difficulty of the task. Each of these four causal elements may be conceptualized along two dimensions: the source controlling the outcome of a given performance (internal versus external) and the stability of the factor influencing performance outcomes over time (stable versus temporary).

Ability and effort are characteristics internal to the individual. Luck and task difficulty are external factors, because the extent to which they influence the outcome of a task may vary as a result of environmental conditions. People have been found to differ in their tendency to attribute their own performance to themselves or to environmental causes (Rotter, 1966, 1975; Throop & MacDonald, 1971).

Ability, effort, luck, and task difficulty also vary in the extent to which they represent relatively stable factors or factors that may be expected to change from one performance situation to another. Ability and task difficulty are relatively stable in that neither should fluctuate dramatically across time. Luck and effort, on the other hand, may change because the individual's luck has changed or because he or she decides to exert more (or less) effort on a task.

The person who attributes success on a task to a stable internal factor such as ability is likely to feel secure that successful outcomes are of her or his own making; thus, that person will approach new achievement situations with confidence. Attributing failure to unstable external factors (bad luck) is also unlikely to inhibit future striving for success. On the other hand, the person who attributes success to external and/or unstable factors such as luck, task difficulty, or effort may be less confident of her or his own ability and feel reluctant to strive for success in new situations. This is particularly true if the same individual readily attributes failure to the stable, internal factor of low ability.

Research on sex differences in causal attributions for performance indicate that the explanations offered by men and women for their success or failure on a task differ markedly. Men generally attribute success to a stable, internal factor (ability) and failure to an external, unstable factor (bad luck) (Mednick & Weissman, 1975). Thus, men tend to give credit to themselves if they succeed and blame something or someone else if they fail. In contrast, women generally rely on external and/or unstable explanations for performance, regardless of whether they succeed or fail (Deaux, 1976; Frieze, 1975).

Overall, women are more likely than men to attribute their performance on a task to external factors such as luck (Feather, 1969; Frieze & Bar-Tal, 1974; McMahan, 1972; Simon & Feather, 1973) or the difficulty of the task (Croke, 1973, Frieze & Bar-Tal, 1974; McMahan, 1972). Unlike men, when women do attribute their success to an internal cause, they are likely to use the unstable factor of effort rather than the stable factor of ability (Bar-Tal & Frieze, 1973; Feldman-Summers & Kiesler, 1974). To the extent that women are more likely than men to view positive outcomes on a task as due to fate and/or extraordinary effort, they may be reluctant to strive for success.

You will recall that, in comparison to boys, girls are more likely to blame themselves when they fail (Crandall et al., 1965). Consequently, it appears reasonable to anticipate that women would also be more likely than men to attribute failure to an internal cause such as lack of ability. Data bearing on this hypothesis are contradictory. In some studies, women have been found to be more likely than men to attribute failure to lack of ability (Deaux & Farris, 1974; McMahan, 1971, 1972). The results of other studies indicate that women are no more likely than men to attribute failure to internal factors (Feather, 1969; Frieze, 1973). However, when Bar-Tal and Frieze (1973) compared the causal attributions for failure made by women who were highly motivated to achieve with those of women who were not, they found that the achievement-oriented group attributed their failures to the unstable, internal factor of low effort. This finding is generally consistent with the view that women are more likely than men to accept personal responsibility for failure.

Further support for this contention was obtained in a study of the effect of group performance on the feelings of pride or shame experienced by female and male group members (Zander, Fuller, & Armstrong, 1972). Females were more ashamed of themselves than males when their group had failed, particularly if they viewed the group's failure as the result of lack of effort. Like ability, effort represents an internal causal explanation for performance. However, effort is an unstable factor rather than a stable one.

The tendency on the part of women to attribute their performance to external and/or unstable factors may undermine their confidence in their ability to predict outcomes accurately. As a result, they may prefer easy tasks or tasks in which the outcome appears to be dependent on chance rather than skill. In a recent study, Deaux, White, and Farris (1975) observed the preferences expressed by women and men for games requiring luck (for example, bingo) versus skill (for example, ring tossing) on the midway of a county fair. As hypothesized, women were more likely than men to "try their luck" on games of chance, while men preferred games that required some degree of skill.

In a subsequent laboratory study, Deaux and her colleagues (1975) gave male and female college students the opportunity to play a game of electric darts. Although the game was actually the same in all conditions, the subjects were told that they could choose between a game of skill and one of luck. Nearly 75% of the men chose to play the game described as requiring skill, while 65% of the women selected the game of chance. Although both women and men thought that it was more important to succeed on a skill game, women's estimates of the probability of success on a game requiring skill were much lower than men's. There were no sex differences in performance estimates on the chance game. Thus, the preference expressed by women for the game of chance was related to their expectancy for success.

These findings indicate that women are less likely than men to view themselves as skilled. Even when they do succeed on tasks that require skill, they are reluctant to accept personal responsibility for their achievements. We have already discussed Horner's contention that for women success may be associated with negative consequences. An alternative explanation (which does not rely on the postulation of a motive) for women's hesitancy to attribute success to their own ability emphasizes the prevalence of a societal norm that dictates modesty among women (Frieze et al., 1975; Vaughter et al., 1974).

It is not unreasonable to suggest that, like men, women too feel proud when they succeed and have higher expectancies for future performances when they know they have done well. However, in order to avoid appearing boastful, they may refrain from acknowledging their success publicly, neither increasing their ability estimates nor attributing their success to superior ability. Whereas males are expected to show self-assurance by displaying confidence in their own abilities, females are taught to present themselves as only moderately competent and "properly" self-effacing. When a man's attitude and behavior reflect the assertion "I'm good and I know it," others react favorably and comment on his "healthy ego." The same behavior on the part of a woman is likely to be interpreted as an expression of conceit.

In comparison to men, who are socialized to be competitive (agency), women are expected to be more interpersonally (communion) oriented (Bakan, 1966). To the extent that women derive satisfaction from their own success without reference to others (Kipnis, 1974; Veroff, McClelland, & Ruhland, 1975), they may be less concerned than men about public recognition of their accomplishments. They may also view the potential cost (envy, hostility, and so forth) associated with such recognition as detrimental to the maintenance of interpersonal relationships that they have been taught to value.

A different explanation for women's failure to attribute their performances to stable, internal causes is provided by Bem's (1972) theory of self-perception. In Bem's view, people's causal inferences about their own behavior are based, in part, on the same kinds of information they use to make inferences about others' behavior. In American society it is widely believed that women are less predictable (stable) and less competent (able) than men.

The available research clearly indicates that women are expected to perform less well than men on a variety of achievement tasks. For example, Feldman-Summers and Kiesler (1974) were unable to find a single occupation in which females were expected to outperform males. Even in the presumably female-appropriate occupations of elementary school teaching and nursing, Sedgwick (reported by Feldman-Summers & Kiesler, 1974) found that subjects of both sexes expected males to be more competent and successful than females.

Moreover, when male and female subjects are asked to evaluate the same performance attributed to either a man or a woman, they tend to agree that the man's performance is superior. For example, the female college students who were asked by Goldberg (1968) to rate professional articles on the basis of value, persuasiveness, profundity, writing style, and competence gave higher ratings to identical papers when they were led to believe that the author was male. Bem and Bem (1970) replicated these findings with male college students. Similar results have been obtained in studies requiring both women and men to evaluate the artistic merit of paintings (Pheterson, Kiesler, & Goldberg, 1971) and the qualifications of student applicants for a study-abroad program (Deaux & Taynor, 1973).

Several attempts have been made to specify the conditions under which a woman's achievement may be regarded as more (or equally) meritorious than that of a man. Taynor and Deaux (1973) found that a woman's behavior in a civic emergency (armed robbery) was rated as more deserving of a reward than that of a man when her behavior was portrayed as somewhat out of role (she remained coolheaded) and her actions were praised by experts (the police). Similarly, Pheterson et al. (1971) found that a woman's artistic achievement was evaluated as favorably as that of a man only when it had been judged superior by experts. Apparently, for a woman's competence to be recognized, her accomplishment must be portrayed as exceptional (requiring unusual drive and dedication) and its worth must be acknowledged by an authoritative source.

Even when a woman's achievement is acknowledged, her success is generally attributed not to her ability but to luck or effort. Deaux and Emswiller (1974) asked male and female college students to evaluate the performance of a fellow student (either male or female) on a task characterized as either masculine or feminine. When the task was presented as one at which males usually excel, both male and female raters attributed a good performance by a male to his skill. The same level of performance by a female was attributed to her luck. Similarly, Feldman-Summers and Kiesler (1974) found that college students attributed the success of a male physician to his ability and that of a female physician to her great motivation. They interpret these findings to suggest that in this society it is generally agreed that those who are number two (women) must try harder.

In the Feldman-Summers and Kiesler study, an attempt was made to affect the subjects' expectation for the physician's success by varying his or her medical specialty; thus, the physician was presented as either a pediatrician or a surgeon. It was hypothesized that males would be expected to be more successful surgeons than females; but no differences in the causal explanations for success were obtained as a result of the sex-role appropriateness of the medical specialty. These results indicate that in this society both males and females associate success with "maleness." If success in a job is tied to being a male, then males will be expected to be more successful than females regardless of the sex-role appropriateness of the occupational context in which success occurs. As a result, a woman's success may always be regarded as unexpected and due to different factors than the (expected) success of a male.

A recent study by Touhey (1974a) suggests that the anticipation of increasing participation by women in high-status occupations generally reserved for males (such as architect, college professor, lawyer, physician, and scientist) results in a tendency on the part of both males and females to reduce the prestige and desirability of these occupations. This decrease in prestige and desirability is accompanied by attributions of increased passiveness, insecurity, and uselessness and of decreased success. In a subsequent study, Touhey (1974b) found that the anticipation of increased proportions of males in traditionally feminine occupations such as nursing, social work, and home economics results in an increase of these occupations' prestige and desirability.

To the extent that women internalize (incorporate into their self-image) the stereotypic assumptions that competence and stability are incompatible with femininity, their tendency to attribute the outcome of their performance to external and/or unstable causes may indeed reflect the belief that women are less able and more unpredictable than men. However, the demonstrated tendency of females to attribute their performance to unstable factors such as effort and luck may also represent a defensive strategy used to avoid being held personally responsible for success and/or failure.

Defensive Externalization

Not only do people differ in the extent to which they attribute success and failure to themselves or to outside forces, but they also differ in a more general disposition to see themselves in control over the events in their lives. In 1966 Rotter devised a test (Internal versus External Locus of Control) to measure the expectancies of people concerning the degree to which they believed they had control over the reinforcements they received. Some people, called externals, characteristically view themselves as lacking control over their environment. Things happen to them; rewards and punishments have little to do with their own behavior. Internals, on the other hand, see themselves as capable of controlling the reinforcements they receive. Thus, internals agree that "getting ahead in life depends on hard work," whereas externals are more likely to concede that "getting ahead in life depends primarily on having the right breaks."

As might be expected, internals are generally more effective in dealing with the environment than are externals (Phares, 1968). Several attempts to relate perceived locus of control to achievement behavior have demonstrated that internals are more achievement-oriented than externals. However, this relationship has been obtained only for male subjects (Weiner & Kukla, 1970; Weiner & Potepan, 1970).

In several early studies of the relationship between locus of control and behavior, Rotter (1966) noted that some subjects performed as if they believed that they had control over their reinforcements but, at the same time, that the outcome of their performance was dependent on luck or chance. In other words, these individuals behaved like internals but scored on the locus-of-control measure like externals. To account for this puzzling inconsistency, Rotter suggested that those individuals who were anxious about failure might have endorsed the view of external locus of control as a defense against anxiety. Although the concept of defensive externalization was originally conceived of as a defense against the impact of continued failure (Hjelle, 1970; Rotter, 1966), it is quite possible that success may evoke anxiety as well (Horner, 1968). Thus, by viewing the events in his or her life as controlled by external forces, the individual is freed from assuming personal responsibility for either failure or success. For example, a competent woman who tries to be successful in a field traditionally dominated by males may seek to avoid taking credit for her own success. If she attributes her superior performance to chance, she can hardly be labeled as competitive, assertive, or unfeminine.

If women's tendency to attribute their achievements to external factors is a learned tactic to avoid negative consequences associated with success, it is not surprising that researchers have failed to find a relationship between internalization and achievement motivation among women. The findings of Thurber (1972) offer some tentative support for this suggestion in that college women classified as external on Rotter's Locus of Control Scale demonstrated superior academic performance in comparison to those classified as internal. Presumably, these women are able to avoid the potentially negative consequences of competitive academic achievement by attributing their success to luck rather than ability.

I often overhear female students discussing their midterm grades as they leave class. Characteristically, the bright young woman reports to her friends with a sigh of relief "Yeah, I got an A. Boy, was I lucky! I studied all the right things." She fails to comment on the fact that she never has gotten a grade lower than a B or that she found the exam easy. Her equally competent and successful male peer (who studied all night) "knew the material cold."

Thurber's results suggest that the global measure of locus-of-control orientation developed by Rotter may not differentiate between the individual who believes that her life is controlled by external forces and the one who adopts this position in order to protect her "feminine" best interests. A number of researchers have criticized the locus-of-control measure on the grounds that it does not afford a distinction between an individual's belief in his or her own ability to control outcomes, the power of others to control, and the influence of chance (Collins, 1974; Levenson, 1972; Prociuk & Breen, 1973).

In a study of the relationship between locus-of-control orientation and political activism among Blacks, Gurin, Gurin, Lao, and Beattie (1969) argued that the dichotomy between internal and external locus of control based on ability versus chance was artificial. In their view, certain groups of individuals are confronted with external obstacles to achievement that have nothing to do with chance. When these researchers refined the concept of internal-versus-external control to reflect beliefs in personal control, control ideology, individual system blame, and race ideology, they discovered that the belief in personal control was the strongest predictor of both achievement motivation and activism among Black males. Beliefs regarding the source of control for other people's outcomes were relatively independent of the individual's own feeling of control. The recognition of external obstacles imposed by the system enhanced rather than inhibited achievement aspirations. Although these findings were obtained in a study of racial differences in achievement motivation, Depner (1974) maintains that they have significant implications for understanding the dynamics of achievement motivation among women.

The woman who feels she cannot succeed because of her own deficiencies (for example, her inability to hold a job and at the same time properly care for her children) rather than because of obstacles in the environment (for example, lack of child-care facilities) may be unlikely to aspire to high levels of competitive achievement. If a woman has low feelings of personal control, the tendency to blame herself rather than the system for her lack of opportunity may further diminish her achievement strivings. Similarly, the woman who believes that she (unlike others) has little control over her life is unlikely to aspire to high-level goals. In order to adequately understand and predict achievement behavior for women, it will be necessary to specify the impact of causal beliefs and attributions on performance more completely.

Horner's assumption that men and women do not differ in the extent to which they are motivated to achieve may indeed prove to be correct. Whether fear of success represents a motive, the reflection of a stereotype, or a tactic to diffuse the impact of taking credit for one's success will not be easy to determine. In a society as achievement-oriented as ours, the intuitive appeal of the defensive explanation is strong, particularly in light of the recent evidence that neither the achievement motivations nor the behaviors of boys and girls differ significantly (Maccoby & Jacklin, 1974).

In our discussion of sex differences in achievement, thus far we have focused on explanations that emphasize differences in achievement motivation, expectancies of success, and causal attributions for performance. Each of these approaches has added to our understanding of why males and females behave differently in achievement situations. However, the origins of these differences has still not been specified. Two recent attempts to explain the failure of women to fulfill their intellectual potential have focused on differences in the way males and females are taught to view success (Hoffman, 1972; Stein & Bailey, 1973). Both explanations emphasize the impact of early childhood experiences and relate sex differences in achievement strivings to the potential conflict between women's need to achieve and their need to affiliate.

Affiliation versus Achievement

Each of us is interested in exerting some kind of control over the environment in order to maximize the rewards that we receive from others. According to Hoffman (1972), the early socialization experiences of boys and girls teach them to use different methods to obtain reinforcement. Boys learn that they are most likely to be rewarded for demonstrating independence and mastery over tasks that require skill. Presumably, as boys grow older, they find the demonstration of mastery reinforcing in and of itself (Crandall, 1963). Thus, they are not dependent on the approval of others to obtain positive reinforcement for their accomplishments. For example, a boy who has just completed a model airplane does not need praise from his father to feel proud of the fact that he assembled the toy correctly and that his plane will fly.

Girls, on the other hand, learn that the most effective way to obtain reinforcement is to seek the help and approval of others. Unlike their brothers, girls are not exposed to situations that promote the development of pride in independent accomplishment. For them reinforcement depends less on performing well than on pleasing their audience. Because affiliation, rather than achievement, becomes the primary source of girls' reinforcement, girls develop stronger affiliative needs than boys. In Hoffman's view, even when females do express achievement striving, it is out of a desire to please rather than to succeed.

Although the results of a number of studies provide support for the hypothesis that girls are more concerned about social approval and more likely to seek help than boys (Crandall & Rabson, 1960; Crandall, Dewey, Katkovsky, & Preston, 1964; Hoffman, 1972; Maccoby, 1966; Walberg, 1969), it is not clear what effect affiliative concerns have on girls' performances. The results of two studies suggest that girls who express a strong desire for love and approval are more likely to strive for success than those who do not (Crandall et al., 1964; Tyler, Rafferty, & Tyler, 1962). However, children of both sexes increase their efforts to achieve when they receive verbal praise for their performance (Maccoby & Jacklin, 1974; Stein & Bailey, 1973). To the extent that both boys and girls view verbal praise as a form of positive reinforcement for performance, it is hardly surprising that they respond by exerting more effort. It is, however, difficult to evaluate the significance attached to verbal praise by females and males.

In two studies, Deci (1972) and Deci, Cascio, and Krusell (1973) found that college males who received verbal reinforcement for their efforts to solve a difficult puzzle were more likely to continue to work the puzzle during a "free" period than those who did not receive such feedback. Females, on the other hand, displayed less interest in the puzzle after they received positive feedback on their performance. Deci interprets these results to suggest that positive feedback for performance is interpreted differently by males and females. Males view positive feedback about performance as information about mastery; thus, their sense of competence and self determination is strengthened by it. In contrast, females, who are socialized to be more sensitive to the reactions of other people, may view the administration of positive feedback as an attempt on the part of the experimenter (male or female) to control their behavior.

As we saw in Chapter Four there is some evidence to suggest that, overall, females are more (not less) susceptible to influence than males. However, working puzzles is a stereotypically masculine task, and the females in Deci's studies may have felt secure in resisting the experimenter's attempts to influence them and in behaving instead in a manner appropriate to their sex role.

Despite the intuitive appeal of the hypothesis that females have greater affiliative needs than males, this difference does not appear to be the result of early socialization. You will recall from our discussion of sex-role development (Chapter Three) and of psychological differences between the sexes (Chapter Four) that there is little evidence to support the contention that girls are encouraged to be more dependent than boys. Nor are adults less likely to reinforce girls for the demonstration of skill and mastery. During early and middle childhood girls achieve well, particularly in school. They value academic achievement and set high standards for their own performance. Reduced achievement striving does not occur among females until they reach adolescence and adulthood. Perhaps the implications of the potential conflict between intellectual achievement and affiliation do not become a reality until societal pressure is exerted to "behave like a lady."

As a graduate of a women's college I have often tried to recall the basis for the achievement behavior of myself and my peers in an institution where competition and academic excellence were overriding concerns. I suspect that many of us who fancied ourselves as intellectually very competitive were striving for academic success to gain the approval of a faculty (predominantly male) who valued such achievement. Those who obtained high grades were not only rewarded with academic honors but also singled out for animated discussions of ideas over coffee. The grade reflected a comment on mastery but was also perceived as an estimate of personal worth—"He cares for me an A's worth." Certainly, acknowledgement of one's intellectual competence was reinforcing, but so was the social approval (and attention) it ensured.

Although the same kind of approval was sought from female faculty, the nature of the emotional relationship with a woman teacher was somewhat different. Grades were perceived as indicative of personal worth and approval, but the approval was from a same-sex model for whom in most cases we had no fantasies of romantic or sexual involvement.

Male faculty did become the target of affiliative concern in a romantic sense. The competition for the affections (attention) of one's tutor was heightened by the intellectual intensity with which senior women approached the writing of their tutorials (or senior theses). In this situation intellectual achievement was certainly not defined as incompatible with femininity. Indeed, many of us married and went on to graduate school.

However, for many young women adherence to the traditional feminine-role definition dictates that one of the most important areas for female achievement is social skill (Stein & Bailey, 1973). Achievement striving and social activity are more closely linked for females than for males. Although this link has frequently been interpreted as evidence that females' achievement striving is motivated by the need to affiliate, it appears equally plausible that the demonstration of social skills reflects achievement concerns. When Friedrich (1976) expanded the method of scoring projective measures of achievement motivation to include achievement in traditionally feminine areas, such as social skills, she obtained the predicted relationship between women's achievement-motivation scores and performance.

It has been recognized that the demonstration of skill and competence need not be restricted to occupational success (Heckhausen, 1967; Rosen, 1956). However, there have been no attempts to measure achievement in child rearing or homemaking. Certainly, baking a cake represents an achievement in an area in which standards of excellence may be applied. But the skill required to bake even the best chocolate cake is not afforded the same status as that required to produce the best automobile. Because the definitions and measures of achievement have focused exclusively on the academic-vocational-masculine model of success (Bardwick, 1971), it is difficult to evaluate the meaning of sex differences in achievement.

Recent work by Veroff and his colleagues (Veroff, 1969, 1973; Veroff & Feld, 1970; Veroff, McClelland, & Ruhland, 1975) demonstrates the importance of distinguishing among a variety of achievement orientations. On the basis of a factor analytic study of interviews conducted with 365 adult females and males, Veroff et al. identified six types of achievement orientation.[3] Males were more likely than females to score high on items measuring assertive-competence motivation (the desire to see themselves as successfully performing valued achievement activity in the society). However, no sex differences were obtained on measures of task-competence motivation (the desire to rise to the challenge of succeeding on a given task). Veroff suggests that because of sex differences in socialization women are taught to

---

[3]The six varieties of achievement orientation identified by Veroff et al. (1975) are assertive-competence motivation, task-competence motivation, fear of failure, social-comparison motivation, future-achievement orientation, and hope of success.

value achievement only under certain circumstances. Unlike males, who are encouraged to express assertive competence (perhaps as a measure of their personal worth in relation to others), females do not learn to value competitive achievement above other goals. However, females are no less likely than males to learn to value task competence.

The implications of Veroff's findings are consistent with Stein and Bailey's suggestion that women's achievement values and goals are different from men's. However, contrary to Hoffman's contention that male achievement is inner-directed whereas female achievement is other-directed, Veroff's data support the opposite conclusion. Indeed, Veroff et al. (1975) as well as Kipnis (1974) have recently argued that the achievement striving of males is more dependent on the presence (and approval) of others.

Further empirical research is necessary to test the validity of these alternative explanations of the effects of differential socialization on the achievement behavior of women and men. It is clear, however, that any comprehensive theory of achievement must take sex differences in achievement values and goals into account. Whether women continue to be less likely than men to achieve in areas requiring intellectual competence and leadership will undoubtedly depend on the prevailing norms defining sex-appropriate achievement and success in this society.[4]

Summary

American society emphasizes striving, accomplishment, and success. Yet, women, who constitute over 50% of the population, are badly under-represented in positions of power and prestige. In this chapter we have examined three general approaches to understanding why women are less likely to achieve than men.

The expectancy-value theory of achievement motivation assumes the existence of three primary determinants of achievement behavior: the tendency to achieve success (T_s), the tendency to avoid failure, (T_{-f}), and extrinsic motivation (T_{ext}). Early studies of achievement behavior showed that male subjects who obtained high scores on the projective measure of achievement motivation performed better on tasks such as anagram solutions and addition problems than those who scored low. Subsequent work using female subjects failed to demonstrate a similar relationship between achievement motivation and performance. The fact that instructions intended to arouse the motive to achieve did not work for female subjects led

---

[4]Although the focus of this chapter is on intrapsychic barriers to women's achievement, it is important to consider the effects of institutional barriers as well. Sex discrimination in hiring and promotion does exist, and institutional barriers are powerful in and of themselves and probably also generate additional psychological barriers. A woman who confronts sex discrimination on the job may be discouraged by the effect that discrimination has on her self-confidence or by the difficulties inherent in striving for success in a hostile environment. Objective barriers breed subjective reactions that may be damaging to career aspirations.

some researchers to conclude that women are not as motivated to achieve as men. The results of more recent research indicate that factors other than motivation, such as the sex-role appropriateness of the task and the sex of the central figure in the cue used to measure the achievement motive, may affect women's expression of achievement imagery and striving. The results also indicate that in general females' expectations of success are lower than males' expectations.

The tendency to achieve success may be inhibited by the tendency to avoid failure. There is some evidence to suggest that males are better able to cope with failure-related anxiety than females. Males are socialized to protect themselves from failure by attributing their lack of success to external factors; females, on the other hand, accept personal responsibility for failure and feel guilty about it. In the original formulation of the expectancy-value theory of achievement motivation, the motive to avoid failure was regarded as the primary source of achievement inhibition. However, Horner (1968) acknowledged the possibility that negative consequences might be associated with success as well as with failure. Thus, she introduced an additional factor into the equation, the tendency to avoid success (T_{-s}).

Horner suggested that the motive to avoid success was likely to be aroused in achievement situations in which the individual felt anxious about competition and its aggressive overtones. Although fear of success was not postulated as a female-specific motive, Horner did suggest that women confronted with the conflict between feminine image and competitively derived achievement are more likely to fear success than men. However, the results of recent research suggest that college men fear, or at least devalue, competitive success. It is difficult to determine whether women's reluctance to strive for success in traditionally masculine occupations is due to personality dispositions, to motives, or to a learned response to social pressures. It does seem clear, however, that women are not less motivated to achieve than men.

Attribution theory deals with the way in which people assign causes for both their own behavior and that of others. Research on sex differences in causal attributions for performance indicate that men generally attribute success to the stable, internal factor of ability and failure to the unstable, external factor of luck. Women tend to attribute their performance to external and/or unstable causes, such as effort or luck, regardless of whether they succeed or fail. The fact that women are less likely than men to accept personal responsibility for success may reflect a societal norm that dictates modesty, or it may be a tactic used to diffuse the potential negative consequences associated with success.

It is widely held that females have greater affiliative needs than males. Males are socialized to demonstrate mastery; females are presumably socialized to seek help and approval. However, there is little empirical evidence to support the notion that females' affiliative concerns conflict with their achievement strivings. For one thing, females do not begin to inhibit achievement behavior until adolescence. Perhaps the potential conflict between achievement and affiliation does not become apparent until adolescence.

The definitions and measures of achievement have focused exclusively on masculine models of success. Also, the achievement goals of males and females may be different. As a result, it is difficult to evaluate the meaning of sex differences in achievement.

Chapter Six

Stereotypes and Conceptions of the Female Role

Ted is very masculine; Kitty is very feminine. Can you describe them? Many of you would probably agree that Ted is strong, independent, active, logical, and self-confident. Kitty is gentle, understanding, warm, nurturant, well groomed, and interested in art and literature. Ted likes sports and cars and plans a career as an engineer or a corporate executive. Kitty likes to cook and sew and is looking forward to marriage and raising a family. The fact that on the basis of a single word—masculine or feminine—we are able to draw such complete pictures of two people we have never met demonstrates the existence of commonly held beliefs and stereotypes about the traits and behaviors that characterize males and females.

Sex-role stereotypes may be viewed as stylized exaggerations of women and men and as widely shared overgeneralizations that are assumed to reflect "a grain of truth" (Unger & Siiter, 1974). Although stereotypes may simplify the task of classifying people on the basis of their membership in a given group (for example, women and men) and thus make the world easier to understand, they are usually inaccurate or partially inaccurate beliefs. For example, many people would probably agree with the statement "Women are gossips," even though they know many women who do not gossip.

Because stereotypic conceptions of women and men are so widely shared, it has been easy to assume that they reflect real differences between the sexes. In American society men are "supposed" to be masculine and women are "supposed" to be feminine and neither sex is "supposed" to be much like the other (Bem, 1975). According to these stereotypes, if Ted is independent and logical and likes sports, Kitty should be warm and understanding and should like to cook. Indeed, the adequacy of Ted's and Kitty's performances in their assigned social roles may be evaluated on the basis of how well those performances conform to expectations defined along stereotypic lines. In this chapter we will review the literature on sex-role stereotypes and examine the influence of these stereotypes on women's definitions of themselves and their roles.

Sex-Role Stereotypes

As we noted in Chapter Four, a person's identity as either male or female exerts a strong influence on his or her social behavior. Depending on one's sex label, there are clearly defined behavioral norms that demand conformity to specific roles. These roles are partially delineated in accordance with prevailing sex-role stereotypes (Tresemer & Pleck, 1974).

The role prescribed for an individual on the basis of sex not only affects his or her own behavior but determines certain expectations concerning the appropriate behavior of others as well. Conformity to stereotypically defined sex-role standards may help an individual to gain acceptance for displaying the "right" behavior and to avoid punishment for engaging in the "wrong" behavior (Tresemer & Pleck, 1974). However, as we shall see, the tendency to define male and female sex roles in opposite terms exaggerates the perception of differences between the sexes and obscures the recognition of similarities.

Studies of sex-role stereotypes, both descriptive (average, or "typical," male and female) and prescriptive (ideal male and female), have repeatedly confirmed the view that men are the opposite of women (Broverman, Vogel, Broverman, Clarkson, & Rosenkrantz, 1972; Elman, Press, & Rosenkrantz, 1970; Fernberger, 1948; Lunneborg, 1970; McKee & Sherriffs, 1959). When subjects of both sexes are asked to characterize men and women, they agree that men are strong, independent, worldly, aggressive, ambitious, and logical, as well as blunt, rough, loud, sloppy, and unable to express tender feelings. In contrast, women are described as weak, dependent, passive, not worldly, not ambitious, and illogical, as well as tactful, gentle, understanding, neat in appearance, and able to express tender feelings with ease (Broverman et al., 1972).

Not only are women and men described in stereotypically opposite terms by subjects of various ages, religious affiliations, educational levels, and marital statuses, but the very dimensions underlying these descriptions are different (Broverman et al., 1972). An analysis of the characteristics commonly attributed to men reveals that the most highly valued masculine traits represent a "competency" cluster that includes objectivity, skill in business, and self-confidence. The traits considered most valuable for women comprise a "warmth-expressiveness" cluster that includes tenderness, understanding, and concern for others (Broverman et al., 1972; McKee & Sherriffs, 1957).

Although subjects of both sexes agree that certain masculine and feminine traits are desirable, they consider the masculine traits more desirable than the feminine traits (Rosenkrantz, Vogel, Bee, Broverman, & Broverman, 1968; Sherriffs & Jarrett, 1953; Sherriffs & McKee, 1957). Furthermore, Broverman and her colleagues (1972) found that, of the 41 positive stereotypic traits identified in their study, 29 were attributed to men. Subjects of both sexes were also more likely to attribute desirable feminine traits to men than desirable masculine traits to women.

The tendency on the part of both men and women to evaluate men and masculine traits more positively than women and feminine traits has been widely interpreted to suggest that, in comparison to men, women hold a negative opinion of their worth. In one study, Rosenkrantz et al. (1968) found that the self-ratings of college women and men corresponded closely to their same-sex stereotypes. The women incorporated into their self-ratings the negative aspects of the female stereotype (relative incompetence, irrationality, passivity, and so on) as well as the positive feminine traits (tenderness, warmth, understanding, and so forth). It is interesting to note, however, that the self-ratings of the female subjects were significantly less "feminine" than their ratings of women in general (Rosenkrantz et al., 1968).[1]

In evaluating the mental health of women and men, even practicing clinicians use different criteria, less favorable to women (Broverman, Broverman, Clarkson, Rosenkrantz, & Vogel, 1970; Neulinger, 1968). In one study, 79 female and male mental-health workers were asked to describe a mature, healthy, and socially competent man, woman, or adult whose sex was not specified. Not only did these mental-health workers agree that the profiles of psychologically healthy men and women were significantly different, but their general standard of psychological health (that is, the standard they used to describe a healthy adult, sex unspecified) was applied to men only. According to these psychiatrists, psychologists, and psychiatric social workers, a healthy woman was *less* independent, adventurous, aggressive, and objective and *more* easily influenced, excitable in a minor crisis, and conceited about her appearance than either a healthy male or a healthy unspecified adult (Broverman et al., 1970).

Assessing Sex-Role Stereotypes

Although the existence of sex-role stereotypes has been demonstrated repeatedly, it is difficult to determine the impact of these beliefs on people's perceptions of themselves. Early attempts to specify the content of sex-role stereotypes (both average and ideal) defined sex stereotypes in terms of those traits that most differentiated between the sexes rather than in terms of those that most characterized each sex (Pleck, in press). As a result, measures used to assess sex stereotypes failed to include traits that were seen as common to males and females. As McKee and Sherriffs (1957) observed, the omission of common traits from paper-and-pencil tests designed to tap sex-role stereotypes may have resulted in an exaggerated view of the differences between men and women.

However, as Spence, Helmreich, and Stapp (1974) have recently observed, when traits found to differentiate between the sexes are measured along a single continuum, the mean ratings of females and males seldom fall on opposite sides of the midpoint of a given scale. For example, although the difference between the mean stereotypic ratings of males and females measured on a 10-point continuum ranging from active (10) to passive (1) may be statistically significant, subjects do not rate males as extremely active (9) and females as extremely passive (2); rather, they rate males as more active than females. As Pleck (in press) recently noted, the female stereotype includes masculine as well as feminine traits, in the sense that ratings of

---

[1]Despite the intuitive appeal of the hypothesis that women have lower self-esteem than men, studies comparing the overall self-esteem scores of women and men on standardized tests have generally obtained no differences (Maccoby & Jacklin, 1974). However, the bases of women's and men's positive self-evaluations may differ. Recent evidence suggests that in contrast to males, who tend to value themselves for their strength and potency, females value themselves for their social orientations (Maccoby & Jacklin, 1974).

females may be on the masculine side of the midpoint (5) for many traits, although the mean value of the ratings of males may be higher than the mean value of the ratings of females (for example, 7.3 versus 6.1). Similarly, the male stereotype includes many feminine traits. When sex-role stereotype measures are used that allow subjects to characterize males and females on the basis of both overlapping and differentiating traits, subjects of both sexes agree that the "most feminine" and the "most masculine" persons they can imagine share many desirable traits (Jenkin & Vroegh, 1969). Finally, the fact that measures of sex-role stereotypes are frequently introduced with the request to rate the "typical" or "average" female and male may encourage subjects to respond stereotypically by exaggerating the differences and minimizing the similarities between them (Lunneborg, 1970).

Because the results obtained in studies of sex-role stereotypes vary so dramatically as a function of the method used to measure them,[2] it is difficult to determine what these stereotypes mean even to the people who believe in them (Brannon, 1976). It is even more difficult to assess the effect of such stereotypes on behavior.

One interpretation of the effect of sex-role stereotypes is that they serve to obscure the similarities among people by exaggerating their differences. Indeed, Steinmann and Fox (1966) hypothesized that women share a similar set of life and achievement values and that these values represent a balance of self-achievement and family orientation.

In order to test this hypothesis they asked 837 American women to respond to three forms of the Maferr Inventory of Feminine Values (Steinmann & Fox, 1974). The inventory consists of 34 statements representing a particular value or value judgment related to women's activities and satisfactions. Strength of agreement or disagreement with each statement is indicated on a 5-point Likert scale. The statements represent a continuum ranging from a traditional, family-oriented concept of femininity (passive) to a nontraditional, self-achieving-oriented concept (active). Each subject responded to three forms of the inventory: Self-Concept, Own Ideal Woman, and Woman's Concept of Man's Ideal Woman. The results indicated that the subjects perceived themselves as having achieved a balance between self-achievement and family orientation. Furthermore, the relatively small discrepancy between the subjects' Self-Concept and Own Ideal ratings suggested that these women were pretty much what they wanted to be. However, they did not think that they were what men wanted them to be; they perceived Man's Ideal Woman as one who was almost exclusively family-oriented—that is, who placed her duties as wife and mother before her needs for personal growth and development.

Steinmann and Fox also asked 423 men to respond to the Maferr Inventory as they believed their ideal woman would. The men's responses for their ideal woman were strikingly similar to the women's ratings of

---

[2]For example, using Peabody's matched-scale methodology, which equalizes the availability of male and female-valued adjectives, Koeske and Koeske (1975) failed to obtain preferences for men and masculine traits. Similar results were obtained by Frieze (1975).

themselves and of their ideal woman. However, the women's ratings of men's ideal woman were more traditionally feminine than men's ratings of their own ideal woman. Similar results were obtained by McKee and Sherriffs (1959). Women apparently believe that men adhere to the traditional feminine myth much more closely than men actually do. In over 20 years of sex-role research Steinmann and Fox have replicated these findings across a large number of Western cultures (Steinmann & Fox, 1974; Steinmann, 1975).

It is interesting to note that the same paradox reflected in the research on the female role is reflected in a recent study of the male role (Steinmann & Fox, 1974). Men and women share ideal male images. However, the discrepancy between the men's perception of women's ideal man and the actual women's rating of their ideal man is quite striking. The ideal man in women's ratings is somewhat more family-oriented than the ideal man in men's own ratings. However, when rating women's ideal man, men erroneously conclude that women want a man who is more family-oriented than self-oriented. Thus, neither women nor men seem to portray accurately the ideal member of their own sex from the perspective of the opposite sex.

Whatever the weight of the grain of truth at the basis of every stereotype, it appears that the extent of the misperception far outweighs the actual divergence between the sexes. Unger and Siiter (1974) have recently suggested that sex-role stereotypes may best be understood as shared misperceptions regarding the values of the opposite sex. Interestingly, the results of several recent studies suggest that males' perceptions of the values of females are less accurate than females' perceptions of the values of males (Garcia & Dingman, 1975; Siiter & Unger, 1975; Unger & Siiter, 1974).

Since sex-role stereotypes influence what is considered appropriate for each sex, thus representing cultural expectations for conformity with an assigned role, they may also influence an individual's self-definition. As we have seen, the literature on sex-role stereotypes appears to support the contention that a woman's place is in the home. Women who adhere to a stereotypic definition of the female role are likely to assume that they lack the necessary "masculine" characteristics to ensure competitive success and are therefore suited to fulfill only their socially defined roles as dutiful wives and devoted mothers. This conclusion is, of course, based on the assumption that, if Kitty views herself as gentle and nurturant, she cannot view herself as independent and logical.

Early attempts to identify trait differences between the sexes were based on the assumption that the differences reflected in the sex-role stereotypes were real. Masculinity-femininity (M-F) was postulated as the central trait around which differences in the personalities of males and females were organized (Terman & Miles, 1936). Tests designed to measure the M-F construct assumed that masculinity and femininity represented opposite poles of a single dimension. The underlying traits assumed to comprise the "essence" of the feminine personality included tenderness, emotionality, passivity, and concern with the well-being of others. In contrast, autonomy, dominance, aggression, and adventurousness were seen as core masculine traits.

Test items were therefore selected on the basis of the items' ability to discriminate the responses of females from those of males (Constantinople, 1973). For example, one section of the Terman-Miles M-F test asks subjects to select which of four words they associate with a standard word. When males and females are presented with the standard word "moon" and asked to choose from among the associative words "light," "month," "round," and "night," males select "light" whereas females select "night" or "round" (Oakley, 1972). An individual's total score reflects the degree to which his or her responses across many items agree with those of other respondents of the same sex. Because bipolarity is assumed, obtaining a high feminine score excludes the possibility of obtaining a high masculine score and vice versa.

Since the tests were comprised of items that would successfully discriminate between the sexes, it is not surprising that females and males characterized themselves in opposite terms. However, recent attempts to relate sex differences in personality traits to the behavior of women and men have met with limited success. As a result, researchers have begun to question the assumption that the sexes are most accurately characterized by the traits that best differentiate between them (Bem, 1974; Bem & Lenney, 1976; Constantinople, 1973; Pleck, in press; Spence et al., 1974).

The historical tendency to define masculinity-femininity on a single bipolar dimension resulted in an artificial dichotomy and encouraged social scientists to define masculinity and femininity in absolute terms. An alternative conceptualization introduced by Sandra Bem maintains that masculinity and femininity represent independent dimensions (Bem, 1974). In her view, a given individual may be both masculine and feminine. Bem labels such individuals "androgynous."

Androgyny

The term *androgyne* comes from the Greek *andro* (male) and *gyne* (female) and means an individual who possesses both male and female physical characteristics. Bem uses the term *androgyny* to refer to individuals who have both feminine and masculine psychological characteristics. In order to measure androgyny, she constructed the Bem Sex Role Inventory (BSRI). The BSRI is comprised of a Masculinity Scale and a Femininity Scale, each of which contains 20 personality characteristics selected on the basis of sex-typed social desirability. Characteristics selected for the Femininity Scale include affectionate, gentle, and understanding; characteristics selected for the Masculinity Scale include ambitious, dominant, and self-reliant. The BSRI also includes 20 items representing personality characteristics generally held to be socially desirable for both sexes (for example, conscientious, sincere, and adaptable).

Subjects indicate the extent to which each of the 60 items characterizes them on a 7-point scale ranging from "almost never or never true of me" to "always or almost always true of me." Respondents are classified on the basis of their scores as sex-typed (masculine or feminine) or androgynous. In order to be classified as androgynous, an individual must endorse an approximately equal number of male and female characteristics as self-descriptive—for example, rate herself or himself as usually analytical, forceful, and self-sufficient *and* usually affectionate, gentle, and tender.[3] In order to be classified as sex-typed (feminine or masculine), a person must endorse only those attributes that characterize one sex and reject those that characterize the other sex.

Psychometric analyses of the BSRI (Bem, 1974) reveal that, as predicted, the Masculinity and Femininity Scales are empirically independent; that is, the responses of a given individual to the 20 items that comprise the Femininity Scale do not predict how that individual will respond to the 20 masculine items and vice versa. A subject's scores on the scale are internally consistent and reliable over time and are not correlated with the tendency to characterize oneself as socially desirable.

Over one third of the college students included in Bem's original sample were androgynous, 50% were sex-typed in the conventional direction (masculine males and feminine females), and the remainder were sex-reversed. The incidence of androgyny in the general population has not yet been assessed. However, studies of masculinity-femininity using traditional measures reveal that an individual's M-F scores change as a function of education. College women obtain higher masculine scores than their less educated peers, and college men score higher on femininity than noncollege men. Thus, it is reasonable to anticipate that the more education an individual has, the more likely she or he is to be androgynous.

It should be noted that, according to Bem's operational definition of androgyny, in order to be classified as androgynous, a person must endorse a balance of masculine and feminine traits as self-descriptive. Given this definition, it is not possible to distinguish between a person who scores androgynous because she or he endorses neither masculine nor feminine traits and a person who defines herself or himself as highly masculine *and* feminine. As Spence et al. (1974) have recently suggested, there is a conceptual distinction between individuals who score androgynous because they endorse neither masculine nor feminine characteristics as particularly self-descriptive and those who characterize themselves as simultaneously highly masculine and highly feminine. Using a methodology that allowed them to distinguish between these two groups, Spence and her colleagues found that approximately half of the male and female college subjects in their sample

---

[3]In order to determine an individual's androgyny score, a student's t-ratio for matched groups is calculated for the difference between a person's endorsement of masculine and feminine personality characteristics. If the obtained t-value is nonsignificant the individual is classified as androgynous. A significant positive t-value indicates a feminine sex-typed score; a significant negative t-value indicates a masculine sex-typed score.

who would have been identified as androgynous with Bem's scaling method scored low feminine and low masculine (Spence, Helmreich, & Stapp, 1975). Furthermore, the mean self-esteem scores were highest for men and women who scored high on both masculinity and femininity and lowest for those who scored low on both masculinity and femininity in the Personal Attributes Questionnaire (Spence et al., 1974). As a result, Spence and her colleagues designate as androgynous only those individuals who score high masculine *and* high feminine. Individuals who endorse neither masculine nor feminine traits as self-descriptive (low masculine/low feminine) are considered to be undifferentiated. Spence's conceptualization of sex-role identification thus yields a four-fold typology: masculine, feminine, androgynous, and undifferentiated. Similar typologies have been proposed by both Berzins (1975) and Heilbrun (1976).

Recently, Bem and her colleagues have acknowledged the utility of distinguishing between androgynous and undifferentiated subjects in studies of the effects of sex typing on behavior (Bem & Lenney, 1976; Bem et al., in press). Thus, it appears that in future research the term *androgynous* will be reserved for those individuals who score high in both masculinity and femininity. Unlike androgynous individuals, who are high in self-esteem and evidence few behavioral restrictions in response to sex-typed tasks, those who are undifferentiated have low self-esteem and suffer from some behavioral inhibition (Bem et al., in press). Interestingly, both androgynous and undifferentiated individuals are alike in that neither group adheres to self-concepts defined as exclusively sex-typed. Androgynous individuals endorse both masculine and feminine traits as self-descriptive, while undifferentiated individuals do not endorse either masculine or feminine traits as particularly self-descriptive.

As traditionally defined, culturally imposed definitions of femininity and masculinity restrict the behavioral alternatives of women (and men). A woman who adheres to the stereotypically defined norms governing feminine sex-typed behavior may fear that any indication of deviance from that role will imply masculinity. Thus, she may perceive the recognition and expressions of those "masculine" aspects of her character as threatening and have strong needs to anchor her self-definition against a masculine "better" half.[4] Indeed, she may measure her success as a woman by her ability to catch (and hold on to) a man. His pleasure is the object of her domestic concern, and he is the source of her reinforcement for domestic tasks. The female role defined in stereotypically "feminine" terms dictates that, in order to maintain her femininity, she must play woman to his "man."

At the opposite end of the bipolar sex-role dimension is the woman who adheres to a stereotypically masculine definition of her role. Such a woman presumably denies the feminine aspects of her character and focuses exclusively on the development of her more "masculine" attributes, such as

---

[4]Ellis and Bentler (1973) obtained some evidence suggesting that it is not a person's view of her or his own sex but, rather, her or his view of the opposite sex that provides the primary frame of reference for a person's conception of himself or herself as sex-typed.

self-assertion, dominance, and competence. According to the stereotype, this woman wears her hair pulled tightly in a bun, dresses in severely tailored gray, and gives up her claims to womanhood by remaining single and childless. (Of course, her career flourishes.)

In contrast, the androgynous woman (or man) subscribes to a self-definition that includes both feminine and masculine traits. Theoretically, androgynous individuals should have the psychological freedom to conform to environmental demands to behave in *either* a feminine or a masculine way, depending on the situation. The results of a series of studies examining the relationship between androgyny and behavior clearly suggest that androgynous women (and men) enjoy a level of psychological and behavioral freedom that their sex-typed and sex-reversed counterparts do not share.

Sex Typing and Behavior

Hypothesizing that sex typing limits a person's behavioral flexibility, Bem (1975) conducted two studies in which sex-typed and androgynous subjects were asked to perform a task that, on the basis of pretests, had been classified as either masculine or feminine. In the first study, resistance to social pressure (presumably a "masculine" characteristic) was assessed in a situation in which subjects could choose to maintain their independence by assigning the label "funny" to objectively funny cartoons and the label "unfunny" to objectively unfunny cartoons or to conform to the opinions of others who were preprogrammed to label funny cartoons as unfunny and vice versa. As predicted, masculine and androgynous subjects (both females and males) were more resistant to pressures to conform than feminine subjects. No differences were obtained between masculine and androgynous subjects who were equally likely to maintain their independence.

In the second study, masculine, feminine, and androgynous subjects were provided with the opportunity to interact with (nurture) a kitten. Results paralleling those obtained in the first study were predicted; that is, feminine and androgynous subjects would spend more time nurturing the kitten than masculine subjects. Feminine and androgynous men did spend more time playing with the kitten than masculine men. However, feminine women spent less time playing with the kitten than either androgynous or masculine women.

Taken together, the results of these two studies suggest that androgynous people feel freer to behave in a manner consistent with the demands of the situation than sex-typed people. In these two studies, androgynous people were able to both maintain independence under social pressure to conform and be nurturant. However, evidence that sex typing imposes stereotypically defined behavioral restrictions was stronger for men than for women. Masculine men were independent but not nurturant, and feminine men were nurturant but not independent. Masculine women were independent, but feminine women were not nurturant—at least not when provided with the opportunity to play with a kitten.

In order to determine whether feminine women's low level of nurturance was specific to animals or reflected a more general behavioral deficit, such as a reluctance to act assertively in interpersonal situations by initiating an interaction, Bem (1975; Bem et al., in press) conducted two additional studies. In one study, subjects were provided with an opportunity to interact with (nurture) a 5-month-old baby (Bem, 1975). As in the kitten study, feminine and androgynous men were equally responsive to the baby and were significantly more nurturant than the masculine men. Although the original analyses of the women's responses did not support the hypothesis, subsequent analyses, in which the non-sex-typed subjects were separated into two groups (androgynous and undifferentiated), revealed that, regardless of sex, masculine subjects were significantly less nurturant than either feminine or androgynous subjects (Bem et. al., in press).

The second study was designed in such a way that subjects could display nurturance without having to accept the responsibility of either initiating or maintaining interaction with an adult (Bem, 1975; Bem et al., in press). Subjects were assigned the role of "listener" in a study of the "acquaintance" process. The "talker" (a confederate of the experimenter) characterized himself or herself as a lonely transfer student. Measures of the subjects' expressed nurturance included facial expressions, nods, and comments such as "uh hum." As predicted, both feminine women and men were more responsive listeners than either androgynous or masculine men and women. The fact that feminine women found it easiest to express nurturance in the one situation in which they were not required to take an active role has been interpreted by Bem (Bem et al., in press) to suggest that adherence to the traditional sex-role stereotype limits women's ability to take action even more severely than men's.

Sex-typed individuals not only feel more compelled than androgynous ones to respond within the confines of their stereotypically defined sex roles but are also more likely to avoid cross-sexed behavior, even if it costs them money to do so. Bem and Lenney (1976) asked sex-typed and androgynous women and men to select which of 60 different masculine, feminine, or neutral activities they would be willing to perform for pay, while being photographed. The activities were presented in pairs, and the less sex-appropriate choice always paid more money. For example, female subjects were asked to choose between "preparing a baby bottle" for 2¢ and "oiling a squeaky hinge" for 4¢. Sex-typed subjects were more likely than either androgynous or sex-reversed subjects (masculine women and feminine men) to avoid cross-sex activities. This was true even when the experimenter was of their own sex, a situation that presumably removed one obvious barrier to cross-sex activity (the presence of a member of the opposite sex).

Once the subjects had made their selections, the experimenter asked them to perform three sex-appropriate, three sex-inappropriate, and three neutral activities and pretended to photograph them. After performing each activity, subjects were asked to indicate how they felt about themselves. Sex-typed subjects reported the greatest discomfort after performing a sex-inappropriate activity and felt worse about themselves after their activity.

Overall, the results of the work of Bem and her colleagues suggest that the behavior of people who adhere to stereotypically defined conceptions of themselves is severely restricted.

These findings clearly call into question the validity of the traditional assumption that masculine men and feminine women typify mental health. Instead of facilitating general psychological or social adjustment, a high level of sex typing may limit not only the behavioral flexibility of individuals but their potential for growth as well (Bem, 1972). As we saw in Chapter Three, high femininity in females has been found to be associated with high anxiety and poor adjustment. Women who define themselves and their roles in traditionally stereotypic terms may be assured of acceptance for displaying the "right" behavior. However, the limitations placed on their ability to respond to the demands of a given situation (initiating interactions with kittens or even babies) suggest that their actions are motivated more by the fear that they will be punished for behaving inappropriately (Bem, 1975) than by their conviction that the "feminine" response is the only appropriate response.[5] There is no evidence to suggest that androgynous women see themselves as less feminine than their more traditionally oriented peers (Hawley, 1971; O'Leary & Depner, 1976).

Recently, Heilbrun (1976) used a four-fold typology of sex-role definition similar to the one proposed by Spence and her colleagues and found that androgynous individuals (both females and males) were better adjusted (that is, less likely to seek treatment at a campus mental-health clinic) than either undifferentiated or sex-typed individuals. People who adhere to androgynous conceptions of themselves appear to show both greater behavioral flexibility and higher levels of psychological adjustment. Feminine women (and masculine men) may fit the stereotypic prescription for "how one ought to be," but they do not appear to function most effectively.

Changing Sex-Role Stereotypes

At the beginning of this chapter it was suggested that sex roles are partially delineated in accordance with prevailing sex-role stereotypes (Tresemer & Pleck, 1974). One would expect stereotypes to change and, consequently, sex roles to change too. And yet most of the recent studies of sex-role stereotypes provide little evidence for such changes (Elman et al., 1970; Neufeld, Langmeyer, & Seeman, 1974; Spence & Helmreich, 1972). Even when evidence exists, it appears to be based on the recognition that endorsing traditionally defined sex-role stereotypes is no longer considered the "socially desirable" response.

O'Leary and Depner (1975), for example, found that, when male college students were asked to characterize their "ideal woman," they generated a profile of "wonderwoman"—a more competent, more successful,

---

[5]Spence, Helmreich, and Stapp (1975) investigating the relationship between sex-role identification and self esteem found that the self esteem scores of traditionally sex-typed women were significantly lower than those of androgynous women.

and more adventurous person than college women's ideal man. It is tempting to interpret these results as an indication that sex-role stereotypes are changing. A more plausible explanation, however, may be that these men were aware of the consciousness-raising attempts of the women's liberation movement and did not want to be labeled "male chauvinist pigs." The results of a study by Komarovsky (1973) lend additional support to this interpretation. When she asked a sample of college males to indicate their role expectations for women, most agreed that women should have the opportunity to pursue careers at all levels and expressed higher esteem for working women than for housewives. However, when asked about the role expectations they held for their own future wives, most men were adamant in their expressed preference for "traditionally oriented" spouses, whose major concerns centered around the needs of husband and family.

Conceptions of the Female Role

Sex-role stereotypes convey cultural expectations for the behavior of people in certain categories or in certain situations. However, we do not always encourage people to act in accordance with these expectations (Brannon, 1976). For example, on the basis of the stereotype we may expect women to gossip, but we do not insist that they gossip. Indeed, we may be pleased to find that they do not.

Roles, on the other hand, may be defined as "any pattern of behaviors that a given individual in a specified (set of) situation(s) is both (1) expected and (2) encouraged and/or trained to perform" (Brannon, 1976, p. 5). In American society the primary roles of women and men are clearly defined: women marry and have children; men work. However, within the last decade we have become increasingly aware that not all women subscribe to a definition of themselves or their roles based exclusively on the stereotypic assumption that "women's place is in the home." Most women do marry and have children, but many of these women also work outside the home. Some even pursue careers in fields traditionally defined as appropriate only for men.

From 1900 to 1974 the participation of adult women in the labor force rose from 20% to 45% (Troll, 1975). In 1969 over 29 million American women (37% of the total labor force) were employed, and 40% of these women were married (U.S. Department of Labor, 1969). Whether or not a married woman works outside the home and the type of job she holds depend on a variety of factors such as her level of education, her husband's income, and her interests. Some employed married women are forced to accept the dual role of wife-mother and worker out of economic necessity (Hoffman & Nye, 1974), but others enter (or remain in) the labor force by choice. The decision of a woman to work or not is influenced by her conception of the female role.

Historically, American women have been encouraged to assume the traditionally feminine roles of wife and mother. Parents who sent their daughters to college encouraged them to become nurses or teachers, so they would have something to fall back on "just in case." For most college women the prospect of finding themselves in the spring of their senior year without an engagement ring was frightening. Career women were portrayed as cold and masculine, and no young woman wanted to be an "old maid." Of course, the possibility that some young women might be interested in pursuing a career was recognized, but such women were advised to adopt an "Is it worth it?" attitude toward career aspirations (Depner & O'Leary, 1976).

For example, in their 1954 publication entitled *How to Be a Woman*, Frank and Frank cautioned:

> Consider your job from every standpoint: the satisfactions it gives you and how necessary they are, the *net* income it contributes after you pay for all the services your job prevents you from doing for yourself, the effect it has on your stamina, your disposition, your relationship with your husband. When you become pregnant, set the time when you feel the job had best be given up. And decide, with your husband, when— and whether—you think you should resume. Perhaps an honest examination of the problem will suggest other solutions: a less taxing part-time job, or a secretarial/typing service you can conduct from your home, or the development of a latent skill, such as painting tiles or hooking rugs, which will help you keep alert and active without disrupting your entire home life or cutting off the extra income you are counting on [p. 69].*

Thus, women were encouraged to imagine all *possible* negative consequences of a career and to weigh them against *assured* positive outcomes. Obviously, in order for a career to be regarded as justifiable, it would have to offer sufficient benefits to cancel out all possible liabilities (Depner & O'Leary, 1976).

During the 1970s a wider range of roles have been defined as acceptable for women. Career women are portrayed by the media as vital and exciting. Children of working mothers, once assumed to be deprived, are currently being characterized as mature and adaptable. The popular press abounds with stories about role innovation and alternative life styles for women. At the same time, the Equal Rights Amendment is being met with strong opposition, and women are flocking to discover Fascinating Womanhood and striving to become Total Women. Given these alternatives, it is possible to classify women on the basis of their role orientation (traditional versus nontraditional).

Nontraditionally Oriented Women

Not surprisingly, women who subscribe to nontraditional definitions of the female role tend to be career-oriented (Alper, 1973; Tangri, 1972; Vogel, Rosenkrantz, Broverman, Broverman, & Clarkson, 1975). Indeed, most

---

*From *How to Be a Woman*, by L. K. Frank and M. Frank. Copyright 1954 by The Bobbs-Merrill Company, Inc. Reprinted by permission.

early attempts to characterize nontraditionally oriented women selected subjects on the basis of their commitment to careers historically regarded as appropriate only for men.

On the assumption that for a woman to succeed in the competitive economic marketplace she must possess traits regarded as stereotypically masculine, a number of studies have compared the personality profiles of professional females with those of their male colleagues and with those of traditionally oriented women. In a study of three generations of women psychologists, Bachtold and Werner (1971) found that these women's responses to Cattell's 16 Personality Factor Questionnaire indicated that they were significantly more aloof, flexible, adventuresome, inner-directed, confident, radical, and self-sufficient than nonprofessional women. Helson (1971) compared the personality characteristics of women mathematicians rated by other mathematicians as creative with a group of women mathematicians not so rated and with a group of creative men mathematicians. The scores of the creative women did not differ significantly from those of the other two groups on measures of cognitive ability. However, in comparison to creative men, creative women mathematicians did manifest greater (1) rebellious independence, narcissism, introversion, and rejection of outside influences, (2) symbolic interests and ability to find self-expression and self-gratification in directed research activity, and (3) flexibility, or lack of constriction, in general attitudes and mathematic work. In turn, the creative men mathematicians manifested higher dominance, sociability, social presence, and self-acceptance than their women colleagues.

Similar results were obtained in a study by O'Leary and Braun (1972) comparing the personality characteristics of academic women (in a variety of disciplines) with men colleagues in the same academic fields and with women who held B.A. degrees but had neither entered graduate school nor worked outside the home. Professional women not only differed from the nonprofessional women in being relatively aloof, dominant, stable, and self-sufficient, but they scored higher on these dimensions than their male colleagues. In addition, the female academicians were similar to their male colleagues but significantly different from their female peers in being imaginative, radical, experimental, and freethinking.

Tangri (1972) investigated the personality characteristics of role-innovative college women. She classified senior women as role innovators on the basis of their occupational choices in fields traditionally considered inappropriate for the female sex role (for example, fields in which fewer than 30% of those employed were women). She found that the self-descriptions of role-innovative college women tended to be characterized by responses scaled as unconventional, intellectual, not too successful, and away from the extreme feminine position. Tangri attributed the low success scores of the role innovators to the fact that the "more innovative women were generally in more competitive fields and dealing with subjects considered 'tougher' than the more traditional women" (p. 187). Overall, the profile of the role innovator emphasized autonomy, self-reliance, and the assumption of responsibility for others.

The recurrent profile of professional and professionally oriented (nontraditional) women depicts an individual who is nonconforming, self-reliant, independent, flexible, self-directed, and high in ego strength. Such a profile is generally antithetical to the traditional feminine stereotype. Since all of these women have been subjected to socialization pressures emphasizing sex typing, it is important to try to identify the origins of their ability to withstand (or ignore) those pressures.

Rossi (1965) has suggested that "deviant choices in adult roles are rooted in other kinds of deviance earlier in the life line" (p. 2). She defines deviance as a departure from a cultural expectation of what is appropriate for a given individual on the basis of age, sex, class, and so on. Among the variables that have been identified as related to early-life differences are a number of demographic characteristics. For example, Graham (1970) and Helson (1971) found a significant number of career women to be either foreign-born or the daughters of foreign-born parents. Tangri (1972), Graham (1970), and Ginzberg (1966) all report a high incidence of daughters of working and/or professionally trained mothers within their nontraditionally oriented female samples. Astin (1969), Helson (1971), and Ginzberg (1966) found that the educational level of both parents of nontraditionally oriented women was higher than average.

There is also some evidence to suggest that religious/ethnic affiliation may be related to the selection of nontraditional occupations among women. Both Ginzberg (1966) and Helson (1971) report that, in relation to the proportion of Catholic and Jewish women in the general population, Catholic women tend to be underrepresented in male-dominated professions, whereas Jewish women are overrepresented. Another frequent finding is that professional women tend to come from small families with one sibling or none (Ginzberg, 1966).

On the basis of the work of Crandall and Battle (1970), which indicated that children who show the greatest intellectual gains are those who have been encouraged to develop independence, O'Leary and Braun (1972) hypothesized that nontraditionally oriented women were more likely than traditionally oriented women to come from families in which early independence was encouraged. Using the Torgoff Developmental Time Table (Torgoff, 1961) to tap perceptions of independence in childhood (recalled retrospectively), they found that the professional women in their sample did report that they were granted the opportunity to be independent at a younger age than the nonprofessional women. Similar results were obtained by Tangri (1972), who found that the parents of role innovators had been more likely to stress early independence training than those of more traditionally oriented women. Tangri relates this finding to maternal employment, pointing out that, because role innovators tend to come from families in which the mother was employed, they received greater independence training. In her recent review of the literature on the effects of maternal employment, Hoffman (1974b) cites a number of studies that have obtained similar results (see Almquist & Angrist, 1971; Birnbaum, 1971; Hartley, 1960). It has been suggested that the impact of a working mother on her daughter's (nontraditional) role orientation is not limited to the acquisition of independence. Working mothers, particularly those who are satisfied with their dual role, may serve as nontraditional female-role models for their daughters (Baruch, 1972).

Nontraditional Role Models

Kemper (1968), utilizing the concept of reference groups (groups with which an individual identifies and that, therefore, provide a basis for social comparison) to explain achievement motivation, suggests that a role model may function as a comparison group (or individual). Such a model demonstrates for an individual (the actor) how something is done in a technical sense. The essential quality of the role model is that she (or he) possesses skills and displays techniques that the actor lacks (or thinks she lacks) and from whom, by observation and comparison, the actor can learn. In Kemper's view, such a role model does not motivate, influence, reward, or persuade the actor but merely provides a technical explanation of how the role is to be performed.

Most women who aspire to careers do not substitute the work role for the more traditional wife-mother-homemaker one but add a 40-hour work week to the 50-60 hours they spend on domestic tasks (Turner, 1964; Warren, 1968). In order to set and strive for realistic occupational goals that emphasize achievement-directed behavior, women may require role models who illustrate how to combine marriage and career successfully (Douvan, 1974).

A number of studies have examined the influence of mothers' occupational choices and role satisfaction on the work orientation (traditional versus nontraditional) of their daughters (Almquist & Angrist, 1971; Astin, 1968; Siegel & Curtis, 1963; Tangri, 1972; White, 1967). In general the findings suggest that nontraditionally oriented mothers who serve as role models, successfully combining family and career and expressing satisfaction with their life styles, have daughters who are similarly oriented (Baruch, 1972). The availability of such a model within the home apparently encourages daughters to adopt the working-mother role.[6]

When asked to indicate the most important source of influence on their occupational choices, nontraditionally oriented women most often name professors and persons in those occupations (Almquist & Angrist, 1971; Tangri, 1972). Traditionally oriented women, on the other hand, are more likely to view family members and friends as influential, although many report that no one influenced their choices (Almquist & Angrist, 1971; Simpson & Simpson, 1963).

---

[6]Although working mothers may serve as nontraditional role models in the technical sense (Kemper, 1968), nontraditionally oriented daughters do not appear to identify strongly with parents of either sex. Tangri (1972) found that role-innovative young women reported maintaining substantial cognitive distance from both parents, although they did express warm feelings toward mother and some perceived similarity with father.

Almquist and Angrist (1971) suggest that faculty role models may provide psychological incentives to select a particular occupation. These incentives include rewards for academic performance or work activity in which the professor aids the student in developing a conception of herself (or himself) as a person capable of operating effectively in a given occupational role. Looking back at my own undergraduate experience, I cannot help but be struck by the extent to which the encouragement of one (male) professor (a social psychologist) shaped my conception of myself as a professional. Because the college I attended had no graduate programs, faculty were forced to rely on undergraduates to help them with their research. As a result, interested students were encouraged to become actively involved in both research and writing. By the end of my senior year I had helped to design and run three studies that were subsequently published. There is probably no more effective means to develop a sense of professional identity as a psychologist than to see one's name in print as the junior author of a journal article. By the time I entered graduate school, I naively regarded myself as a social psychologist.

Unfortunately, the number of professional women available to serve as role models is limited even in academic settings. This is particularly distressing in light of the results of a study conducted by Joesting and Joesting (1972) suggesting that qualified female role models may enhance the self-images of women students. Male and female college students were asked to rate the value of being a woman. Half the students were enrolled in a class taught by a qualified male and half in a class taught by a qualified female. In the class taught by a male instructor 26% of the women thought there was "nothing good about being a woman." In contrast, only 5% of the women enrolled in the class taught by a female instructor thought there was nothing good about being a woman. It is possible, of course, that some of the women students were reluctant to admit in the presence of a qualified woman that they did not value the female role.

Even when professional women are potentially available in a given setting to serve as role models, they are not always interested in helping other women "learn the ropes." Such women have been labeled by Staines, Tavris, and Jayarante (1974) "queen bees." Queen bees are women who have achieved professional success and are antifeminist. They are strongly individualistic and deny the existence of discrimination based on sex. Despite the fact that they often hold positions of power and could help other women advance, they do not offer their support.

A number of reasons have been postulated for the existence of the queen-bee syndrome (Staines et al., 1974). First, the very organizational settings in which these women have experienced success may reward them for their unwillingness to advance the cause of other women. Second, these women may identify more with the male colleagues that surround them than with women as a group or class. Third, they may enjoy their unique positions as successful women in male-dominated fields and be unwilling to compete with young (female) "upstarts," whom they may view as unduly advantaged by the vocal support of the women's movement. Historically, the privileged members of any minority have tended to be resistant to social change that promised to improve that status of all its members. Fortunately, such resistance is usually short-lived, and Staines and his colleagues conclude that there is already evidence that the queen-bee phenomenon is becoming less common.

As we noted earlier in this chapter, most women do marry and have children. Thus, women who strive for nontraditional occupational success are more likely than their more traditional peers to perceive nontraditional careers as compatible with the satisfaction of their social and marital needs. In a recent study, Trigg and Perlman (1976) found that, compared with women whose career choices were traditionally feminine (nursing and medical rehabilitation), women whose career choices were nontraditional (medicine and dentistry) were less prone to view marriage as incompatible with career commitment. Consistently with results obtained by Tangri (1972) and Hawley (1971, 1972), nontraditionally oriented women were more likely to view the attitudes of significant others (boyfriends and parents, particularly mother) as supportive of their career choices. The availability of support from significant others is probably crucial in determining a woman's role orientation, because the decision to perform multiple roles necessarily results in some degree of role conflict.

Role Conflict

Because many of the female participants in the labor force are married, current discussion has focused on how women do (or should) perform in both career and family roles. All of us fulfill a variety of roles in pursuing our everyday activities; in the course of any day each of us may function in the roles of parent, student, employee, and daughter or son. Each of these roles carries with it a set of role relationships with other people. The requirements of the role itself, as well as the expectations of others who hold positions in our various role sets, make behavioral demands on us. When the behavioral demands of multiple roles are incompatible, we are likely to experience role conflict. Intrarole conflict occurs when multiple demands for behavior within a given role are incompatible. For example, as a student you may want to spend more time working in the library on a term paper, but your professor thinks you should spend more time studying for the weekly quiz. Interrole conflict occurs when the demands associated with two or more roles are incompatible. For example, your final exam is scheduled at the same time that your youngest child is starring as a tree in the kindergarten play.

Both intra- and interrole conflicts may originate from the incompatible demands placed on you by others (role senders). However, the most common source of role conflict is role overload (Herman & Kuczynski, 1974); that is, you may recognize the legitimacy of the expectations of all your role senders but be unable to satisfy these expectations within the time available to you. Time constraints force most of us to set priorities and risk the disapproval of some of our role senders on some occasions.

Recently, Hall (1972a) has proposed a model of strategies women use to cope with role conflicts (O'Leary, 1974b). On the basis of the results of a survey of college-educated women, Hall identified 16 behavioral strategies commonly used by women to cope with role conflict—strategies that can be grouped into three general behavioral responses. Type-1 coping, or structural role redefinition, involves altering the expectations imposed on us by others. This type of coping is probably the most effective means of dealing with role conflict, although it necessarily involves the approval of role senders, which may be difficult to obtain. For example, not all professors are willing to excuse a student from a final exam in order to allow a parent to attend a kindergarten play. Type-2 coping, or personal role redefinition, involves changing our own expectations and behavior, rather than attempting to change the environment. Thus, a married woman attending night classes may unilaterally decide that she will not cook dinner for the family on the nights that her class meets. Whether this strategy proves effective will depend in part on the reactions of her role senders. Personal role redefinition may not be effective if one's role senders continue to demand conformity to their expectations. Type-3 coping involves an attempt to meet all the role demands by planning, scheduling, organizing better, and working harder.

Examining the relationship between coping style and satisfaction among women, Hall (1972b) found that Type-1 coping was positively related to satisfaction, while Type-3 coping was negatively related to satisfaction. In accordance with Kroeker's (1963) suggestion that attempts to respond to all the demands associated with multiple roles reflect a defensive rather than a coping behavior, Hall views Type-3 coping as maladaptive. The fact that he found the incidence of Type-3 coping to be highest among women employed part time and who performed a limited number of roles lends some credence to Hall's interpretation of Type-3 coping as defensive. Objectively, part-time work probably does involve less potential role conflict than full-time work, as does performing one or two roles as compared to three or four or more. Women who work part time and who perform a limited number of roles may expect themselves to handle conflict successfully. However, if they adopt defensive behavioral strategies to cope with role conflict, they may feel less adequate than women who cope actively with a greater number of conflicts. On the other hand, I have yet to meet a professional married woman with children who is familiar with Hall's work who does not categorize herself as a Type-3 coper.

When Hall (1972b) examined the role pressures, coping behavior, self-image, satisfaction, and happiness as functions of age, life stage, and number of life roles, he found that women's stage in life was related to experienced role conflict and pressure and that age was not. Since life stage was measured in terms of the ages and number of children in the family, the results indicate that children are a major influence on a married woman's perceived role pressures. For example, her satisfaction with the way she manages her role(s) decreases with the addition of each new child to the family (Lopata,

1966) and then rises again when the children begin to leave home. As the number of roles a woman plays increases, she experiences more conflict, feels more time pressure, and relies more on Type-2 coping (personal role redefinition).

Hall and Gordon (1973) report that among married women, employed or not, home pressures are the most important contributors to experienced role conflict, (low) satisfaction, and (low) happiness. Apparently, home-related activities are of prime concern to married women, regardless of their personal orientation (traditional versus nontraditional). Furthermore, the role conflicts experienced by women are strongly related to their perception of what men expect from women (Gordon & Hall, 1974).

In a recent study, Herman and Kuczynski (1974) compared the perception of interrole conflict of men and women employed in similar occupations. Interestingly, the women reported a lower level of career-family conflict than did the men. The authors suggest that these women may consider multiple-role demands on their time as a way of life and thus more readily tolerate a higher level of role overload than men. The women did, however, express conflict between their jobs and home-maintenance responsibilities. Home maintenance is, of course, a stereotypically feminine activity. Home pressures contributing to the experience of interrole conflict among employed married women may be specifically related to their perception that they are unable to combine home maintenance and career and still demonstrate appropriate feminine concerns.

American society has assigned the role of breadwinner and status giver to the male and that of homemaker to the female. In a study of 54 professional couples, Poloma and Garland (1971) found that the assumption of a professional role by the wife did not result in a dramatic change in family roles. Their data yielded no indication that either women or men desired an equal sharing of traditionally masculine and feminine tasks within the family. Similar results have been obtained by a number of other investigators (Bryson, Bryson, Licht, & Licht, 1976; Holstrom, 1972; Poloma, 1972; Rapaport & Rapaport, 1972). While society may be approaching the day when the average married woman is employed outside the home, it does not appear that any dramatic increase in the prestige of the feminine role (Touhey, 1974a) or any reversal of male-female roles within the family will result. Blood and Wolfe (1960) found certain differences in the division of labor in families in which the wife was employed outside the home, but they did not find any indication that the "relative balance" of domestic roles had been upset.

Similar results were obtained in a recent study of husband and wife psychologists (Bryson et al., 1976). The wives of the professional pairs were more productive (as measured, among other things, by articles and books published) than professional women who were not married to other psychologists, but they were less productive, more likely to feel discriminated against, and less satisfied with their careers than their husbands. Among these couples the conflict between career and home demands was resolved in a traditional fashion and was accepted by both members of the pair; wives assumed greater responsibility for traditionally feminine, domestic activities.

Women who combine marriage and motherhood with full-time careers in male-dominated fields appear to be close to having realized the androgynous ideal (Bem, 1976). And some have. But for others the attempt to respond simultaneously to the cultural demands associated with both femininity and masculinity may culminate in what has been labeled the "superwoman syndrome" (Stein & Bailey, 1973).

Superwomen presumably incorporate stereotypically masculine characteristics into their self-description, but the core of that description remains essentially feminine in the traditional sense. The strength of commitment to both sets of traits and behaviors may be strong, but one is not exchanged for the other. Thus, superwomen strive for competitively derived success in careers while, at the same time, feeling compelled to maintain full control over the social-domestic sphere of their lives (O'Leary & Depner, 1976). Models for such dual achievement currently abound in the media; an example is the popular breakfast-drink commercial that presents Dr. X, biochemist, lecturer in a large university, dutiful wife, and the devoted mother of four beautiful, healthy, and well-adjusted children.

As a new female stereotype, superwoman does not represent the androgynous ideal, because it falls short of providing a realistic alternative to the restrictions imposed by sex-role stereotypes. Women should not be encouraged to feel that they are subject to behavioral restrictions because of their biological sex, but neither should they feel compelled to display the traits and enact the roles of both sexes in order to "atone" for a self-definition that incorporates characteristics of men and women. The freedom to endorse traits and behaviors of the opposite sex as sex-role appropriate must also imply the freedom to establish priorities in accordance with realistic goal setting.

I was married one week after I graduated from college, and I entered graduate school that fall. Looking back, I wonder if I would have felt as comfortable about pursuing graduate study had I not been the recipient of a "ring by spring." My orientation had been clearly nontraditional from an early age; at 11 my dreams for the future included a divinity degree and a pulpit (at that time women were not yet allowed in the pulpit of the Methodist church). But I also wanted to marry and raise a family. Having demonstrated my ability to "catch" a man, I think I felt secure in my decision to obtain a Ph.D.

You will recall from our discussion of sex differences in early childhood in Chapter Four that there is little reason to believe that the behavioral potentials of females and males differ significantly. However, the socialization experience of girls and women is different from that of boys and men. These experiential differences result in a willingness to accept adult social roles assigned on the basis of biological sex.

The range of alternative role definitions deemed acceptable for women has increased in recent years. And yet it appears that for many women the realization of the benefits of choosing a nontraditional role remains contingent on the demonstration that they can meet the traditional criteria for femininity.

Summary

Although stereotypes simplify the task of classifying people on the basis of their membership in a given group, they are usually based on inaccurate or partially inaccurate beliefs. Because stereotypic conceptions of men and women in American society are so widely shared, it has been easy to assume that they reflect real differences between the sexes. Furthermore, the tendency to define male and female stereotypes in opposite terms exaggerates differences and obscures similarities. Measures used to assess sex stereotypes, by omitting common traits in testing, contribute to this exaggerated view of differences between men and women.

Sandra Bem offers an alternative to the historical tendency to define masculinity-femininity on a single bipolar dimension. Bem maintains that masculinity and femininity represent independent dimensions and that a given individual may be both masculine and feminine. She labels such individuals "androgynous."

Studies examining the relationship between sex typing and behavior clearly suggest that androgynous women (and men) enjoy a level of psychological and behavioral freedom that their sex-typed and sex-reversed counterparts do not share. They display "masculine" independence under pressure to conform, as well as "feminine" nurturance when interacting with kittens, babies, and lonely students. They are also less likely than masculine or feminine individuals to display evidence of psychological maladjustment and have higher scores on measures of self-esteem.

Most recent studies of sex-role stereotypes provide little evidence to suggest that these stereotypes are changing. When changes are shown, they appear to be based on the recognition that endorsing traditionally defined sex-role stereotypes is no longer considered the "socially desirable" response. Within the last decade it has become apparent that not all women subscribe to the American stereotypic assumption that "woman's place is in the home." During the 1970s a wider range of roles has been defined as acceptable for women. Nevertheless, large numbers of women still make very traditional choices. Whether or not a woman chooses to work and pursue a career appears to be influenced by her conception of the female role.

Those women who subscribe to nontraditional definitions of the female role tend to be career-oriented. The recurrent profile of professional, nontraditional women depicts an individual who is nonconforming, self-reliant, independent, flexible, self-directed, and high in ego strength. Education, religious/ethnic affiliation, and even size of family have been indicated as variables in producing nontraditionally oriented women. It has also been suggested that parents of role innovators are more likely to stress early independence training than those of traditionally oriented women.

Most career women do not substitute the work role for the traditional one but usually add the 40-hour work week to their domestic responsibilities. Realistic goal setting for these women may require role models who illustrate how to combine marriage and career successfully. Studies have shown that mothers who serve as role models, successfully combining family and career, have daughters who are similarly oriented. The availability of significant others is probably crucial to the nontraditional woman's role orientation, because the choice of multiple roles necessarily results in some degree of role conflict.

When the behavioral demands of multiple roles are incompatible, the result is role conflict. While the range of alternative role definitions deemed acceptable for women is expanding, there is no current indication that the conflict between career and home demands will be resolved in any way other than the traditional fashion. It seems that for most women the realization of the benefits of the nontraditional choice is contingent on the demonstration that their core identity remains feminine in the traditional sense.

Chapter Seven

Black Women

In 1944 the Swedish sociologist Gunnar Myrdal observed a parallel between the oppression of Blacks and the oppression of women in American society. Seven years later Helen Hacker (1951) published an extensive analysis of the sociological and psychological characteristics shared by women and minorities. What are the implications of these observations for the status of Black women, who are both members of a minority and females?

Beale (1970) has argued that the inferior racial and sex status of Black women has placed them in a position of "double jeopardy"; that is, as a result of their visible minority status, Black women are subject to discrimination on two counts: racism and sexism. In contrast to this view, Epstein (1973a, 1973b) has suggested that the doubly negative (Black/female) status of Black women may have a "double whammy" effect; that is, the Black female may achieve more than would be predicted on the basis of either her sex or her race. However, if there is indeed such an effect, it is restricted to a small number of Black professional women who offer a double-barrelled combination for employers seeking to comply with affirmative action programs.

As a Black woman I have played a number of socially prescribed roles throughout my adult life. I am a wife and a mother. Since 1970 I have pursued a full-time career as a developmental psychologist. In reading the work of Beale and Epstein, I find it difficult to characterize my experience as representative of either the double-jeopardy or the double-whammy phenomenon. I share the same conflicts over my wife-mother and career roles expressed by my White female colleagues. But I am also aware that my experiences are in some ways different from theirs because I am Black.

Much of the available empirical literature relevant to our understanding of women is based on studies of White middle-class American women, many of whom are college-educated. Relatively little is known about the experience and behavior of women representing other racial, ethnic, socioeconomic, or even cultural groups. In this chapter we will examine the available psychological literature on one such group—Black women. Unfortunately, this literature is not extensive. Moreover, the majority of studies that have been conducted with Black women have focused on the lower class. As a result, because of the confounding of race and class variables, it is difficult to draw direct comparisons between studies of Black and White American women.

This chapter was contributed by Algea O. Harrison.

We will begin our discussion by examining several myths about Black women generated by social scientists and popularized by the media. These myths, generally subsumed under the heading of Black matriarchy, have evolved from the failure to critically examine the findings of the relatively few studies of Black women that do exist, as well as from the tentative nature of these findings. Next, we will review the results of empirical studies relevant to sex-role stereotypes and definitions of the female role within the Black community. Then we will consider alternative models that Black women use to define their feminine identity and the implications of these models for the development of self-esteem. Finally we will consider the way in which the maternal role is viewed within the Black community.

Black Matriarchy

Until recently most analyses of the role of the Black woman focused exclusively on what was assumed to be her unique position of dominance within the family. The fact that comparative studies of the family status of Black and White women revealed a significantly higher proportion of Black female heads of households was widely interpreted as evidence for the existence of a matriarchal social structure within the Black community. On the assumption that female-headed households were by definition less stable than male-headed ones, it was argued that Black matriarchy was a major source of instability within the Black community. And even within intact families it was assumed that the Black woman played a dominant role resulting in the emasculation of Black men and encouraging pathology within the Black family (Moynihan, 1965; Rainwater, 1967, 1970).

Some contemporary Black writers have echoed the matriarchal theme. For example, Chappelle (1970) believes that the historical role of Black women results in the psychological castration of Black men. She views the Black Power movement as instrumental in reasserting the Black males' right to function in the manner defined as traditionally masculine in the dominant culture. Indeed, Chappelle (1970) believes that Black women should encourage Black men, even at their own expense.

> It may happen that a talented black woman is offered a post on the Negro College campus because the administration is convinced that a qualified black male cannot be found at a price the college is able to afford. Should this happen, the black woman has an obligation to refuse the position and force the institution to continue the search (even if it means compromising by changing the definition of "qualified" or by raising the price it is willing to pay) [p. 38].*

Why have White (and Black) writers been so willing to accept the assumptions underlying the theory of Black matriarchy? Let us examine the

*From "The Black Woman on the Negro College Campus," by Y. Chappelle, *The Black Scholar*, January–February, 1970, pp. 36–39. Reprinted by permission.

nature of the empirical evidence used to support the view that Black women dominate the Black community.

The primary sources of empirical evidence that have been used to support the notion of Black matriarchy are contained in the U.S. census statistics. Compared to White women, Black women are overrepresented as both heads of households (U. S. Bureau of the Census, 1972) and as participants in the labor force (Harwood & Hodge, 1971). On the basis of these statistics it has been argued that Black women have traditionally enjoyed both social and economic advantages over Black men.

As recently as 1974, 34% of all Black households were headed by females, as compared to 10% of White households (Clay, 1975). There are a number of pragmatic reasons for the disproportionately high number of Black households headed by women. Historically, Black men have found it difficult to find and maintain the types of employment necessary to support their families. Also, the structure of the welfare system encourages low-income men to live apart from their families. Finally, the ratio of Black men to Black women is low, because Black males generally die earlier than Black females. It is difficult to interpret any of these reasons as evidence that Black women have greater social power within the Black community than Black men. It should also be pointed out that analyses focusing on racial differences in the proportions of Black and White households headed by women frequently fail to acknowledge that both spouses are present in the majority (61%) of Black families (U.S. Bureau of the Census, 1975b).

The argument that Black women have been economically advantaged over Black men is based on the contention that Black women have always had greater access to work than their male counterparts, even if work generally meant a low-status, low-paying job. However, there is no evidence to support this contention. Not only have Black males consistently outnumbered Black females in the employed labor market (Jackson, 1972), but the median income of Black males has always been substantially higher than that of Black females (Aldridge, 1975; Harwood & Hodge, 1971). For example, in 1970 the wage or salary income of fully employed Black men was 29% greater than that of Black women (Aldridge, 1975). This income discrepancy is even more notable when we compare the median income of Black female heads of households ($4441) with that of Black male heads of households ($7329) (U.S. Bureau of the Census, 1972).

It is, however, true that in comparison to Black men, a greater proportion of Black women have been and are employed in occupations labeled "professional" (Billingsley, 1971; Epstein, 1973a). But the advantage enjoyed by Black professional women is primarily due to the fact that they are allowed greater access to occupations considered appropriate for women (for example, teaching and nursing) than Black men to occupations considered traditionally masculine (for example, middle management). These findings, therefore, do not refute the fact that, although a slightly higher proportion of Black professionals are women, most Black women are employed in low-paying, low-status jobs. Since 1890 every census has revealed that Black men are employed in a greater variety of occupations than Black women (Harwood & Hodge, 1971). It should also be kept in mind that employed Black men have benefited from the protection of labor-union contracts—an advantage denied to Black women, who swell the ranks of domestic and service workers.

Thus, although Black women are more likely than White women to assume the role of head of household, there is little evidence to support the view that they maintain an economic advantage over Black men. If the Black woman holds any power advantage within the Black community, we must look elsewhere to find its source.

It has been suggested that Black women play a more dominant role within the family than do White women. The results of one study do indicate that lower-class Black urban women assume more responsibility for making major family decisions than their White counterparts (Blood & Wolfe, 1971). This may be due to the fact that many lower-class Black women have more formal schooling than their husbands and that, because these women are frequently employed in domestic and service positions, they may have more experience in dealing with the White system (Hannerz, 1969). Recognizing this reality, lower-class Black men may sometimes afford their wives major decision-making responsibilities. However, as Staples (1970) points out, Black women rarely make decisions in opposition to their husband's wishes.

According to Jackson (1971), for a variety of reasons there is a disproportionately low ratio of males to females within the Black community, particularly during the peak marriage years (18 to 44). As a result, a married Black woman is at a disadvantage if her attempts to control her spouse lead to irresolvable conflict and end in divorce.

Of course, decision-making responsibility is only one measure of the power relationship between husbands and wives. In an extensive review of the literature relevant to patterns of spouse dominance, Jackson (1973) found little evidence to support the contention that Black women play a more dominant role than White women in solving domestic problems. As a matter of fact, the most common pattern for couples of both races was an equalitarian one. Jackson did, however, find some differences in the patterns of spouse dominance as a function of socioeconomic class and geographic location. Southern lower-class Black couples are more likely to endorse male dominance than Whites, while the reverse is true in the North.

Another argument that has been used to support Black matriarchy is the observation that Black families have been more likely to educate their daughters than their sons (Moynihan, 1965). Historically this has been true, but the suggestion that this was an expression of Black mothers' preference for their daughters is clearly untenable (Staples, 1970). Black parents have always been concerned with providing the best possible protection for their children. And since the greatest perceived threat to their daughters' safety was the prospect of sexual exploitation by White males in the homes where they served as domestics (Harrison, 1974), Black families sought to give female children economic freedom through education. As Grier and Cobb (1968) so aptly observe, "If school is seen as a refuge from the white aggressor, and if the black family places its women and children within such safe confines, and if the men turn to face the enemy—pray show me that critic of the weak Negro family'' (p. 124).

In addition, following emancipation, the Black family's primary source of income was farming and sharecropping. Because of the nature of the work, many male offspring were forced to terminate their formal schooling early in order to help support the family. Therefore, if any member of the family was to be educated, it was the female. Moreover, limited resources were a reality, and this usually meant that the males of the family pooled their money and sent their females to school.

The theory of Black matriarchy, which holds that the Black woman's dominant (and dominating) position in the family is the key factor in the social disorganization of the Black community, cannot be substantiated on empirical grounds. The stereotype of the Black female as a matriarch does not reflect reality. Indeed, Black matriarchy is a myth.

Black matriarchy was postulated as an explanation for observable differences between the social structures of the Black and the White communities of the United States. As we have seen, the assumptions on which this explanation is based cannot be substantiated empirically. However, the persistence of the myth of Black matriarchy dramatically illustrates the biases inherent in viewing one culture from the perspective of another. Only by viewing the experience and behavior of women (and men) within the social context in which they occur can we begin to appreciate the influence of stereotypically defined social expectations on human behavior. The results of a number of recent attempts to specify the context of sex-role stereotypes within the Black community further demonstrate this point.

Stereotypes and Conceptions of the Black Female Role

According to the commonly held female stereotype, women are (or should be) weak, passive, dependent, and submissive. As was pointed out earlier, stereotypically feminine traits are valued less than stereotypically masculine ones. However, these stereotypically feminine traits do not reflect accurately those characteristics that are most highly valued in Black women within the Black community—strength, independence, and resourcefulness.

As a member of a minority group, the Black woman has had to assume a central role in the economic structure of her community. Forced to compete in the economic marketplace, often in the role of sole provider of financial resources for her family, the Black woman adopted behaviors and attitudes characteristically assumed to be ''masculine.'' Submission, passivity, and dependence were for many Black women dysfunctionally related to the reality of their lives and roles.

Within the context of the stereotypes held by the larger society, the Black woman may appear less ''feminine'' than her White counterpart. The very traits that ensure her survival and that of her family have made her the subject of Whites' scorn and ridicule. Originally portrayed in the media as a docile servant, when the Black woman finally emerged from "the White man's kitchen," she was characterized as cunning, domineering, and castrating. For example, the portrayal of Sapphire, the loud, sarcastic, and tyrannical wife on the "Amos and Andy Show" of two decades ago, was both unflattering and unfeminine. In contrast, the White woman's public image has been, if not highly valued, at least stereotypically feminine.

The majority of research on sex-role stereotypes has focused on sex-role standards ascribed to and shared by White men and women. Relatively little is known about the stereotypic images of the Black male and female within their own culture. In an attempt to determine whether Black college women shared White women's misperception of men's ideal women, Steinmann and Fox (1970) administered their Inventory of Feminine Values to 100 Black and 126 White college females and to 100 Black and 82 White college males. Neither the self-perceptions nor the same-sex ideal profiles of the Black and White women differed significantly. However, Black and White women did differ with regard to their perceptions of men's ideal woman. As revealed in previous studies (Steinmann & Fox, 1966, 1974), White women felt that men preferred a family-oriented woman. In contrast, Black women believed that men wanted a woman with a balance of familial and self-achieving orientations. Furthermore, Black males and females agreed that the ideal (Black) woman was very much like what the Black woman was and wanted to be.

In a recent study, O'Leary and Harrison (1975) compared the sex-role stereotypes of Black and White men and women and found that Blacks endorsed significantly fewer items that discriminated between the sexes than did Whites. Even when Black females and males agreed that a given trait was more characteristic of one sex than of the other, they were less likely than Whites to devalue females on traditionally stereotypic grounds. The White adult female was rated more negatively by White subjects of both sexes than was the adult Black female by Black men and women. These results are consistent with the suggestion that the Black woman's social role has been traditionally perceived as more valued in the Black community than that of the White female in the White community.

The fact that Blacks are less likely than Whites to differentiate between the sexes on the basis of stereotypic conceptions of masculinity and femininity may reflect the dual nature of the Black woman's traditional social role. Most Black women marry, have children, and work as well. Approximately two-thirds of the wives in Black families work, as do three-fifths of the Black women who are heads of households (Hill, 1972). Indeed, most unmarried Black females expect and want to work outside the home after marriage and even after the arrival of children (Kuvlesky & Obordo, 1972). Furthermore, Black college women do not perceive work as incompatible with family goals (Fichter, 1967; Gurin & Katz, 1966; Mednick & Puryear, 1975; Turner, 1972). It should be noted, however, that a commitment to work does not necessarily involve a commitment to a career (Mednick & Puryear, 1975).

The results of studies of Black males' attitudes toward the female role suggest that Black men are generally supportive of working wives. For example, Alexson (1970) found that 68.7% of Black males, as compared to 48.1% of White males, believed that a wife should work if she chose. Similarly, Entwistle and Greenberger (1972) found that Black adolescent boys were less opposed than their White counterparts to women working outside the home.

The fact that Black men are generally supportive of working wives probably stems more from their perception of economic necessity than from their feminist ideology. Indeed, the educational and career aspirations of Black women appear to be influenced by the recognition that their potential earning power may improve their marriage prospects (Harrison, 1974). For example, Turner (1972) found that the career aspirations of Black college women were related to their belief that holding a good job would help them to attract a high-status husband. Incidentally, the results of a comparative analysis of the marital status of Black and White female teachers reveal that Black teachers are more likely to marry than White teachers (Reed, 1970).

You will recall from the discussion of female achievement in Chapter Five Matina Horner's (1968) postulation that women who regard achievement and femininity as incompatible may fear success. To the extent that Black women view a commitment to work as compatible with the roles of wife and mother (Mednick, 1973), it is reasonable to anticipate that Black women will be less likely to fear success than White women. This hypothesis was confirmed by Horner (1970), who reported that the proportion of Black women who responded to "Anne's success in medical school" with fear-of-success imagery was substantially lower than that of White women—29% versus 64%. Similar results were obtained by Weston and Mednick (1973). These studies also indicated that lower-class Black women were no more likely to fear success than middle-class Black women. Apparently, Black women do not perceive competitively based achievement as incompatible with their concepts of femininity.

However, in a subsequent study of fear of success among Black women, Puryear and Mednick (1975) found that high fear-of-success imagery was related to women's involvement in the Black Power movement. Advocates of Black Power view female independence and assertiveness as detrimental to the survival of the Black community. They advocate the assumption of the dominant role by Black men and urge Black women to aid in the struggle by assuming a traditionally stereotypic supportive role. You will recall that in Horner's view the motive to avoid success is aroused only in those situations in which the individual feels anxious about competitiveness and its aggressive (and presumably unfeminine) overtones. The fact that Black women are less likely than White women to respond to female competitive success with fear-of-success imagery suggests that most Black women view competitively derived achievement as sex-role appropriate.

To the extent that increasing numbers of young Black women have been influenced by the philosophy of the Black Power movement, they may be confronted with new pressures to redefine their public roles along more traditionally (White) stereotypic lines.

In a study conducted in 1972 and 1973, Dansby (1974) asked Black college women to list at least three advantages and three disadvantages of being a Black woman as compared to being a White woman and to being a Black man. At that time, the majority of respondents listed the following as advantages of Black women over White women: pride, complexion and beauty, slower aging process, degree of family concern, and inner strength (traditionally feminine attributes). They saw White women as having an advantage in employment, economic security, respect, and equal rights and opportunities (traditionally masculine concerns). However, when Black women compared themselves to men, the majority of these women saw themselves as advantaged in the traditionally "masculine" areas of employment opportunity, parental status, strength, determination, and independence. In a replication of this study a year later, Dansby (1975) found that her Black female respondents were less likely to describe themselves as holding any advantage over Black males. Dansby (1975) interprets these findings as evidence that young Black women view both sexes as "struggling to make it" (p. 36). An alternative and equally plausible explanation is that Dansby's results may be due, at least in part, to the impact of the myth of Black matriarchy within the Black community.

Black Feminine Identity

As we have seen, the stereotypes and conceptions of the female role endorsed by the Black community differ from those found in the broader (White) culture. Recall that one primary means of acquiring sex-role identity is through modeling. If the Black female accepts the stereotypic feminine image held by Whites as an ideal and attempts to emulate it, she cannot live up to the expectations of the Black community (Harrison, 1974). If, on the other hand, she accepts her community's definition of Black femininity, she cannot measure up to the stereotype held by the broader culture. Where, then, does the Black female look for appropriate models to help her define her sex-role identity? We will consider the influence of these alternative sources of feminine identity in order to understand how Black women view themselves.

The White Model

In their analysis of the Black female, Grier and Cobb (1968) suggest that the Black woman rejects herself because she cannot meet the White criteria of femininity. The demands of her culture militate against the adoption of those personality traits assumed to define the feminine role, and certain physical characteristics associated with the White feminine ideal—such as blond hair, blue eyes, fine facial features, and a peaches-and-cream complexion—are impossible for the Black woman to attain. The influence of the White feminine ideal on the self-image of Black girls is poignantly revealed in this comment by a Black woman:

> Because I was dark I was always being plastered with vaseline so I wouldn't look ashy. Whenever I had my picture taken they would pile a whitish powder on my face and make the lights so bright I always came out looking ghostly. My mother stopped speaking to any number of people because they said I would have been pretty if I hadn't been so dark. Like nearly every little black girl, I had my share of dreams of waking up to find myself with long blond curls, blue eyes and skin like milk [Marshall, 1970, p. 26].*

The fact that Black men have traditionally viewed light-skinned women as more desirable girl friends, beauty queens, and wives (Grier & Cobb, 1968; Liebow, 1967; Silberman, 1964; Staples, 1973) has served to perpetuate the acceptance of the White feminine ideal within the Black community. So much so that Grier and Cobb (1968) conclude that it is difficult, if not impossible, for a Black female to achieve a healthy, mature view of herself as a woman. However, this conclusion is based on the assumption that the White feminine ideal is the primary source of Black women's identity. As we shall see, the validity of this assumption is a matter of some controversy.

The Black Model

A number of social scientists have recently suggested that young Black females look within the Black community for their definition of the feminine role (Barnes, 1972; Billingsley, 1968; Ladner, 1972; Powell, 1973; Stack, 1974; Staples, 1972; Watson, 1974). In an extensive study of the attitudes and behaviors of lower-class urban adolescent Black females, Ladner (1972) found no evidence that her subjects had any desire to be White. Furthermore, the most prevalent conception of womanhood that existed among the preadult females she interviewed was that of strength and resourcefulness. Most of the girls expressed great admiration for their mothers and other Black female models whom they viewed as independent, self-reliant, and successful. Thus, their conception of femininity focused on the ability to accept responsibility, and the traits they valued most highly in women were strength, resourcefulness, and self-reliance. Similar results have been obtained by a number of other researchers (Kandel, Lesser, Roberts, & Weiss, 1968; Scanzoni, 1971; Schulz, 1969).

It appears that the young Black female is exposed to a highly valued model of feminine behavior that incorporates characteristically "masculine" stereotypic traits—a model with which she identifies and that she attempts to emulate. It should be noted, however, that most of the research on Black females has focused on the lower class. Thoye (1969) found that the concep-

---

*From "Reena," by P. Marshall. In T. Cade (Ed.), *The Black Woman* (New York: Signet, 1970). Copyright 1970 by Paule Marshall. Reprinted by permission of the author.

tion of femininity among upper-income Black families was closer to the traditional feminine stereotype than that of the middle- and lower-class Black families.

The question of which community, Black or White, provides the criteria for the feminine identity of Black women has recently been addressed by Myers (1975). Among a sample of Black women drawn from a medium-size Midwestern city, Myers found that 40% reported identifying with a Black woman they knew and 54% reported identifying with Black women in general. Only 2% of Myers's subjects reported identifying with a specific White woman, and 4% said they identified with White women in general. Myers also found that 92% of the women in her sample listed the positive qualities of their own mothers as those that they most hoped to emulate. Thus, Grier and Cobb's assumption that the White feminine stereotype provides the dominant model for Black feminine identity may be outdated. Two decades ago it was not uncommon for Black parents to prize their light-skinned children (Harrison-Ross & Wyden, 1973). As teenagers, my friends and I did admire Lena Horne's fine features and fair skin. Yet, even then not all the physical attributes considered attractive by Whites were equally valued among Blacks.

When I listen to White women reminisce about their adolescent struggles to trim their legs and hips, I cannot help but be amused and a bit incredulous. While they were madly exercising to reduce their thighs and hips, we were exercising to reduce our waists so that our hips would look fuller in contrast. When I attended my 24th high school reunion last summer, several of us eagerly compared legs in the ladies' room to see whose had maintained the fullest shape.

Interestingly, a recent survey of Black beauty queens on Black college campuses conducted by *Ebony* magazine ("Campus Queens," 1975) reveals that negroid features have become a valued asset in the criteria used for selection. Thus, the physical standards of beauty in the Black community appear to be changing in response to the recognition that Black beauty is qualitatively different from White beauty.

Self-Esteem

As we have just seen, there is little empirical evidence to support the contention that Black women base their feminine identity on the stereotypic White ideal. Whether or not this adversely affects the self-esteem of Black women is a matter of some controversy.

Traditionally, it has been assumed that Blacks have lower self-esteem (one's overall positive evaluation of self) than Whites. The major source of empirical evidence for this notion was provided by the results of a study by Clark and Clark (1947). The Clarks found that Black children preferred White over Black dolls. When asked to choose which dolls (Black or White) were nicer and which was the "nicer color," children of both races expressed a preference for White dolls. These results were widely interpreted as evidence for the negative effects of segregation on the developing self-esteem of Black children. However, subsequent attempts to replicate these findings (after the "Black Is Beautiful" movement) have yielded inconsistent results and have failed to support Clark and Clark's findings (Gregor & McPherson, 1966; Hraba & Geoffrey, 1970; Johnson, 1966; Morland, 1958). Recently, McAdoo (1974) found that Black children of both sexes were able to place a high value on themselves, while at the same time acknowledging that within the broader culture White was more valued than Black.

If, as Cooley (1956) suggested, our self-images are perceived and defined in terms of others' reactions to us, it is reasonable to anticipate that Black women (who live in a predominantly White world) see themselves as less valuable than White women. But it has also been suggested (Watson, 1974) that the Black community represents the primary reference group for Black women and provides a different standard for self-evaluation (Gurin & Epps, 1975). This standard serves as the basis for the realistic enhancement of self-esteem among Black women (Dobson, 1970; Ladner, 1972; Wright, 1975; Yates & Collins, 1974). In a recent study of the primary basis of self-esteem among Black women, Wright (1975) found that Black women stress concerns about self and individual action as important aspects of their feminine identification. As Wright observes, these results are contrary to those usually obtained in studies of the self-esteem of White women, who stress heterosexual relationships and physical standards of beauty as the primary bases of their feelings of self-worth (Bardwick, 1971).

Thus, the relative rank order of self-esteem among Black and White men and women may depend on the specific criteria used by the researcher to evaluate self-esteem (Baughman, 1971). The traditional assumption that, because of Black women's double-jeopardy position (Beale, 1970), their self-esteem must necessarily be lower than that of White women and of men of both races has not been substantiated by the results of empirical research (Blair, 1972).

It should be noted, however, that both the church and the extended family have traditionally provided a strong base of emotional support for the Black woman within her community. Now these institutions on which Black women have so long depended are eroding. Deprived of her ties to the church and to the extended family, the contemporary urban Black woman has been left to struggle alone with her feelings of powerlessness within the broader society (Slater, 1973). It has been suggested (Slater, 1973) that the recent dramatic increase in depression and suicide among Black women may be attributed, at least in part, to the decline in the strength of the Black church. Furthermore, many Black men have begun to accept the view that Black women are too threatening, too castrating, and too independent and unwilling to submerge their own self-interests in order to promote the advancement of Black men (Moynihan, 1965; Prendergass, Kimmel, Joesting, Peterson, & Bush, 1976). As a result, the Black woman may be less sure of herself and her identity today than she was 20 years ago. Much of this uncertainty stems from the fact that the traditional role of women within the Black community is undergoing public reexamination.

Black women do not tyrannize Black men, nor are they the helpless (and romanticized) victims of poverty, self-hate, prejudice, and irresponsible male providers (Ladner, 1972). Black women, like their White counterparts, derive a positive sense of self from many of the traditional aspects of the feminine role (Bonner, 1974). Black women may, however, define ther social roles differently than the majority of White women.

As we have seen, Black women expect to and do work after marriage and the birth of children. For many, this may reflect a current economic necessity. However, economic independence has historically characterized the role of Black women (Billingsley, 1971)—both during slavery and, before then, on the African continent. There is also some evidence to suggest that Black women are more likely than their White counterparts to value the role of mother over that of wife (Bell, 1965). The mother-child bond is an important aspect of the structure of the Black community, and it, too, has its roots in the African culture (Billingsley, 1971).

The Black Mother

The role of mother is central to the Black woman's definition of self. Children are highly valued by the Black community. Although pregnancy outside of marriage is not encouraged, neither unwed mothers nor their illegitimate offspring risk social rejection. Indeed, Ladner (1972) has observed that lower-class Black females view the birth of a child as the "rite de passage" into womanhood.

Ladner's observation, however, does not imply that Black females view pregnancy outside of marriage as desirable. When Himes (1964) asked a sample of unmarried Black women how they would react if they found themselves pregnant, the overwhelming majority felt that they would be deeply ashamed and embarrassed. Furstenberg, Gordis, and Markowitz (1969) obtained similar results in a study of adolescent Black unwed mothers. Most of the young women in their sample reported that they had been extremely upset when they discovered they were pregnant. Although few considered giving their infants up for adoption, many believed that the birth of their child diminished their chances to get married and to pursue their education.

Grier and Cobb (1968) have suggested that in her role as a mother (nurturing and protecting her young) the Black woman has been the salvation of many a family. As we have seen, Black women function as heads of households more than do White women. Moreover, it appears that, because Black women possess both stereotypically feminine characteristics (for example, warmth and expressiveness) *and* stereotypically masculine ones (for example, strength and resourcefulness), they are better equipped than White women to cope with the demands of child rearing in the absence of a father (Hartnagel, 1970). Gurin and Epps (1975) report that growing up in a home without a father did not adversely affect the academic performances, future aspirations, or achievement goals of Black college students. Again, this may be the result of the dual nature of the definition of the Black woman's role as mother and provider. The strength and resourcefulness for which the Black woman has been traditionally valued may have prepared her to respond adaptively to her life circumstances (Rhodes, 1971).

You will recall that we concluded the discussion of the theory of Black matriarchy by suggesting that it represents a myth rather than a fact. However, the lower-class urban Black woman may have been forced by economic necessity to adopt an important role in the domestic structure of the Black community.

Recently, Stack (1974) has suggested that the structure of the lower-class Black family is not the same as that of the middle-class nuclear family. Rather, it is based on an extended cluster of kin, related primarily through children but also through marriage and friendship, who align to perform domestic functions.

Because they are poor, lower-class Black young women with or without children do not perceive any choice but to remain at home with their mothers or other female relatives. Even when these women are collecting welfare for their children, they benefit from the opportunity to share goods and services within the extended family. Similarly, men who are unemployed or working only part time often remain at home with their mothers or brothers and sisters. This pattern of residence continues long after the men become fathers, long after they establish sexual relationships with women who are, in turn, living with their own kin or friends or living alone with their children. As a result of this living arrangement, most female-headed households are not composed exclusively of women. Male relatives, friends, and boyfriends are available to aid in child rearing and household maintenance.

According to Stack (1974), lower-class urban Black women have assured their own survival and that of their children by adopting a kin network. The evolution of extended kin networks has allowed these women to maximize their independence, acquire and maintain domestic authority, limit (but positively value) the role of husband and father, and strengthen ties with kin. When economic resources are limited, people must rely on all the resources available to them. Economic pressures serve to strengthen relationships among kin, and sometimes active attempts are made to prevent the loss of either males or females from the kin network through marriage or other lasting relationships. My unmarried brother recently alluded to the existence of this type of domestic network when he observed that women who still lived with their mothers were poor prospects as wives.

Stack's analysis of the domestic network characteristic of the urban lower-class Black family provides insight into the structure of one segment of the Black community. It is a structure based not on the dominance of Black women but on an effective strategy for survival in the urban ghetto. It should, however, be noted that the domestic network Stack described is an urban phenomenon that is not characteristic of the structure of either the lower-class rural Black community (Young, 1970) or the Black middle class.

As we have seen, there is some reason to view the female experience as different for Black and White women. Certainly, the stereotypic image of, and roles played by, Black women within their culture are not the same as those used to define White femininity. However, when Dansby (1975) asked Black college women to describe what it meant to them to be a Black woman, most felt that it meant "being beautiful and feminine under conditions of hardship and oppression" (p. 36). If White women were to mention hardship and oppression in similar self-descriptions, they would likely be referring to the oppression of sexism, not racism.

As we noted at the beginning of this chapter, most of the research cited in this book has been conducted with White women. Where possible, we have tried to compare the responses of Black and White women directly. However, until further research is done, many interesting hypotheses remain untested. For example, sex-role stereotypes appear to be less well differentiated in the Black community than within the broader culture. Thus, it seems reasonable to suggest that Blacks are more likely than Whites to define themselves as androgynous (see Chapter Six). On the other hand, the incidence of sex-typed self-definitions may be greater among certain other age and socioeconomic groups than among predominantly middle-class college students. As Mednick (1976) has so aptly suggested, in order to understand women we must study variations of the female experience within groups and across time. Although an intensive review of the literature of cross-cultural differences in the behavior and experience of women is beyond the scope of this chapter (and this book), such comparative analyses are essential to our understanding of the behavior of both women and men.

Summary

Although it has been argued that the inferior race and sex status of Black women places them in a position of great disadvantage (double jeopardy), another view considers this doubly negative status as an advantage ("double whammy" phenomenon). There have been very few studies of Black women, and the majority have focused on the lower class. In the absence of extensive information about the Black Woman, several myths have been generated by social scientists and popularized by the media.

The fact that there is a higher proportion of female-headed households among Blacks than among Whites has been interpreted as evidence for the existence of a matriarchal social structure within the Black community. Although it is true that Black women have always had greater access to work (in the form of low-status, low-paying jobs) than Black men, there is no evidence that Black women have enjoyed any economic advantage over Black men. Comparative studies of the average income of Black men and women reveal that at all educational levels Black females earn less than Black males. Black matriarchy cannot be substantiated.

Recent research on sex-role stereotypes reveals that Blacks perceive fewer differences between females and males than Whites. This may be due to the dual nature of the Black woman's social role, since it appears that neither Black men nor Black women view working as incompatible with being a wife and a mother. However, the rise of the Black Power movement may be exerting new pressures on Black women to redefine their public roles along more traditionally stereotypic lines.

Within the Black community women are valued for their strength, independence, and resourcefulness—traits that have traditionally been part of the American masculine stereotype. Thus, there may be conflict for the Black woman between the culturally approved definition of femininity in the Black community and the traditional feminine stereotype held by the White majority of American society.

There is evidence of the influence of the White feminine ideal on the self-image of Blacks. Black men have traditionally viewed light-skinned women as more desirable girl friends, beauty queens, and wives. If, as some social scientists suggest, the Black woman is identifying with the White model as a basis for her own femininity, she may be at a disadvantage. However, studies of lower-class young Black females have shown that these women have no desire to be White. Their conception of femininity appears to be drawn from their mothers and other Black models whom they admire and view as independent, self-reliant, and successful.

The traditional assumption that, because of their double-jeopardy position, Black women must have lower self-esteem than White women or men of either race has not been substantiated by recent research. As a matter of fact, the value placed on the Black woman within her own community may have strengthened her sense of self.

The role of mother is central to the Black woman's definition of self. Forced by economic necessity to assume the dual role of mother and provider, the characteristic strength and resourcefulness of urban lower-class Black women has encouraged the evolution of extended domestic networks as one strategy for survival (Stack, 1974).

The social experience of Black women is undoubtedly different from that of White women. However, most of the differences between these two groups of women (who are in many respects similar) are probably not due to race per se but, rather, to the political, social, and economic conditions in this society that have encouraged the existence of a separate Black community within the broader culture. In order to understand the many variations of the female experience, we must study these variations both within and across cultures.

Chapter Eight

Female Sexuality

Most contemporary women were socialized to view themselves as sexy but not sexual. The ability to look and act sexy has long been considered an appropriate, even necessary, part of a female's repertoire of man-catching gimmicks. But the notion that women are, and should be, sexual is of relatively recent origin.

Teenage magazines assure adolescent females that the ability to create a "sexy" illusion is an important tool of womanhood. One's smile should have sex appeal, one's body should be alluring. Ads for bust-line developers (shipped in plain wrappers) promise to add inches to flat chests and to ensure more active social lives. Such ads frequently feature interviews with girls like Cathy, who "was really flat . . . felt cheated somehow . . . never had any dates . . . [until] with Mark Eden it all changed" ("Life Is More . . .," 1976). The image of sexy women is presumably so compelling (and desirable) that it dominates the media and is used to promote a variety of products ranging from perfume to tuna fish. Adolescent girls in this society cannot help but be impressed with the importance of acting sexy, but relatively few are equally impressed with the importance of their sexuality.

In recent years female sexuality has received widespread attention in the scientific as well as in the popular literature. The combination of the Women's Liberation Movement and the publication in 1966 of Masters and Johnson's landmark work, *Human Sexual Response*, has provided the major impetus for both our current interest in and knowledge about female sexuality.

In this chapter we begin by reviewing the female reproductive anatomy; then we examine the physiology of the sexual-response cycle; and finally we look at female sexuality as a social-psychological phenomenon.

Female Reproductive Anatomy

Although a discussion of the reproductive anatomy of women may seem too basic for a book of this kind, a brief review of the medical terms used to describe such anatomy seems in order, because these terms— necessary to a discussion of the physiology of the sexual-response cycle— are often confusing. Also, many women have never actually examined their own external genitalia. Few of us, of course, are supple enough to view our own genitals without the aid of a hand mirror, but this is a relatively minor technical problem. Much more important are the societal prohibitions

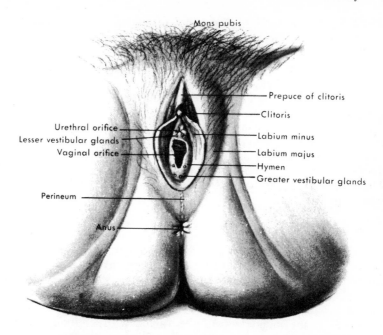

Mons pubis

Prepuce of clitoris

Clitoris

Urethral orifice

Lesser vestibular glands

Vaginal orifice

Labium minus

Labium majus

Hymen

Greater vestibular glands

Perineum

Anus

Figure 8-1. Female genitals: Outer organs. (From *Basic Human Anatomy and Physiology*, by C. M. Dienhart. Coypright 1967 by W. B. Saunders Company. Reprinted by permission.)

against examining the genitals; if it is "not nice" to touch yourself "there," it logically follows that you should not look either.

The outer genitals of women are referred to as the *vulva*. In the adult female the most obvious feature of the vulva is the presence of pubic hair, which covers the pubis, and of the labia majora (outer lips) of the vagina. The pubis (mons veneris, or "mountain of Venus") is the rounded fatty mass where the pubic bones meet. At the top of the labia majora is the clitoris, a small organ of erectile tissue functionally analogous to the male penis. Like the penis, the clitoris is composed of a shaft and glans (or top); the shaft is hidden under the clitoral hood, but the glans protrudes.

The clitoral hood is part of the labia minora (inner lips) of the vagina, which extend down from the clitoris to frame the sides of the vaginal opening. The area between the labia majora and the perineum (the area between the vagina and the anus) is called the *vestibule*. Housed within the vestibule are the urinary and vaginal openings.

The inner organs of the female reproductive system include Bartholin's glands, the vagina, the cervix, the uterus, the fallopian tubes, and the ovaries. Bartholin's glands are located on either side of the vaginal opening. They produce small amounts of mucous and were at one time believed to be the primary source of lubrication within the vaginal canal. However, as we shall discuss in greater detail later, this notion has been challenged by Masters and Johnson (1966).

The vagina, or birth canal, is located between the bladder and the rectum and extends inward from the outer genitals and upward beyond the cervix toward the back. The cervix is the narrow end of the uterus that extends into the vagina. The os is the small cervical opening through which the uterine lining is shed.

Although the fallopian tubes and ovaries are part of the female's reproductive anatomy, neither organ plays a role in the sexual response cycle. However, significant and dramatic physiological changes in the reproductive organs we have described do occur in response to sexual stimulation. We will now examine the nature of these changes at each of the four stages of the sexual-response cycle.

Female Sexual Response

On the basis of an intensive 11-year study of natural sexual activity in a laboratory setting, Masters and Johnson (1966) divided the sexual-response cycle into four phases: excitement, plateau, orgasm, and resolution.[1]

The excitement phase. In the female the onset of the excitement phase is signaled by the moistening of the vagina with a lubricating fluid. The secretion of this fluid occurs within 10 to 30 seconds after the beginning of effective sexual stimulation. What constitutes "effective" stimulation varies, of course, from person to person. For some women erotic thoughts or fantasies may be the source of "effective" stimulation; for others direct genital manipulation may be necessary. In males the most noticeable response during the excitement phase is the attainment of the penile erection.

Although the lubricatory response of the female is less dramatic than the male erection, Masters and Johnson (1966) suggest that both responses are the result of vasocongestion, or engorgement of the genital tissues with blood. Contrary to earlier notions that had located the source of lubrication at the cervix or in Bartholin's glands, Masters and Johnson hypothesize that the engorgement of the vagina causes some of the fluid in the tissues of the genital area to pass through the vaginal wall.

Historically, the presence of this lubricatory fluid in the vaginal canal was assumed to be female ejaculate, analogous to the discharge of semen in males. During the Middle Ages the belief that "female ejaculate" was

[1]Masters and Johnson (1966) based their descriptive schema on their observation of approximately 600 men and women, ranging in age from 18 to 89, during more than 10,000 cycles of sexual response. The initial participants in this research were prostitutes, but most of the studies were done with more conventional volunteers. Masters and Johnson do not claim that their subjects were average people representing a cross section of the population (many were from the university community). But they were sexually responsive people. Although their educational characteristics may not have been representative, there is little reason to believe that their physiological responses were systematically different from those of other groups.

necessary for conception led to religious tolerance for female masturbation when orgasm did not occur during coitus.

The presence of vaginal lubricant, which marks the beginning of the excitement phase of the female sexual-response cycle, is followed by other physical changes as tension mounts. The clitoris becomes engorged with blood and may be visibly erect in some women. The inner two-thirds of the vagina lengthens and distends in preparation for penetration. The uterus also enlarges and elevates, pulling the vagina upward and making it wider. Engorgement of the blood vessels in the labia minora causes them to enlarge, and their purplish-red color darkens.

Later in the excitement phase the nipples become erect in response to a concentration of blood serum in the breast tissues. A measles-like rash, or "sex flush," may be observed, appearing first under the rib cage and extending rapidly across the breasts. Masters and Johnson report observing the sex flush in 75% of the women they studied. It was most noticeable among fair-skinned brunettes.

The plateau phase. The plateau phase is a state of increased arousal immediately preceding orgasm. During this phase the focus of physiological change shifts from the inner two thirds to the outer third of the vagina, which becomes so engorged with blood that the vaginal opening narrows to two-thirds of its normal size. Masters and Johnson have labeled this area the *orgasmic platform* (see Figure 8-2). Here is where the rhythmic contractions associated with orgasm are most pronounced.

The clitoris, which had become congested during the excitement phase, now retracts under the clitoral hood. Nipple erection appears to diminish during the plateau phase because of the swelling of the tissues that surround the nipples.

The color change in the labia minora, which began during the excitement phase, becomes more pronounced during the plateau phase. Masters and Johnson report that a female's orgasm is always preceded by this dramatic color change, or "sex skin reaction."

The orgasmic phase. During the plateau phase high levels of sexual arousal are indicated physiologically by increases in muscle tension (myotonia) and in edema, or swelling of the blood vessels (vasocongestion), particularly in the target organs of the genitals. When vasocongestive distention reaches a certain point, a reflex stretch mechanism in the responding muscles is set off, causing them to contract vigorously. These contractions release the blood trapped in the tissues and create the sensations associated with orgasm. The precise mechanism responsible for the onset of orgasm is not known, but it begins with rhythmic contractions starting in the orgasmic platform, which occur at intervals of about eight-tenths of a second. The number of orgasmic contractions ranges from 3 to 15, and the first few are the strongest.

The muscles involved in a woman's orgasmic response are exactly the same muscles that produce orgasm and ejaculation in men. Masters and

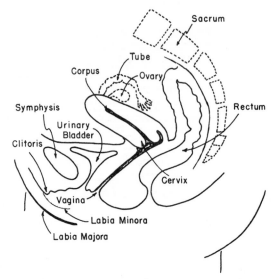

Figure 8-2. Female pelvis: Orgasmic phase. (Adapted from *Human Sexual Response*, by W. H. Masters and V. E. Johnson. Copyright 1966 by Little, Brown and Company, Publishers. Reprinted by permission.)

Johnson's discovery that contractions of the orgasmic platform are produced by the movement of extravaginal muscles against the vaginal walls provided the necessary physiological evidence to dispel the myth of the vaginal orgasm perpetuated by psychoanalytic theory.

As we said earlier, Freud (1933) had theorized that women experience two types of orgasm: vaginal and clitoral. According to his theory, during the early stages of psychosexual development the clitoris is a girl's primary site of sexual stimulation and gratification. In order to achieve sexual maturity, a female has to shift her primary sexual focus from the clitoris to the vagina. According to Freud, if this transfer does not occur, the woman remains fixed at the phallic stage of development and is not capable of the mature vaginal response assumed by Freud to be characteristic of the final (genital) stage of female psychosexual development. In the eyes of a psychoanalyst, a woman unable to achieve vaginal orgasm is frigid.

Those of you who received your sex education after the publication of Masters and Johnson's work may view Freud's theory as very old-fashioned. However, as recently as 1964 many authoritative marriage manuals subscribed to Freud's dual-orgasm theory. As an undergraduate I read one such book, borrowed from one of my college professors, in which frigidity among women was attributed to masturbation. It was argued that female masturbation results in clitoral fixation, which inhibits the transfer of sexual gratification to the vagina and, in turn, results in the inability to achieve orgasm during coitus. From my perspective such a consequence was much more dire than the appearance on my palms of either hair or warts!

As a result of Masters and Johnson's work, it is now clear that women experience only one kind of orgasm. Regardless of the source of stimulation—digital manipulation of the clitoris, intravaginal thrusting during coitus, or even breast stimulation alone—orgasm is physiologically defined as contractions of the orgasmic platform. Furthermore, clitoral stimulation is a major source of sexual arousal for most women. Even during coitus the movement of the penis within the vagina provides stimulation by drawing the fold of skin that comprises the clitoral hood across the clitoris.

The contractions of the orgasmic platform during orgasm are accompanied by uterine contractions as well. The pattern of uterine contractions is less definite, and many women are not aware of any specific uterine response. Other physiological responses to orgasm include increases in respiratory rate, heartbeat, and blood pressure.

As we have seen, orgasm may be defined physiologically as a release of myotonia and vasocongestion built up in response to sexual stimulation. Subjectively, orgasm is experienced as peak physical pleasure. Women's descriptions of the intensity of orgasm tend to correspond to the number of actual contractions in the orgasmic platform. Orgasms subjectively labeled as intense are characterized by a high number of contractions. According to Masters and Johnson, most women label 5-to-8-contraction orgasms as average or typical, 8-to-12-contraction orgasms as intense, and 3-to-5-contraction orgasms as mild. Among postmenopausal women 3 to 5 contractions are considered typical. It should be noted that postmenopausal women do not report a decrease in satisfaction with the average orgasm.

When Masters and Johnson asked their female subjects to describe the sensations they experienced during orgasm, they found that these sensations could be divided into three phases. The onset of orgasm is characterized by a feeling of momentary suspension. This feeling is then either accompanied or immediately followed by a sensation of warmth that begins in the area of the clitoris and then spreads throughout the pelvic area.

Stage two is described as a feeling of enveloping warmth. Initially this sensation is focused in the pelvic area and then spreads through the entire body.

The third and final stage of orgasmic progression was characterized by all of the women as a feeling of involuntary contractions within the vagina. The term "throbbing" was frequently used to describe the experience. It is interesting to note that the sensation of throbbing corresponds directly to the rhythmic contractions of the orgasmic platform.

The resolution phase. Following the cessation of orgasmic contractions, which signals the end of the orgasmic phase, the sex flush and swelling of the breast tissue rapidly disappear. The clitoris, which had remained retracted under the clitoral hood during the orgasmic phase, returns to its normal position five to ten seconds after orgasmic contractions stop.

Vasocongestion in the orgasmic platform disappears quickly. As a result, the vaginal opening widens and the labia majora return rapidly to their unstimulated size. Within three to four minutes after orgasm the inner two-thirds of the vagina returns to normal and the cervix descends to its unstimulated position.

Sex Differences in Sexual Response

Perhaps the most dramatic finding reported by Masters and Johnson was the extent of similarity in the physiological sexual-response cycles of men and women. There are, of course, some differences.

Although the sexual-response cycles of women and men may be divided into the same four phases, in men these phases are not as clearly defined. The excitement phase in males is typically much shorter than in females, although it can be prolonged through the deliberate use of delaying techniques. These techniques include concentrating on nonerotic distractors, such as reciting the alphabet backwards. If deliberate distractors are used, partial penile tumescence and detumescence may occur many times.

Perhaps the most striking difference between the sexes is the male ejaculatory response. The first of the orgasmic responses in men is the sensation of the inevitability of ejaculation. There does not appear to be a parallel reaction in women. Indeed, once ejaculation begins, orgasmic contractions continue involuntarily whether or not stimulation continues. In females orgasmic contractions cease if stimulation stops.

As a general rule, the duration of effective orgasmic contractions is about twice as long for a woman than for a man. The implications of this fact for the subjective experience of orgasmic intensity are not understood. Certainly, folklore suggests that men experience more intense orgasms than women. However, Masters and Johnson's observations indicate that there is little difference in either the physiological or the psychological reaction to orgasm between men and women whose orgasmic platforms are "fully developed," with elaborately distended veins and tissues.

Masters and Johnson suggest that, if sex differences in the experience of orgasmic intensity do exist, they may be related to the more localized vasocongestion in the male pelvic area. Interestingly, the six pregnant women in Masters and Johnson's sample reported increased sexual responsiveness. During pregnancy the uterus enlarges and puts pressure on the veins in the pelvic area. As a result, chronic excitement-phase vasocongestion may be symptomatic of pregnant women.

Unlike most men,[2] women have the capacity to achieve multiple orgasms within a short period of time. Multiple orgasms do not differ in any substantial way from single ones. In fact, most multiorgasmic women report that the later orgasms in a series are more satisfying than the initial one.[3]

Women's potential to achieve multiple orgasms appears to depend on the type of stimulation used to effect arousal. The average female with

[2]Some young men are capable of repetitive ejaculations. After the initial ejaculation the erectile chambers return to a plateau-level refractory period, and within a few minutes a full erection is regained. This capacity for multiple orgasms is typically lost around the age of 30. Masters and Johnson report one young male subject who achieved three orgasms within a ten-minute period.

[3]Multiorgasmic men usually associate the first orgasm in a series with the most pleasure. In males the amount of ejaculate is associated with the intensity of the orgasmic experience. The amount of semen expelled during the first orgasm in a series is objectively greater. This fact may explain males' preference for the first orgasm.

optimal arousal will usually be satisfied with three or four manually induced orgasms. However, if a less tiring mechanical means of stimulation, such as a vibrator, is used, she may be induced to continue for sessions of an hour or more, during which she may have 20 to 50 consecutive orgasms (Masters, cited in Sherfey, 1972, p. 109). Thus, human females appear to enjoy a much greater orgasmic potential than human males.[4] Sherfey (1972), following Masters and Johnson's findings, notes that the more orgasms a woman has, the stronger they become and that the more orgasms she has, the more likely she is to attain orgasm on subsequent occasions of effective stimulation. From this Sherfey concludes "to all intents and purposes, the human female is sexually insatiable in the presence of the highest degrees of sexual satiation" (p. 112). In other words, the closer to orgasmic satiation the female gets, the greater her desire to experience more orgasms. Sherfey refers to this phenomenon as the satiation-in-insatiation hypothesis. In support of this hypothesis, Sherfey points to the fact that in peak periods of estrus female primates have been observed to perform coitus as many as 50 times in a single day. She goes on to suggest that, were it not for the cultural restrictions imposed on the sexual activity of human females, their behavior might parallel that of these primates.

In Sherfey's view, women are not biologically built for the monogamous marital structure imposed upon them by society. Monogamy represents the evolution of a cultural norm that was necessary to ensure (1) the survival of human offspring, who remain helpless for so many years, and (2) the development of an agrarian economy with clearly delineated property rights and kinship ties. Of course, Sherfey's speculation is difficult to substantiate, since the data necessary to support it lie beyond the reach of recorded history. Nevertheless, the hypothesis that women possess a biologically determined sex drive that is even by traditional male standards inordinately high can give rise to endless speculations regarding the social consequences of a "new sexual freedom."

Interestingly, the belief that women are sexually insatiable was used to justify witch-hunts during the Middle Ages. In 1486 the *Malleus Maleficarum* (The Hammer of Witches) was published by two Dominican inquisitors as a manual for witch-hunters. Women were primary suspects for heresy and witchcraft because "all witch-craft comes from carnal lust, which is in women insatiable" (Sprenger & Krämer, 1486/1968, p. 47).

The physiological investigations of the female sexual response conducted by Masters and Johnson clearly indicate that most women are biologically capable of achieving orgasm. Whether or not a given woman's biological potential is realized appears to be determined in large part by the social-psychological context in which her sexuality is expressed. For example, the average woman is able to reach orgasm during masturbation less than four minutes after the onset of effective stimulation. Males require an

---

[4]Moreover, Masters and Johnson (1966) found only one sequence of sexual response that is characteristic of the male cycle. In contrast, they were able to identify three different patterns of female sexual response. This indicates that women experience a greater variety of responses to effective stimulation than do men.

average of two to four minutes of self-stimulation to reach orgasm (Katch-adorian & Lunde, 1975). Yet, from 30 to 50% of women report difficulty in achieving orgasm in heterosexual relationships, despite the fact that nearly all women are readily orgasmic when (and if) they engage in masturbation or lesbian relationships (Fisher, 1973; Masters & Johnson, 1966, 1970). Furthermore, as we shall see, the majority of cases of sexual malfunction in women (and men) are psychological rather than biological in origin. As is true of most human behaviors, the expression of sexuality is influenced by past experience and learning.

Sexuality as a Social-Psychological Phenomenon

In the same sense that females learn through practice to act sexy, they also learn to be sexual. Indeed, much of the conditioning of a woman's sexual behavior comes from the culture in which she is reared (Bernard, 1968). For example, in an intensive study of a rural Jamaican community, Cohen (1955) found that the majority of adolescent females he interviewed reported attaining orgasm during coitus. The adolescent members of this community did not regard affection for one's sexual partner as a prerequisite for sexual involvement; rather, most early sexual encounters were initiated for the physical satisfaction of both partners. If either failed to satisfy the other sexually, the relationship dissolved. In contrast, the results of a study of the sexual behavior of a sample of American women conducted at approximately the same time (Kinsey, Pomeroy, Martin, & Gebhard, 1953) revealed that only 20% of the women surveyed reported coital experience between the ages of 15 and 20. And of those women who had engaged in premarital sex during adolescence, one-third had never experienced orgasm during coitus. These results clearly suggest that patterns of sexual behavior are, at least in part, culturally determined.

Until the publication in 1974 of Morton Hunt's *Sexual Behavior in the 1970's*, most of what was known about the patterns of human sexual behavior in the United States was based on the survey data gathered by Alfred Kinsey and his associates (Kinsey, Pomeroy, & Martin, 1948; Kinsey et al., 1953). The Kinsey sample was comprised of 5940 female and 5300 male respondents, representing a wide variety of ages, marital status, educational levels, occupations, and religious backgrounds. However, despite its impressive size, the sample cannot be regarded as representative of the general population. All the participants were volunteers, and the sample was not randomly selected. In addition, the data were collected in face-to-face interviews and are thus subject to criticism on the grounds of interviewer bias and self-report distortion on the part of the subjects. As a result of these methodological problems, Kinsey's findings must be interpreted with some caution. It should be noted, however, that a number of less extensive but more methodologically sophisticated investigations conducted during the 1960s generally supported the accuracy of Kinsey's major findings (Gottheil & Freedman, 1970; Offer, 1972; Rainwater, 1966; Shope, 1968, 1971, 1975; Shope & Broderick, 1967; Simon, Gagnon, & Carns, 1968).

Chief among Kinsey's general findings was empirical verification of a double standard concerning premarital and extramarital sex. Of the males surveyed, 85% reported having engaged in premarital intercourse, and 50% of all married males reported engaging in extramarital relations (Kinsey et al., 1948). In contrast, only 48% of the women sampled reported having engaged in premarital intercourse, and about one-fourth (26%) of the married females in the sample had had extramarital coitus by age 40 (Kinsey et al., 1953).

In the two decades between the collection of the Kinsey interview data and the nationwide survey of adult sexual behavior and attitudes conducted by Hunt[5] (1974), premarital intercourse has become both more acceptable and more common. This shift toward increased permissiveness is particularly evident among females. According to Kinsey's data, by age 25 one-third of the females sampled (single and married combined) had engaged in premarital intercourse, while over two-thirds of the women in this age group surveyed by Hunt reported engaging in premarital sexual relations. It should be noted, however, that the obvious increase in the number of women willing to initiate sexual activity before marriage has not resulted in a dramatic increase in the number of women willing to participate in sexually intimate relations outside of the context of a loving or affectionate relationship. For example, Kinsey found that 46% of all married women in his sample who had engaged in premarital intercourse had had only one partner, their fiancé.

As Hunt (1974) observes, the absolute number of women who are willing to engage in intercourse in the absence of emotional ties to their partners has undoubtedly increased over the last 20 years. However, for most young women the shift toward greater sexual permissiveness can be defined as "permissiveness with affection" (Reiss, 1967). The results of a number of studies clearly suggest that women tend to equate sex with love (Bardwick, 1971; Biller, 1966; Kaats & Davis, 1970; Reiss, 1967). For example, in a series of studies at the University of Colorado, Kaats and Davis (1970) found that 70% of the women college students they sampled approved of sexual intercourse for themselves if they were in love but that less than 40% felt that their premarital sexual involvement would be acceptable if their relationship with their partner were based only on affection. It is interesting to note that, in two different studies, from 10 to 20% of the college women who endorsed premarital coitus when in love had not yet experienced intercourse.

The sexual attitudes and behaviors of the population have changed. However, the increased liberalization of sexual standards, particularly among women, is not sufficiently dramatic to warrant the label of revolution. What we appear to have witnessed during the last two decades is, rather, a sexual evolution. The range of sexual variations used by both married and

---

[5]In 1972 Morton Hunt was commissioned by the Playboy Foundation to conduct a survey of Americans' sexual attitudes and behaviors. Although the Hunt sample reportedly "closely parallels the U. S. population of persons 18 years old and over" (Hunt, 1974, p. 16), it was not a true probability sample and is subject to a number of methodological criticisms. For example, of the total number of individuals asked to participate in the study, four out of five refused. Thus, self-selection is clearly a problem.

unmarried people seems to have increased since Kinsey's time (Hunt, 1974). Oral-genital relations are generally accepted as natural, and attitudes toward anal stimulation are much more permissive than at the time of Kinsey's study. On the other hand, mutually sanctioned extramarital affairs, mate swapping, and marital swinging are not widely endorsed, nor is any type of sexual activity performed outside some emotional context or with strangers. And men, who frequently profess an ability to separate sexual gratification from love, are no less likely than women to agree with the statement "Sex cannot be very satisfying without some emotional involvement between the partners" (Hunt, 1974, p. 38). In one recent study of college students, Avery and Ridley (1974) found a high rate of agreement regarding the relative importance of interpersonal factors in determining appropriate levels of sexual intimacy. Both males and females felt that affection was the most important factor at all levels of intimacy, ranging from kissing to heavy petting.

The extent to which the shift in societal attitudes toward sex has affected the women's motives for engaging in intercourse has not yet been determined. The results of several studies suggest that many women do not engage in coitus for their own physical satisfaction but, rather, to gratify the sexual needs of their partners. For example, Bardwick (1971) found that the majority of college women she interviewed viewed coital involvement as a means of either securing love or ensuring that they would not lose it. Although very few of the young women Bardwick interviewed reported attaining orgasm, almost all indicated that their sex lives were satisfactory. Similarly, Wallin (1960) and Schaefer (1964) reported that orgasmic attainment in women was not necessarily associated with sexual satisfaction. In a recent survey of *Redbook* readers (Levin & Levin, 1975), 81% of the women who reported being orgasmic almost all the time evaluated their sex lives as good or very good. However, 52% of those who were only occasionally orgasmic and 29% of the women who were never orgasmic also rated their sex lives as good or very good. Apparently, for a considerable number of women other pleasures experienced during intercourse are enough to create a sense of sexual satisfaction. It is unfortunate that data bearing on the level of sexual arousal reached by such women during their sexual encounters are not available. For the woman who derives her primary sexual satisfaction from the knowledge that she has pleased her partner, vasocongestion in the genital area may not be labeled as unresolved arousal. However, the ability to separate emotional from physiological satisfaction may be greater among inexperienced and/or preorgasmic women (Burgess & Wallin, 1953; Gebhard, 1966; Shope, 1975).

Orgasmic attainment has always been considered a male prerogative; but, as we have seen, Masters and Johnson's work clearly indicates that it is the biological prerogative of women as well. Yet, it appears that not all women define their sexual satisfaction in physiological terms.

During the 18th and 19th centuries sexual responsiveness among women was largely discounted or ignored. Marriage manuals published during the 1800s portrayed women as reluctant participants in sexual activity, and it was assumed that women viewed intercourse as an unpleasant duty, justifiable only as a reproductive necessity (Gordon & Shankweiler, 1971). By the first quarter of the 20th century marriage manuals were beginning to recognize the existence of female sexuality, although it was generally believed that the sexual desires of women were qualitatively different from those of men. Thus, contemporary women have not been provided with a basis for learning to recognize orgasm as an integral part of their sexual role (Gagnon, 1973).

Most young children's knowledge about sexual functioning is limited to the recognition of anatomical differences between the sexes. Such knowledge may be acquired within the family by observing naked parents or siblings, but it is probably more often acquired clandestinely during sex play with peers.

Many children satisfy their natural curiosity about the genitals of others by playing "doctor." On the assumption that parents do not approve of such games, "doctor" is almost always played in secret, and many children feel guilty about participating. Thus, a child's early associations with her or his own genitals (and those of others) may be negative. To the extent that adult sexuality is learned, this kind of early experience is certainly not conducive to the development of positive (healthy) orientation toward one's own sexuality. Also, cultural prohibitions against the expression of sexual curiosity among children may be stronger for girls than for boys.

Parents are unlikely to tolerate early masturbatory behavior on the part of children of either sex, but the curiosity of boy "doctors" may be more readily accepted as natural than similar interest displayed by girls. The subtle ways in which parents suggest that female genitalia are unclean or untouchable are dramatically illustrated in Mother's insistence that little girl's bedtime attire include clean underpants. In contrast, little boys are encouraged to handle their penises in order to urinate "like men." Thus, the association between one's genitals and one's gender role may be stronger for boys than for girls.

These associative differences are further elaborated during puberty. During early adolescence boys learn to associate their awaking sexuality with orgasmic gratification, typically achieved through masturbation. Masturbation is widely discussed, accepted, and practiced by adolescent males. According to Kinsey's data, by age 20, 92% of the males sampled had masturbated to orgasm. Nearly all males reported having heard about masturbation before they tried it, and approximately 40% indicated that they had first observed others masturbating (Kinsey et al., 1948).

In contrast, only 33% of the 20-year-old females in Kinsey's sample had ever masturbated to orgasm. Of those women who had masturbated, most had learned to do so through accidental discovery. It appears, therefore, that females are not only less likely to masturbate than males but also less likely to talk about their masturbatory experiences if they do.

In four college years of close residential contact with female peers during the early 1960s, I can recall hearing reference to female masturbation on only one occasion. The suggestion was met by a unanimous expression of surprise, if not disbelief. In that setting, confidences regarding the details of one's heterosexual experience were rarely exchanged. When the general topic of sexuality was broached in large gatherings, even the most sexually experienced group members responded to issues such as petting with objective and moral disdain.

As a result of the general societal shift toward increased sexual permissiveness, the incidence of female masturbation appears to have increased. Hunt (1974) found that two out of every three women in his sample disagreed with the statement "Masturbation is wrong." Although the actual incidence of masturbatory behavior reported by these women was not substantially higher than that obtained by Kinsey (63% versus 62%), the age of first experience appears to have declined markedly over the last two decades. In Kinsey's study, only 15% of the females had masturbated to orgasm by age 13, whereas Hunt found early masturbatory experience to be more than twice as common in his sample (33%).

The growing recognition that female masturbation is a normal and acceptable means of obtaining sexual gratification does not imply that it is a preferred means. Indeed, it has been suggested that, even when young women do masturbate, they may not associate the experience with their developing sexuality (Gagnon, 1973). When women masturbate, they generally manipulate the entire mons area or the clitoral shaft. Vaginal insertions with either one's fingers or objects such as candles or bananas is relatively rare. Thus, the association between heterosexual intercourse, which involves penile penetration of the vagina, and clitoral manipulation may not be clear.

It is a well-known fact that peak orgasmic responsiveness occurs much later for females than for males. Whereas almost 100% of the males in Kinsey's sample had achieved orgasm by the age of 17, maximum orgasmic response among females was not reached until the mid-30s (Kinsey et al., 1953). In Masters and Johnson's view, the lack of orgasmic response on the part of younger women is the result of the repression of natural urges.

> During her formative years the female dissembles much of her developing functional sexuality in response to societal requirements for a "good girl" facade. Instead of being taught or allowed to value her sexual feelings in anticipation of appropriate or meaningful opportunity for expression, thereby developing a realistic sexual value system, she must attempt to repress or remove them from their natural context of environmental stimulation under the implication that they are bad and dirty. She is allowed to retain the symbolic romanticism which usually accompanies these sexual feelings, but the concomitant sensory development with the symbolism that endows the sexual value system with meaning is arrested or labeled—for the wrong reasons—objectionable [Masters & Johnson, 1970, pp. 215-216].*

According to Masters and Johnson, successful sex therapy involves the release of natural sexual processes.

*From *Human Sexual Inadequacy*, by W. H. Masters and V. E. Johnson. Copyright 1970 by Little, Brown and Company, Publishers. Reprinted by permission.

Gagnon (1973) suggests an alternative explanation for the slower development of full sexual potential among women than among men. He sees female sexuality as a learned phenomenon that occurs within cultural and historical tradition. Female orgasmic responsiveness develops more slowly because women have not been provided with the opportunity to learn that it is their prerogative to be sexually responsive. The culture allows, indeed encourages, boys to accept their sexuality and to value those factors that enhance it. Girls, on the other hand, are often denied societal permission to learn their sexual role.

Thus, Masters and Johnson view the primary influence of past experience and learning on female sexual behavior as inhibitory. Gagnon, instead, sees social learning as an integral part of sexual development. In order to assess the validity of these alternative hypotheses, further empirical research is required. However, the success of Masters and Johnson's program for the treatment of female (and male) sexual malfunction does demonstrate the influence of learning on adequate sexual functioning.[6]

Sexual Dysfunction

It is generally agreed that most sexual malfunctions are psychologically rather than physiologically based. But in contrast to most psychoanalytically oriented therapists, who view sexual malfunctions as symptoms of deep-seated neurotic conflicts, Masters and Johnson view the primary cause of sexual inadequacy as the result of learned (negative) attitudes and ignorance of sexual physiology. Consequently, their short-term sex-therapy program combines sex education and supportive psychotherapy directed at releasing the repression of natural urges from culturally imposed constraints. Before turning to a detailed discussion of Masters and Johnson's approach to sex therapy, let us first consider the most common types of sexual malfunction among women: failure to attain orgasm, dyspareunia (painful intercourse), and vaginismus (conditioned spasm of the vaginal entrance preventing penetration).

Orgasmic malfunction. The inability to experience orgasm (sometimes referred to as frigidity) is the most common complaint of women seeking sex therapy. Masters and Johnson (1970) suggest that the psychological origins of orgasmic malfunction include (1) religious values that severely restrict or prohibit sexual expressions, (2) emotional immaturity, (3) inability to identify (psychologically) with one's partner, and (4) marriage to a sexually inadequate male.

Orgasmic malfunctions are exhibited in a variety of ways. Some women have never experienced orgasm by any means. This type of malfunc-

---

[6]Interestingly, many women also have difficulty expressing their aggressive impulses. Assertiveness training helps women to overcome their learned inhibitions with regard to aggression. In American society more stringent standards for the control of both sexual and aggressive actions are applied to females than to males (Kipnis, 1974). This parallel in learned control is particularly interesting because females have been generally assumed to be more passive than males and less inclined to display basic "animal" impulses.

tion is classified as *primary orgasmic dysfunction*. Others are readily orgasmic in some situations but not in others. Three types of *situational orgasmic dysfunction* have been identified. Coital orgasmic inadequacy refers to the inability to experience orgasm during coitus; orgasm, however, may be readily achieved through manual or oral-genital manipulation. The reverse of coital orgasmic inadequacy is masturbatory orgasmic inadequacy, which refers to the inability to experience orgasm with direct clitoral manipulation; however, the person is able to experience orgasm during coitus. The third type of situational orgasmic dysfunction is classified as random, in that orgasm is experienced on some occasions (or with some partners) but not on others.

On the basis of her clinical observations, Kaplan (1974) estimates that only 8 to 10% of sexually active women never experience orgasm. However, less than half of these women reach climax during coitus without additional clitoral stimulation. Some clinicians place little significance on how orgasm is achieved and regard many cases of situational orgasmic dysfunction in an otherwise responsive and orgasmic woman as a normal variant of female sexuality. But as women (and men) have become better informed about women's orgasmic potential, increasing numbers of women are seeking treatment for all types of orgasmic dysfunction.

Dyspareunia. The technical term for painful intercourse is *dyspareunia*. Although the experience of pain during intercourse may be psychological in origin, it may also be the result of organic factors. Vaginal pain resulting from penile penetration often occurs when there is insufficient lubricant within the vaginal canal, a condition that may result from inadequate sexual arousal. Among older women the normal decline in production of estrogen following menopause is often the cause of insufficient vaginal lubrication. A variety of artificial lubricants are available, or (less commonly) hormone replacements may be prescribed. Other sources of vaginal pain include infections or biochemical reactions to various forms of contraceptives. Pain in the vaginal entrance may be caused by the presence of a partially intact hymen or by scars resulting from vaginal injuries incurred in childbirth, rape, or criminal abortion. When pain is experienced deep within the pelvis, it may be due to tears in the ligaments that hold the uterus in place, infections of the cervix, or endometriosis—a condition in which the tissue that normally lines the uterus implants and grows in other areas of the pelvis. All of these organic problems can be treated medically. Psychological causes for painful intercourse include fear of pregnancy and pain and guilt associated with sex.

Vaginismus. Vaginismus is a relatively rare but clearly defined clinical problem, in which attempts at penetration during intercourse—or even a pelvic examination—result in an involuntary tightening, or spasm, of the outer third of the vagina. The physiological response is real and often severe enough to prevent vaginal penetration. However, vaginismus is psychogenic in origin. Masters and Johnson (1970) suggest that some of the common causes for this condition are marriage to an impotent man, prior history of painful intercourse due to a physical problem, a traumatic sexual experience such as rape, and negative attitudes toward sexuality.

Once a couple becomes aware of the physical reality of the symptom, vaginismus appears to be amenable to successful treatment. In the early phases of treatment vaginal dilators in graduated sizes are used to decondition the involuntary constriction of the muscles at the entrance of the vagina. Of course, the patient's fear of penetration must also be alleviated.

Sex Therapy

Sexual malfunctioning may be mild and of short duration, or it may be severe and persistent. Available treatment for sexual inadequacies range from relatively simple educational programs and self-help to long-term, intensive psychotherapy.

Masters and Johnson's two-week program for dealing with sexual inadequacy combines sex education with supportive therapy provided by a team of female and male cotherapists. Because of Masters and Johnson's conviction that satisfactory sexual functioning requires both anatomically functional sex organs *and* a functional interpersonal relationship, one partner is never treated individually.

After giving a detailed personal history, each partner undergoes a thorough physical examination in order to identify potential organic sources of the difficulty. The cotherapists stress the importance of regarding sex as a natural function rather than as an achievement situation. Pressures to perform inhibit the ability to relax and to give way to the pleasurable sensations associated with sexual arousal. Focusing on performance casts an individual in the "role of spectator" rather than in that of involved participant.

Once therapy has begun, the couple is instructed not to have intercourse but, instead, to explore each other's bodies in order to learn more about what each finds pleasurable. At first the gentle exploration of sensory experience is nongenital. The importance of communication is stressed. Since most people find it easier to "do" sex rather than talk about it, each partner is instructed to actively participate in his or her own pleasure by guiding the other's caressing hands. Gradually, the focus shifts to the genitals and finally culminates in intercourse.

These physical activities constitute the couple's "homework." Each day during the two-week period the partners discuss their feelings and analyze their successes and failures with the cotherapist team. Success in rapid treatment depends on each partner's ability to be accessible (and vulnerable) to the other. Masters and Johnson consider the relationship, rather than the individual, as the patient.

Using charts and models, the cotherapists provide detailed information about the physiology of the sexual-response cycle. For example, a woman previously unresponsive to her husbands' attempts at clitoral manipulation may be easily aroused once the husband has learned that she finds direct manipulation of the head of the clitoris painful.

Masters and Johnson have carefully evaluated the success of their approach to the treatment of sexual dysfunction. Of the 342 women treated for sexual dysfunction, the overall rate of failure was 19.3% (Masters & Johnson, 1970). All 29 cases of vaginismus were successfully reversed. Success rates for orgasmic dysfunction vary; 83% of the 193 women treated for primary orgasmic dysfunction responded successfully. The success rates for two of the three classifications of situational orgasmic dysfunction—clitoral and masturbatory—are also high (84 and 91%, respectively). Random orgasmic dysfunction was found to be less easily reversed. Of the 32 women treated for this type of sexual malfunction, 12 (37.5%) were not helped. Since Masters and Johnson identified an organic cause in most of the cases of dyspareunia, medical referrals were made, but therapeutic success is not reported.

The overall success of Masters and Johnson's program for the treatment of sexual dysfunction among women is impressive and clearly underscores the importance of the interaction between the physiological and social-psychological determinants of female sexuality.

Sexual Arousal in Women

Learning to act sexy is different from learning to be sexual. Sexy women know how to arouse men, but this does not imply that they are easily aroused themselves. Orgasmic attainment depends on the ability to abandon oneself to the physical sensations associated with sexual arousal. For the female who was taught to maintain sexual control in order to avoid premarital intercourse, the transition from being a good, sexy girl to being a sexy (and sexual) woman may not occur automatically with the issuing of a marriage license. Indeed, it may take years for that female to shed her early inhibitions and respond orgasmically to sexual arousal. The ability to abandon oneself to any sensation in the presence of someone else requires trust. In this society females are socialized to value emotional intimacy based on trust as an integral part of interpersonal relationships (Douvan, 1976). Married or not, women may be less likely than men to respond in a physically uninhibited way if they do not feel emotionally secure.

We have seen earlier that, as society's attitudes toward sexual behavior have become more permissive, women have become freer to feel and express their sexuality. However, societal expectations continue to impose constraints on the social contexts in which female sexuality is "legitimately" expressed. For example, despite recent evidence suggesting that women are as likely as men to be sexually aroused by erotic stimuli, they are less likely to acknowledge their arousal.

Until recently it was widely assumed that women are less likely than men to become sexually aroused in response to pornographic stimuli. Kinsey et al. (1953) reported that men were sexually stimulated more often than women by pictures of the genitals or of sexual scenes and that women were aroused almost as often as men by movies and literary materials containing sexual references. Consequently, it was assumed that women are aroused by romantic rather than sexual stimuli.

However, the Kinsey data were based on self-reports. The results of several recent studies suggest that whether or not women recognize and/or acknowledge their own sexual arousal, even when they are physiologically aroused, depends on the situation in which the arousal occurs.

In one study (Siguisch, Schmidt, Reinfeld, & Weidemann-Sutor, 1970), the reports of female subjects exposed to erotic photographs indicated that they were less sexually aroused than men. This was found to be true, despite the fact that these women did experience physiological reactions in the genital area (warmth, pulsations, or vaginal lubrication) and did increase their sexual activity (petting, masturbation, and coitus) within 24 hours of viewing the pictures. In an extension of this study, Mosher (1973) found that male participants reported a significantly higher level of sexual arousal after viewing explicitly sexual films. However, the type of erotic material presented (coitus versus oral-genital relations) differentially affected the level of arousal reported by males and females. Males found the film depicting oral-genital relations more arousing than the one depicting coitus; the reverse was true for females. These results suggest that women are likely to acknowledge their sexual arousal only when they feel assured that such arousal represents a socially appropriate response.

For example, Kaats and Davis (1970) found that college women's awareness of sexual desires was related to their dating status. Of the women steadily involved with one man, 56% acknowledged "urges" to engage in some form of sexual activity at least once a week. In contrast, only 19% of the women who were not dating regularly acknowledged such urges. In the absence of a sexually capable, socially sanctioned partner, women may be hesitant to acknowledge to themselves or to others the existence of their sexual desires[7] (Kennedy, 1973; Norris & Lloyd, 1971; Pfeiffer & Davis, 1972).

The recent invention of a device called *photoplethysmograph* (Sintchak & Geer, 1975) has made it possible to obtain accurate physiological measures of sexual arousal in women. The photoplethysmograph is an acrylic cylinder that contains a photocell and a light source. The photocell registers diffused light as vaginal pressure and blood volume change in response to the presentation of sexual stimuli. Inserted into the entrance of the vagina, the photoplethysmograph can be used to detect relatively low levels of sexual arousal.

---

[7]Androgens have been found to stimulate sex drive in women. Physiologically, androgens exert an effect on the clitoris, increasing its sensitivity to stimulation. Individual reactions to increased clitoral awareness resulting from the administration of testosterone vary. Sexually experienced women who have no access to a sexual partner at the time of androgen therapy may find such increase annoying. Among sexually inexperienced women clitoral awareness may be increased without any corresponding recognition of elevated sex drive. The effectiveness of androgen therapy in the treatment of women who do not experience orgasm appears largely dependent on psychological factors (Kennedy, 1973; Norris & Lloyd, 1971).

Heiman (1974) exposed male and female college students to a series of four-minute taped sequences depicting different levels of erotic activity. The content of each sequence represented erotic, erotic-romantic, romantic, or control (neither erotic nor romantic) material. Within each content category the sex of the initiator and that of the recipient of the activity were varied. After listening to each tape, the subjects were asked to indicate their level of sexual arousal. In addition, physiological measures of arousal were recorded.

Both males and females reported that the erotic and romantic-erotic tapes were equally arousing; the romantic and control tapes were equally unarousing. Subjects' subjective reports of arousal were consistently related to the physiological measures obtained. These data suggest that explicit sex, not romantic content, is critical in eliciting the recognition of sexual arousal from both men and women.

An interesting finding of the Heiman study was that 42% of the women who showed the most dramatic increases in vaginal blood volume (indicative of physiological arousal) failed to identify any change in physiological arousal when either the romantic or the control tapes were presented first. Perhaps women find it difficult to legitimize (and thus report) feelings of sexual arousal in the absence of clear erotic cues. For men the reality of an erect penis in response to even the most ambiguous erotic stimulus is difficult to interpret as anything other than a sign of sexual arousal.

The complex effects of attributing differential labels to states of physiological arousal are just beginning to be examined. As we saw in Chapter Two, expectancies play a role in determining the meaning ascribed to behavioral events such as menstruation. If a woman expects menstruation to be painful, she may well find her expectations confirmed. Similarly, if a young woman expects her first coital experience to result in peak physical pleasure, she may be rewarded.

As the differences between male and female premarital-experience rates begin to decrease, we may begin to see a convergence in sexual-maturity rates (Gordon & Shankweiler, 1971). To the extent that females must learn to act sexual as well as sexy, the general shift in sexual permissiveness documented by Hunt may encourage women to learn to appreciate (and enjoy) their full sexual potential at younger ages.

Lesbianism

Up to this point our discussion of female sexuality has focused on women's sexual behavior within a heterosexual context. Female homosexuality, or lesbianism, provides an alternative dyadic relationship within which a woman's sexuality may be expressed.

If, as we have suggested, female sexuality is learned, so is the context in which it is expressed. Human beings are pansexual: they are capable of

responding to a variety of sexual stimuli. Sexual preference and sexual out-
lets often shift during an individual's lifetime. Kinsey and his colleagues
acknowledged this fact when they introduced a 7-point heterosexual-
homosexual rating scale that allowed for the classification of sexual behavior
along a continuum, from exclusive heterosexuality to exclusive homosexuality.

A female homosexual, or lesbian, is a woman whose primary erotic,
physiological, emotional, and social interests are in a member of her own sex
(Martin & Lyon, 1972). Despite the prevalence of myths regarding the
pathological family backgrounds and bizarre sexual practices of lesbians,
there is little evidence to suggest that homosexually oriented women differ
substantially from their heterosexual peers on any criterion other than their
choice of love object (Freedman, 1971; Rosen, 1974).

As we have seen, women are more likely than men to emphasize the
importance of the emotional context in which their sexuality is expressed.
This is as true for homosexually oriented women as for heterosexually
oriented ones: sex is secondary to emotion (Freedman, 1971). Both
homosexual and heterosexual women regard sexual gratification in the absence of romantic involvement as unsatisfactory (Gundlach & Riess, 1968;
Martin & Lyon, 1972). Indeed, lesbians are no more likely than heterosexual
women to engage in sexual liaisons with many partners (Freedman, 1971;
Gundlach & Riess, 1968; Kinsey et al., 1953).

Overt expressions of sexuality within lesbian relationships closely
parallel those of heterosexual partners. Kissing, caressing, fondling, oral
stimulation of the breasts and genitals, and mutual masturbation represent
the primary means of attaining sexual gratification. Tribadism (the stimulation of one clitoris against the other) is relatively rare. Contrary to popular
belief, vaginal penetration with penis substitutes (dildoes) is seldom practiced.

Despite the commonly held stereotype, most lesbian couples do not
assume rigidly defined male (butch) and female (femme) roles; rather, the
gender identification of both partners is predominantly feminine (Freedman,
1971; Mannion, 1976). Wolff (1971) notes the facility with which culturally
prescribed sex roles may be exchanged between partners in a lesbian relationship. In her view, the possibility for such exchange contributes a rich-
ness and variety to homosexual relationships that cannot be paralleled
within the confines of traditional heterosexuality.

Consistent with a concern for establishing and maintaining warm, affectionate, and lasting interpersonal relationships is the tendency of most
lesbian couples to practice monogamy. Sexual infidelity is discouraged, and
group sex is uncommon.

American society has generally been more tolerant of intimate friend-
ships between women than between men. The sexual orientation of women
who form emotional attachments to each other, travel together, or even live
together for many years is seldom questioned; they are assumed to be
heterosexually oriented. In contrast, adult men who share homes and rarely

entertain women are often assumed to be homosexual. As a result, Lyon and Martin's (1976) recent estimate that one out of every ten American women prefers other women as sexual partners may appear high.

Theories of Female Homosexuality

Traditionally, homosexuality was regarded as a deviant, or abnormal, form of sexual behavior. Psychiatrists and clinical psychologists accepted the term *homosexuality* as a diagnostic label describing a complex set of personality factors that connoted or implied psychopathology (Riess, 1974). On the assumption that homosexuality was a form of mental illness, attempts were made to devise "cures" and several psychological theories were proposed to explain its cause.

The first comprehensive theory of homosexuality was introduced in Vienna by Freud in 1910 and later translated into English (Freud, 1930). In Freud's view, all human beings are inherently bisexual and the origins of bisexuality are biological. However, Freud maintained that bisexuality is also expressed psychologically, in that initially everyone is able to develop sexual feelings toward objects of either sex. In the course of normal psychosexual development, the object choice becomes more or less limited to the opposite sex.

You will recall from our discussion of psychoanalytic theories of identification in Chapter Three that Freud attributed the development of heterosexuality to the successful resolution of the Oedipal complex. For boys the normal course of psychosexual development results in identification with the same-sex parent and the adoption of the female (mother) as the love object. For girls heterosexual development is more complicated, because their first attachment is to a homosexual object (mother). In order to achieve a positive resolution of the Oedipal complex, a girl must transfer her early attachment for mother to father (Freud, 1932). Freud viewed feminine identification as contingent on the girl's rejection of her early clitoral (masculine) sexuality. A girl's failure to accept the reality of her deprived (passive) sexual nature and to identify with her mother was seen by Freud as one cause of lesbianism. He also suggested that the inability of some females to transfer their Oedipal attachment from father to another man is a possible cause of female homosexuality. Interestingly, Freud did not regard homosexuality as an illness, but, rather, as a variation of the sexual functions (Freud, 1930).

Most neo-Freudian theorists regard homosexuality as a manifestation of psychological immaturity stemming from fixations during psychosexual development. For example, Deutsch (1944) viewed female homosexuality as symptomatic of a deep-seated neurosis resulting from penis envy and a pathological attachment to mother. Similar theories have been proposed by a number of other writers (Bieber, 1965; Caprio, 1954; Ellis, 1965; Romm, 1965).

According to Charlotte Wolff (1971), lesbianism may best be understood as one strategy for coping with the fundamental dilemma of being born female (the second sex). In Wolff's view, all females are aware of their inferior status. Mother, the girls' first and greatest love, values her husband and sons more than her daughters (or herself). Thus, the girl is relegated to second place in her mother's affection. Realizing this, she has two choices: she may (1) attempt to secure her mother's love by ingratiating herself to her mother and becoming like her or (2) identify with the male, thereby attaining independence from his superiority.

The first alternative is the most common. It serves two unconscious purposes: it pleases the male (father) and provides the daughter with a means of retaliating against her mother by outdoing her. Most girls deal with their fundamental insecurity by pursuing heterosexuality in an attempt to satisfy their need to be loved, first by their father and then by a husband or lover.

Masculine identification is a less common strategy for dealing with the female dilemma. By identifying with the male, the homosexually oriented girl attempts to compete, on an equal footing with men, for her mother's love. In Wolff's view, the essence of lesbianism is emotional incest with mother. Indeed, she suggests that lesbians expect from one another nothing less than the wish fulfillment of an incestuous mother-daughter relationship—an all-enveloping union from which males are excluded.

Unlike most psychoanalytic writers, who based their observations regarding the origins of female homosexuality on patients they had treated in therapy, Wolff's theory of lesbianism grew out of a research program with nonpatient lesbians. The theory is provocative, and the extensive interviews on which it is based provide insight into an area in which there has been little empirical study. However, the assumption that the underlying dynamic governing women's choice of sex object (homosexual or heterosexual) is motivated by a primary attachment to mother is difficult to substantiate. Furthermore, Wolff's suggestion that female homosexuality implies a masculine identification has not been supported by recent empirical research (Freedman, 1971; Mannion, 1976).

In contrast with most psychoanalytic theories of homosexuality, which regard predominant (or exclusive) interpersonal sexual relations between members of the same sex as a clinical entity or at least a clinical symptom, social-learning theorists view homosexuality as the result of positive associations with homosexual stimuli. In this view, a learned preference for sexual involvement with members of one's own sex is not necessarily accompanied by psychological disturbance.

There is evidence that a person's sexual orientation is based on past experience and present circumstances. According to the behaviorists, all animals (including humans) possess a diffuse sexual energy (or pansexual drive) and are inherently bisexual (Ford & Beach, 1951). The context in which sexual urges are expressed depends on environmental factors. Observations of the sexual behavior of lower animals support the view that sexuality is an amorphous force that can be used in a variety of ways, depending on the circumstances. Animals have been observed to engage in sexual activities to establish dominance hierarchies and to gain the protection of more dominant members of the same species. Sexual contacts between members of the same sex are widespread among mammals. In some species these contacts are limited to sniffing or licking of the genitals of same-sex peer or to playful mounting. However, in other species—for example, the stump-tailed monkey—homosexual contacts are prolonged and intense (Duberman, 1976).

Situational factors, such as restricted availability of opposite-sex partners, increase the frequency of homosexual contacts among animals. Similarly, human homosexual experiences are often the result of situational opportunities, such as those afforded by college or military living arrangements. Prisoners, isolated from members of the opposite sex, frequently express their sexuality with people of their own sex. In one study of female prisoners in California, 75 to 80% of the women interviewed had engaged in homosexual activities while institutionalized (Riess, 1974). Outside of jail, only 7 to 10% of these same women exhibited homosexual behavior. Deprivation, though, is not a necessary condition for homosexual activity among either animals or humans (Katchadorian & Lunde, 1975). Reviewing the anthropological literature relevant to patterns of sexual behavior among primitive peoples, Ford and Beach (1951) found that, of 76 societies surveyed, 49 (or 64%) recognized some forms of homosexuality as an acceptable variant of sexual functioning. However, there is no human society or animal species in which homosexuality is found *in opposition to* heterosexuality.

Behaviorists emphasize the importance of social learning and reinforcement as causal determinants of homosexual and, by implication, heterosexual orientations. Thus, according to this view, the basis of an individual's sexual preference is a positive association with homosexual (or heterosexual) stimuli.

A theory of lesbianism based on sex-role rejection has recently emerged from the feminist perspective (Mannion, 1976). The feminist view of lesbianism emphasizes the limitations imposed on women by society's definition of the female role. Women who feel compelled to reject the constraints of the female role as traditionally defined may find close intimate relationships with other women more rewarding than heterosexual relationships. Thus, a woman's choice of love object will be influenced by her perception of the likelihood that she and her partner (female or male) can maintain an equalitarian relationship based on mutual respect and the potential for individual growth.

The oldest theory of homosexuality maintained that homosexuality reflects a biologically or biochemically based predisposition. Indeed, Freud acknowledged the importance of constitutional determinants of homosexuality. Yet, attempts to identify physiological differences between heterosexuals and homosexuals have not been successful. Physical examinations, chromosomal studies, and endocrine studies have so far failed to identify any particular biological difference between homosexuals and heterosexuals (Katchadorian & Lunde, 1975). Hormones do influence the sex drive but not the direction of sexual behavior (Freedman, 1971). For example, administering testosterone to homosexual men does not increase their interest in heterosexual activity, but it does increase their desire for other men (Perloff, 1965).

Most studies of lesbians have been predicated on the assumption that lesbianism is a form of psychopathology. Only within the last few years has homosexuality (both male and female) been recognized as a normal alternative pattern of sexual functioning.[8] Early studies of homosexual populations drew subjects from therapeutic settings. As a result, it was easy to conclude, as most researchers did, that homosexuality is pathological. More recent comparisons of heterosexual and homosexual women that have not relied on patient populations have failed to support the homosexuality-as-psychopathology position.

Research on Lesbians

The results of recent research comparing the personality characteristics of homosexual and heterosexual women have generally failed to support the contention that there is a lesbian personality or that lesbians are more likely than heterosexually oriented women to display evidence of psychopathology (Armon, 1960; Brown, 1975; Freedman, 1971; Hopkins, 1969; Liddicoat, 1957; Wilson & Greene, 1971). For example, Armon (1960) compared 30 self-identified lesbians and 30 heterosexual women on several projective measures (the Rorschach and the Draw-a-Person tests). Independent clinical judges were asked to do a blind evaluation of the test protocols. None of the judges was able to distinguish "homosexual" Rorschach's or figure drawings significantly better than chance. These results led Armon to conclude that homosexuality cannot be regarded as a clinical entity.

In another study, Freedman (1968) compared the responses of 81 self-identified lesbians who were affiliated with the Daughters of Bilitis (a national homosexual organization) with those of 67 heterosexual women who were affiliated with a women's volunteer division of a national service organization. The test battery consisted of two personal-data sheets containing questions about demographic characteristics (age, marital status, education, and so on) and job motivation and satisfaction, as well as two personality inventories. There were no significant differences between the groups of homosexually and heterosexually oriented women in ratings of psychological adjustment and in measures of neuroticism, variability of results, and self-acceptance. The tests indicated, however, that homosexually oriented women were significantly more inner-directed and self-actualizing[9] than heterosexually oriented ones.

---

[8]Recently, the American Psychiatric Association has removed homosexuality from its official list of psychopathologies and has relabeled it as a "sexual-orientation disorder." As such, homosexuality becomes pathology only when it interferes with the emotional or personality functioning of the individual.

[9]Freedman's finding that lesbians are more self-actualizing than heterosexual women may be due to the fact that his sample was drawn from the Daughters of Bilitis. One of the stated aims of the society is to enable its members to understand themselves and make their adjustment to society in all its social, civic, and economic implications.

Several other investigators, employing paper-and-pencil measures of neuroticism, failed to obtain differences between homosexually and heterosexually oriented women (Brown, 1975; Hopkins, 1969; Siegelman, 1972). As a matter of fact, in one study, Wilson and Greene (1971) found that heterosexuals scored somewhat higher on neurotic traits than homosexuals. Contradictory results have been reported in one large sample study by Kenyon (1968), who found lesbians to score higher on Eysenck's neuroticism scale than heterosexual women.

Three studies attempting to specify female homosexuals' developmental histories are now available (Gundlach & Riess, 1968; Saghir & Robins, 1973; Wolff, 1971). The largest study of this type was conducted by Gundlach and Riess in 1968. In this study, the responses of 226 adult self-identified homosexual women, obtained through the cooperation of the Daughters of Bilitis, were compared with those of 234 adult heterosexual women, obtained through friends of the investigators. Subjects were matched for age, educational level, geographic area, and size of place of residence. None of the subjects were patients, although 41% of the lesbians and 43% of the heterosexual women had had some psychotherapeutic experience. Each subject answered an extensive questionnaire designed to assess early life experience and sexual behavior.

Comparisons of the subjects' responses to the questionnaire revealed surprisingly few statistically significant differences between homosexually and heterosexually oriented women on items tapping family history and parent-child relationships. Homosexually oriented women did appear less likely than heterosexually oriented ones to date during their teenage years. They also expressed less favorable attitudes toward their first menses. As adults the homosexually oriented women viewed themselves as less feminine than their matched heterosexual controls. Although lesbians reported themselves to be more easily aroused to orgasm than heterosexual women, they were significantly less concerned about their need for sexual gratification and engaged in sexual activity less frequently.

Responses to questions about family relationships and attitudes toward men and women failed to differentiate between homosexually and heterosexually oriented subjects. These findings contradict those of Wolff (1971), who found that family relationships, particularly with mother, exerted a strong influence on the sexual orientation of lesbians. In Wolff's sample more lesbians than heterosexual women reported that their mothers were indifferent or neglectful and expressed the view that their mothers would have preferred them to be a male and preferred their brothers to themselves. Among Wolff's lesbian group, family instability was relatively common. The proportion of lesbians who reported their parents to be unhappily married was higher than that of the control group, and parents of lesbians were more frequently divorced.

Wolff (1971) as well as Saghir and Robins (1973) report that more lesbians than controls expressed the desire to be boys and exhibited tomboyish behavior when they were children. However, tomboyism is frequently observed among preadolescent girls, and Saghir and Robins's suggestion that it may be a precursor of lesbianism is questionable. Only a small number of the lesbians in Wolff's study retained into adulthood their desire to be male. This desire was not motivated by the wish for a penis but, rather, by the recognition that in this society males enjoy greater status than females.

In a recent comprehensive review of research on female homosexuality, Mannion (1976) concludes that there is little evidence to support the psychoanalytic contention that lesbianism represents either a fixation at an early stage of psychosexual development or a denial of feminine identity. Attempts to differentiate between homosexually and heterosexually oriented women on various measures of psychological adjustment have been generally unsuccessful.[10]

The results of studies attempting to specify common antecedents and correlates of the development of homosexuality in the biographical histories of lesbians have been inconsistent. However, three elements that emerge relatively often are (1) disruption in family life, (2) prevalence of cross-gender behavior (tomboyishness) in childhood, and (3) recognition of homosexual orientation before adolescence (Mannion, 1976). Since these three factors have emerged in several studies, they warrant further investigation. However, no single factor that determines a woman's sexual orientation has been identified.

Overall, the results of comparative studies of nonpatient lesbians and heterosexuals suggest that the two groups are strikingly similar. Both groups are diverse. The factors that, for each group, determine the choice of the love object's sex have not yet been identified. Rosen (1974) has suggested that a woman's first sexual experience is an important influence on her sexual orientation. A positive first experience with a woman or a negative first experience with a man may lead to a preference for members of the same sex. This suggestion, is, of course, consistent with the social-learning view that the context in which a woman's sexuality is expressed reflects a learned preference. As women, both lesbians and heterosexuals emphasize the emotional context in which their sexuality is expressed.

Summary

Traditionally, American women have viewed themselves as sexy but not as sexual. In recent years the pioneering work of Masters and Johnson as well as the Women's Liberation Movement have provided the major impetus for our current interest in and knowledge about female sexuality.

On the basis of data collected during an intensive investigation of natural sexual activity in a laboratory setting, Masters and Johnson divided the human sexual-response cycle into four phases: excitement, plateau, orgasm, and resolution. Physiologically, orgasm may be defined as a release of

---

[10]As a matter of fact, comparative studies of homosexually and heterosexually oriented women, using paper-and-pencil measures of adjustment, often suggest that homosexually oriented women are better adjusted than heterosexuals. But, when similar comparisons are made on the basis of interview data, there is some evidence for greater pathology among lesbians, often related to alcohol.

myotonia and vasocongestion built up in response to sexual stimulation. Regardless of the source of stimulation, the orgasmic response involves contractions of a set of muscles known as the orgasmic platform. Thus, in contrast to Freud's view, it appears that women experience only one kind of orgasm.

Perhaps the most dramatic finding reported by Masters and Johnson is the extent of similarity in the physiological sexual-response cycles of men and women. There are, of course, some differences. Females do not ejaculate. Unlike most men, women have the capacity to achieve multiple orgasms within a short period of time, and it appears that, the more orgasms a woman has, the stronger they become and the more likely she is to attain orgasm on subsequent occasions. These observations led Sherfey to conclude that women are not biologically built for monogamy. The hypothesis that women possess a biologically determined sex drive that is, even by traditional male standards, inordinately high gives rise to interesting speculations about the social consequences of a new "sexual freedom."

However, research evidence suggests that female sexuality is primarily a social-psychological phenomenon. Just as females learn through practice to be sexy, they also learn to be sexual. Much of the conditioning of sexual behavior comes from the culture in which a woman is reared.

Until the 1970s most of what was known about the patterns of human sexual behavior was based on the survey data gathered by Alfred Kinsey and his associates over two decades ago. Chief among Kinsey's findings was the empirical verification of the double standard. In 1974 Morton Hunt found evidence of increased sexual permissiveness. Although this shift toward permissiveness is particularly evident in the sexual attitudes and behavior of females, most women continue to equate sex with love.

Despite the fact that Masters and Johnson's work clearly suggests that orgasm is the biological prerogative of both women and men, many women continue to engage in coitus to satisfy their partners' physical needs. Even more striking, in view of Masters and Johnson's findings, is the fact that a considerable number of women who have never experienced orgasm report that their sex lives are satisfactory—even good.

Peak orgasmic responsiveness occurs much later for women than for men. Masters and Johnson suggest that women repress their natural urges. Another hypothesis is that, while boys are encouraged to accept their sexuality, girls are often denied societal permission to learn their sexual roles. The results of several studies suggest that women recognize their own sexual arousal only when the situational cues suggest that such arousal is socially appropriate.

Contrary to popular myths regarding the pathological family backgrounds and bizarre sexual practices of lesbians, there is little evidence to suggest that homosexually oriented women differ from their heterosexually oriented peers on any criterion other than their choice of love object. Indeed, the historical assumption that homosexuality represents a deviant or abnormal form of sexual behavior has recently given way to a view of homosexuality as a normal alternative pattern of sexual functioning.

Chapter Nine

Women's Roles:
A Life-Span
Perspective

The traditional female role is clearly defined. American females have been, and continue to be, encouraged to accept the social roles assigned to them on the basis of sex—those of wife and mother. Little girls are often encouraged to "help" with housework and to "nurture" their dolls in preparation for their adult roles. As teenagers these same girls devote endless hours to thinking about, talking about, and pursuing boys. If, as Stein and Bailey (1973) suggest, affiliation is a primary achievement goal for women, most are successful; the vast majority of American women marry and have children.

Despite the significance of marriage and child rearing as major life goals for most women, the demands and responsibilities associated with the traditional feminine role shift across a woman's life cycle. Also, neither the role of wife nor that of mother can be accurately characterized as a unitary role. Rather, the label "female role" refers to a constellation of roles that women play at given stages in their lives (Angrist, 1969; Glick & Parke, 1965; Hill & Rogers, 1964).

Life-cycle analyses focus on the natural history of social development across the life span. From this perspective it is possible to trace the development of the so-called female role from that of child in the family, through single adult, wife, mother, and grandmother (Angrist, 1969). The progression through these roles is determined in part by demographic factors such as age, marital status, education, and employment history. During any given stage in the life cycle, some roles may overlap (for example, student and employee). Some roles are relatively enduring (for example, daughter or mother), while others may change over time (for example, college student or even wife).

In this chapter we will trace the development of the constellation of female roles from adolescence through aging. Although our focus will be on the "natural" progression of a woman's roles through her life span, we will also consider the effects of some critical events, such as widowhood or divorce, that may disrupt this progression.

Adolescence

As we noted in Chapter Three, boys are more likely than girls to be subjected during early and middle childhood to socialization pressures to behave in a fashion that is appropriate to their sex role. If 8-year-old Timothy does not like baseball and prefers to read instead, he may be labeled a "sissy." Although the label "tomboy" may be applied to his 9-year-old sister, Mary, because she plays ball with the boys and climbs trees, the social implications inherent in these two labels are quite different. It is assumed that Mary will outgrow the tomboy stage; sissihood, on the other hand, is seen as a more permanent state.

The fact that before puberty fewer behavioral restrictions are placed on the feminine role has led Bardwick (1971) to suggest that the early identification of girls is bisexual. During childhood girls are unconditionally rewarded for athletic and academic achievements that may later be defined as masculine. In contrast to boys, who must earn their masculinity early, girls are not pressured to earn their femininity until puberty. Before puberty "femininity" is a verbal label, a given attribute that is awarded on the basis of biology alone (Bardwick & Douvan, 1971). As a result, for girls the tasks of searching for identity, achieving autonomy, and developing internal criteria for self-esteem are delayed (Bardwick & Douvan, 1971).

The name of the feminine game is not clearly articulated until puberty, when girls are encouraged to turn their attention to the serious business of preparing for their future roles of wives and mothers. Most of this preparation focuses on learning how to catch, and presumably hold, a man.

According to the developmental theorist Erik Erikson, the primary concern of adolescence is the quest for identity (Erikson, 1950). Erikson implies that sexual identity crystallizes during this period (Gallatin, 1975). By as early as 14 years of age, boys begin to express concern with their future identity in occupational terms (Gallatin, 1975). The attempts of adolescent girls to integrate their current and future worlds is not as specific. From the age of 10 upward, girls hold a more positive attitude toward marriage than do boys (Broderick, 1965; Garrison, 1966; Monks, 1968). However, apart from a general expectation concerning marriage, girls' future plans are not clearly formulated. As Douvan (1970) observes, adolescent girls appear to develop a self-system that is more fluid and vulnerable to environmental influences than the self-system developed by boys.

Angrist (1969) suggests that flexibility about future plans is built into the process of female socialization as contingency planning. Marriage may be a goal, but the achievement of that goal is not guaranteed. In a society that encourages women "to know their place" (Bem & Bem, 1970) and defines that place as the home, establishing a clearly articulated sense of identity in adolescence may adversely affect a girl's opportunity to marry. Since most females are expected to commit themselves exclusively to marriage, it is important that a girl remain malleable enough to fit the value system of a potential spouse (Douvan, 1960). Implicit in this observation is the suggestion that for girls an incomplete resolution of the adolescent identity crisis may prove advantageous in maximizing the number of marriage options available.

During adolescence the girl who was rewarded for superior academic and athletic achievement in grade school may find herself encouraged to behave less competitively. Most teenage girls do not regard straight As as a satisfactory alternative to an invitation to the junior prom. Indeed, the prospect of heterosexual dating in adolescence may exaggerate a girl's feelings of ambivalence toward her developing femininity.

Teen books and magazines abound with advice on how to become popular with members of the opposite sex. Girls are cautioned not to appear to be "too smart" and *never* to play to win. The summer after I graduated from high school, a girl friend and I made the acquaintance of a very attractive young man. We were both interested in dating him and were pleased when he invited us to go swimming. Both of us were good swimmers. When he suggested a race to the dock, I carefully paced my efforts to lose. My friend won. The next evening I was invited for another swim; she was not. Triumphant in my "victory," I could not help but consider my rival's loss of her own making. She should have known that "boys don't like to be beaten." Yet, female successes such as this heighten the distinction between a sense of "self as I am" and "self as (male) others want me to be."

In a study of cultural contradictions and sex roles, Komarovsky (1946) found that 26% of the college women in her sample experienced conflict over the contradictory role expectations held for them by individual members of their families. For example, one student observed

> How am I to pursue my course single-mindedly when somewhere along the line a person I respect is sure to say, "You are on the wrong track and are wasting your time." Uncle Jack telephones every Sunday morning. His first question is "Did you go out last night?" He would think me a "grind" if I were to stay home Saturday night to finish a term paper. My father expects me to get an A in every subject and is disappointed by a B. He says I have plenty of time for a social life. Mother says, "That A in Philosophy is very nice, dear, but please don't become so deep that no man will be good enough for you" [p. 185].*

Although 74% of the students in Komarovsky's study did not feel that the role expectations their families had for them were ambiguous, 40% did indicate that they had occasionally "played dumb" on dates. It can, of course, be argued that sex-role expectations are changing and that women are no longer pressured to adhere to traditional, stereotypically feminine self-definitions. However, in a more recent study of the attitudes of 53 college men toward intellectually oriented women, Komarovsky (1973) found that 30% of the young men in her sample considered social interactions with bright college women difficult to handle. One young man observed "I enjoy talking to more intelligent girls, but I have no desire for a deep relationship with them. I guess I still believe that the man should be more intelligent" (p. 874).†

*From "Cultural Contradictions and Sex Roles," by M. Komarovsky, *American Journal of Sociology*, 1946, 52(3), 184–189. Reprinted by permission of The University of Chicago Press.

†From "Cultural Contradictions and Sex Roles: The Masculine Case," by M. Komarovsky, *American Journal of Sociology*, 1973, 78(4), 873–884. Reprinted by permission of The University of Chicago Press.

Of the 37 college men in Komarovsky's study who said that intellectual relationships with dates were not a problem, 11 believed themselves to be intellectually superior to their female friends and the others were not concerned with intellectual issues. Of the 8 men who did acknowledge dating women whom they considered their intellectual superiors, 7 cited some female weakness (dependency, instability, or plain appearance) that gave them a compensatory advantage. Apparently, traditional feminine deference remains an adaptive strategy for maximizing one's prospects of marriage. There are, of course, men who do value and actively seek nontraditionally oriented women, but as yet such men appear to represent a minority.

According to Douvan and Adelson (1966), the ability of adolescent girls to integrate a concept of adult femininity is central to their adjustment. On the basis of data obtained from interviews with 2005 girls in grades 6 through 12, Douvan and Adelson were able to isolate two general patterns of adolescent identification—feminine and nonfeminine. The critical factor differentiating between these two groups was the focus on marriage as a future goal.[1] Of the two types of feminine patterns of identification (unambivalent and ambivalent), the unambivalent feminine pattern was the more typical. Unambivalent feminine girls were interpersonally oriented, based their self-esteem on helping others, preferred security to success, and were actively concerned about popularity, marriage, and family goals. Although ambivalent feminine girls, too, emphasized the importance of marriage, motherhood, and social development, they were concerned with personal achievements and individual development as well.

Of the four nonfeminine patterns of development identified by Douvan and Adelson (antifeminine, achievement-oriented, boyish, and neutral), only the antifeminine girls, who comprised 5% of the sample, indicated that they did *not* want to marry. All the antifeminine girls expressed the desire to be boys and showed some signs of psychological deviance. Both achievement-oriented and boyish girls did want to marry, but their ideas about marriage were less well developed than those of feminine girls. Neutral girls were nonfeminine only in the sense that their current activities and future plans did not focus on marriage or feminine roles; these girls neither wished to be boys nor aspired to masculine occupations, and they accepted the idea of marriage when questioned directly.

Despite the 4% decline in marriage rates between 1974 and 1975 (U. S. Bureau of the Census, 1975a) and the trend to marry later, most women do marry. It has not been determined whether today's young women are as likely to postpone identity formation until they know whom (or if) they will marry as were their counterparts 20 years ago. However, there is some

---

[1]Douvan and Adelson's (1966) analysis was based on data collected in 1956. Their assumption that a girl's femininity is contingent on her interest in marriage was generally accepted at the time they were writing. Were they to reinterpret those same data today, they might well use different criteria for femininity. However, more recently Bardwick (1971) made a similar assumption when she observed that girls who do not hold the feminine goals of marriage and motherhood are neurotic. We will question the validity of this assumption later in this chapter.

evidence to suggest that adherence to traditional sex-role behaviors is breaking down in the middle class, largely as a result of higher educational attainments (Bardwick, 1971). As increasing numbers of women (and men) obtain college degrees, we may anticipate some changes in women's role orientations; but, as we have seen, for the time being the impact of such changes has not been dramatic.

Adulthood

It is difficult to specify a single event that marks the transition from adolescence to adulthood. In the eyes of the law entry into adulthood coincides with attaining the age of majority. But celebrating the 18th or 21st anniversary of one's birth does not necessarily result in the automatic assumption of adult roles and responsibilities. From a social-psychological perspective early adulthood may be delineated in terms of mastery of particular tasks, such as selecting a mate, starting a family, and entering the labor force (Havighurst, 1972), or in terms of a higher level of ego development, characterized by Erikson (1968) as the capacity for love and work.

Sheehy (1974) views the primary tasks of young adulthood (the decade of the 20s) as a time for preparing oneself for the "shoulds" imposed by society; men "should" pursue career goals, and women "should" marry and have children. If, as Neugarten and Moore (1968) suggest, marriage defines maturity within the family, many young women enter adulthood on their wedding day.

Marriage

The primary social role assigned to women in this society is that of wife. Only 14% of American women never marry, and the average woman becomes a wife at age 20 (Troll, 1975). Young women are socialized to regard the choice of a marriage partner as the most important decision they will ever make (Deckard, 1975). Apparently, they learn this lesson well, since women appear to fall in love less readily and out of love more readily than men (Hill, Rubin, & Peplau, 1976; Rubin, 1973). To the extent that women view their emotional and financial security as inextricably tied to their spouses, it is not surprising that they try to choose judiciously.

Prompted by dreams of ultimate personal fulfillment as wives (and mothers), most young women elect to marry in their early 20s (or younger) and look forward to devoting their energies to caring for others. Sheehy (1974) labels such women as "caregivers." At the time they marry, most caregivers assume that their primary source of satisfaction will always be family- rather than self-oriented.

For the majority of American women (and men) marriage is the preferred status (Norton & Glick, 1976). Despite the growing recognition that marriages need not (and often do not) last forever, most couples regard their marriage vows as expressions of lasting commitment. Their expectations for marriage focus on the pleasures of shared activities and interests, as well as on the exclusive involvement with each other (Troll, 1975). Unfortunately, for many these expectations are never fully realized.

As one would expect, honeymooning couples are more satisfied with their marriages than any other group (Troll, 1975). Young wives, who typically attach value to intimacy and shared activity, are particularly likely to find the early years of marriage rewarding (Campbell, Converse, & Rodgers, 1975; Feldman, 1964). Young husbands are less likely than their wives to view the early years of marriage as very satisfying, perhaps because they find the demands of constant and sustained intimacy difficult to handle (Douvan, 1976). As time passes, women find their marriages less satisfying than men do (Luckey, 1961; Veroff & Feld, 1970). One prominent source of marital stress is the arrival of children.

Most couples enter marriage with the expectation of having children (Duvall, 1971). Indeed, most do—many within the first year of marriage— and couples who cannot have children are the objects of sympathy. Voluntarily childless wives are viewed with suspicion (Veevers, 1973) and often labeled selfish or neurotic (Bardwick, 1971). Social pressures to reproduce remain considerable, despite the fact that married couples without children tend to be more satisfied with their relationships than those who have children (Burr, 1970; Campbell et al., 1975).

For many women the transition from wife to mother is a source of considerable stress. Newborns demand constant care and, for the first few months, give little in return. The new mother often finds herself feeling tired, frustrated, and even resentful of the child whose arrival she so eagerly awaited. For many these negative feelings are a source of guilt or embarrassment. As a friend of mine so aptly observed shortly after the birth of her first child, "No one told me they didn't respond." The loving smile of a 6-month-old is reinforcing, but newborns do little more than eat, sleep, and cry (often, if appears, without cause). As children grow, the nature of their demands change, but they continue to require a great deal of attention. Most young mothers feel tied down and yearn for adult companionship. Two-year-olds are fascinating people, but they are not very good conversationalists.

Housework and child care occupy the majority of most young married women's time and attention. Within the traditionally defined roles of wife and mother, a woman's sole source of gratification is her family (Gove, 1972). Married men, instead, have two sources of gratification: family and work. If a male finds one of these roles unsatisfactory, he can focus his interest and concern on the other. Most women do not share this advantage. Even though many women now work, those who channel their energies into work-related achievement are likely to be accused of neglecting their families. In contrast, husbands and fathers who devote themselves to their careers are likely to be applauded for their commitment to their families' welfare.

Although a creative approach to mothering may provide a major source of satisfaction (Troll, 1975), keeping house can be a source of frustration (Gove, 1972; Oakley, 1974). Housework does not require a great deal of skill; most women, whether educated or not, are at least moderately competent housewives; and the job itself is of relatively low prestige (Komarovsky, 1973; Oakley, 1974).

Oakley (1974) conducted intensive interviews with 40 London housewives and found that 70% were dissatisfied with the "housework" aspect of their domestic role. Among the reasons given for dissatisfaction were monotony, loneliness, long hours (the average work week was 77 hours), and lack of structure. The most frequently mentioned "advantage" of the housewife role was autonomy.

Marriage appears to be more advantageous to men than to women (Bernard, 1973). Comparative data from a variety of sources (community surveys, first admissions to mental hospitals, psychiatric treatment in general hospitals, psychiatric outpatient clinics, private outpatient psychiatric care, and the records of general physicians) clearly indicate that women are more likely to be mentally ill than men (Gove & Tudor, 1973) and that the incidence of mental illness among married women is substantially higher than that among married men. Single women, instead, are less likely to experience emotional difficulties than either married women or single men (Birnbaum, 1971; Gove, 1972; Gurin, Veroff, & Feld, 1960).

It has been suggested that the higher rates of mental illness observed among women may be a function of the differential criteria used to evaluate the mental health of women and men (Broverman et al., 1970; Neulinger, 1968). Indeed, there is ample evidence to suggest that most of the concepts of what constitutes a woman's mental health were formulated by men and have been accepted by women (Chesler, 1971, 1972). As Chesler (1972) notes, psychotherapy is a male-dominated profession practiced primarily on females. The fact that women are more likely than men to seek therapy may have several origins. You will recall that women are more likely than men to acknowledge and disclose their emotions and that help-seeking behavior is considered more appropriate for women than for men. Also, deviant behavior on the part of women (wives and mothers) is less likely to be tolerated than deviant behavior on the part of men. Only recently have practicing therapists (most of them women) begun to recognize the possibility that many of the symptoms associated with emotional disturbances among women—such as depression, paranoia, and anxiety—may emanate from their dissatisfaction with their social roles and environments rather than from some deep-seated personality problem (see Franks & Burtle, 1974).

As Gove and Tudor (1973) observe, the higher incidence of mental illness among married women than among single women may reflect the difficulties inherent in coping with traditional roles, which are neither well defined nor highly valued. Role ambiguity is always a source of stress, and the role of housewife is relatively unstructured and invisible. Even if a woman's wash is "whiter than white," the probability that anyone will notice (or comment) is slight—unless the comment is a negative one.

Because of the lack of structure of the housewife's role, it is difficult to evaluate one's success at the task. Despite the commercials, how do you determine how clean a dish must be to be regarded as "really clean"? The criteria for successful motherhood are no less elusive. Historically, the number (and sex) of a woman's children was used as a measure of her success as a mother (Russo, 1976). More recent attempts to define the quality of a mother's job focus on the outcome of her child-rearing efforts; good mothers have well-adjusted children who grow up to be productive (economically successful) citizens. Even if an adequate definition of "well-adjusted" children existed (and it does not), 20 years is a long time to wait to see if your offspring prove to be productive. For working men periodic raises and promotions provide objective standards for evaluating performance. Most wives and mothers do not enjoy the benefits of such consistent (or immediate) feedback.

Overall, women evaluate their performance as parents more negatively than do men (Troll, 1975). This is particularly true of less-educated mothers, although Lopata (1971) found that nearly all mothers thought that child-rearing was a difficult and often thankless task (perhaps because the criteria are so poorly defined). Most people want to do what they do to the best of their abilities. To be a good wife and mother is an achievement of no small significance.

Feminist writers recognize the importance of the roles of wife and mother (Freeman, 1975), and it is unfortunate that much of the current emphasis on reexamining the status of women in American society has been misinterpreted. The social consequences of encouraging women to develop an independent sense of self, separate from their identities as wives and mothers, need not pose a threat to either the family as a social institution or those women who derive pleasure and satisfaction from performing those roles exclusively. The goal of feminism is equality for both women and men; and such equality implies the freedom to choose the life style to which one is best suited.

As traditionally defined, the roles of women have been limited to those of wife and mother. However, not all women who marry do so with the expectation that their domestic commitment will continue to be their only commitment forever. There are numbers of women who elect to spend their young adult years nurturing but also intend to pursue some extrafamilial activity, such as a career, after the children are in school. Sheehy (1974) classifies such women as nurturers who defer achievement. Unfortunately, the decision to postpone serious career aspirations for an extended period of time is risky; 15 years after graduating from college one's academic training may be inadequate and one's professional skills obsolete. Other women, instead, defer nurturing in order to establish a career. Such women devote the decade of the 20s to their careers and postpone marriage and/or childbearing until their early or mid-30s.

As Sheehy (1974) observes, both deferred achievers and deferred nurturers feel required at some point to choose either love and children *or* work and accomplishment. This is true despite the fact that some women try to satisfy both needs—a difficult task indeed, particularly if a woman attempts to establish herself as a wife, mother, and professional simultaneously, since each of these roles require time, energy, and commitment. In Sheehy's

(1974) view, the degree of personal integration necessary to handle these commitments has not been developed yet by most women in their 20s. Role integration is possible, but an appropriate balance is more readily attained if new roles are not introduced until one is confident in one's ability to perform existing roles adequately. Nurturance and achievement need not be seen as incompatible goals; but the successful integration of these goals may depend on the recognition that it is not necessary to achieve, find a mate, and have a child all in the same year or even decade. Many young women who attempt to respond to the demands of selfhood and motherhood simultaneously end up by letting something go—their husbands, their careers, or their children (Sheehy, 1974).

Of course, not all women marry. Despite the stereotype of the "spinster" who would have given anything to marry but was never asked (Brown, 1970; Fromme, 1972), not all women want to marry. Indeed, many women who remain single have chosen an alternative life style (Baker, 1968; Seaman, 1972). A significant portion of women who never marry fall within the group of highly educated, successful career women (Bernard, 1973). Although several writers have suggested that career women are too independent to be desirable to men (O'Brien, 1973; Rosenteur, 1961), it is equally plausible, as Bernard (1973) suggests, that a woman with a successful career may be less likely to look at marriage as a necessary means of fulfilling her need for financial security. Many women who do not marry may value other goals more than marriage (Ginzberg, 1966). There is no evidence to suggest that single women are socially isolated (Gurin, Veroff, & Feld, 1960; Knupfer, Clark, & Room, 1966). As a matter of fact, single men are much more likely to become socially isolated and antisocial than single women (Knupfer et al., 1966).

Marriage is not the only means of establishing a mutually satisfying long-term relationship with a member of the opposite sex. Increasing numbers of women (and men) establish interpersonal relationships to satisfy mutually negotiated needs for intimacy and welfare without legal or religious sanction (Smith & Smith, 1974). Cohabitation is particularly appealing to young adults who value the opportunity for both interpersonal intimacy and autonomy. Group marriage is another alternative to the restrictions of monogamy (Bernard, 1973).

Wives and husbands, too, are exploring alternative ways to meet their needs for intimacy and autonomy. Some are attempting to achieve a more equitable division of domestic labor by periodically exchanging home and job roles (Rossi, 1964). Others are experimenting with open marriages (O'Neil & O'Neil, 1974) based on a commitment to their own and each other's growth, equal freedom, and identity. Still others have acknowledged the restrictions inherent in the monogamous ideal of exclusive sexual commitment to a person for life and have become involved with mate swapping or group sex (Smith & Smith, 1974).

Marriage may represent the American ideal for womanhood, but, as we have seen, the results of research on the effects of marriage on women suggest that many find the state of matrimony far from ideal. Many women who choose or are forced to relinquish the role of wife through divorce or widowhood find that not all of the consequences associated with the change in roles are negative.

Widowhood

As we said earlier, 86% of American women marry at some time during their lives. The marriages of many of these women are terminated by the death of their husbands. The 9.6 million widows in the United States comprise approximately 12% of the total female population (Troll, 1975). As one would expect, the distribution of widows within this society is related to age, ranging from 1% of the female population between the ages of 30 to 34 to close to 70% of the females aged 75 and over (U. S. Bureau of the Census, 1972).

But, despite these figures and the assumption that widowhood is a status reserved for the elderly, death can (and does) interrupt the marriage cycle at almost any age. I was widowed at 28 and had been married six years. Half of all widows (not including those who have remarried) are under 60. According to these statistics, three out of every four married women can reasonably expect to spend some portion of their lives as widows (Lopata, 1973). And because the average age of widows is 56 and the life expectancy for women is 75, the average woman who is widowed will be single for at least 20 years. The chances that she will remarry are only one out of 100.[2]

Unfortunately, this phase of the female life cycle has been largely ignored by society and social science alike. In this society women are prepared to assume the roles of wife and mother but not the role of widow, despite the probability that most will be forced to play that role at some time in their lives.

Major role transitions are seldom easy, and the transition from wife to widow is complicated by the psychological effects of the grieving process. The death of a spouse inevitably disrupts the attachment bond (Bowlby, 1969) formed by most adults in the course of marriage. This bond is similar to the attachment bond that children form to their parents, and its dissolution is manifested psychologically as "separation distress" (Parkes, 1972).

The natural reaction to the loss of a loved person or object is grief. Thus, bereavement is almost always accompanied by grief. Much of what we know about the effects of adult bereavement is based on the research of Collin Murray Parkes and his associates (Glick, Weiss, & Parkes, 1974; Parkes, 1964, 1970, 1972). According to Parkes (1970), the grieving associated with bereavement is a process of realization, of coming to grips with (and accepting) the reality of an external event that was not desired and for which no plans for coping existed. Although the needs and adjustment prob-

---

[2]Mortality rates among women are lower than among men. Furthermore, most wives are younger than their husbands and consequently are likely to outlive them. Even women who are five years older than their husbands have only a 50% chance of being outlived by them.

lems of a widow are affected to some extent by her age and by the cause of her spouse's death (chronic versus acute), the process of grieving follows a general pattern. Parkes conducted extensive interviews with widows one, three, six, nine, and twelve months after their spouses' deaths; as a result, he was able to identify a common pattern that included numbness, yearning and protest, disorganization, mitigation or defense, and identification.

The knowledge that these reactions are common may be reassuring for the person. Even as they grieve, most widows watch themselves and evaluate the extent to which they are dealing effectively with their grief (Glick et al., 1974). Unfortunately, information regarding grief is rarely shared, and, as a result, it is difficult to evaluate one's own reaction against an objective standard.

For most widows the intense distress associated with grieving is preceded by a period of shock or numbness. Among the widows interviewed by Parkes the most frequent reaction to the news of their husband's death was a form of shock or numbness. Most reported feeling cold ("I actually shivered"), numbed, dazed, or empty. A number described themselves as devoid of feeling for anywhere from five to seven days after their husband's death, although for many the period of numbness was interspersed with brief episodes of weeping.

Many of the widows viewed their numbness as a blessing because it allowed them to cope with the details of notifying family and friends, making burial arrangements, and so on. For example, I attended to those details with a kind of detached efficiency. I felt as if I were observing my own behavior from a distance and repeatedly wondered when the pain of realization would begin. The period of numbness did not last long, and, as the shock dissipated, pangs of intense pining for the lost person began.

Preoccupation with thoughts of the deceased is common among the recently bereaved. Parkes (1970) believes that, until such preoccupation and pining occur, grieving has not yet begun. During this period, memories of the dead person are clear and intense. Much of the time spent focusing on memories of the deceased involves the recall of happy moments the couple spent together. However, most widows also devote time to a compulsive review of the events that surrounded their spouse's death (Glick et al., 1974) in an attempt to explore hypothetical alternatives. Most of these alternatives take the form of "if, then" propositions. My husband died in the crash of a single-engine plane that he was piloting. I spent considerable time trying to reassure myself that I could not have prevented him from taking flying lessons.

During this period of yearning, attention is often directed toward places and objects associated with the deceased. Some of the widows in Parkes's study reported visiting the cemetery frequently in order "to be near him" (Parkes, 1970, p. 448). Others focused their attention on objects that their husbands had treasured, although many of them also avoided photographs and intimate objects, such as clothing, that could evoke intense pining. I lavished attention on my late husband's dog but put away all of his photographs and asked friends to remove his clothes from the closets the day after his death.

During this period of intense mourning, crying is common, but after the first few weeks most widows restrict this overt expression of grieving to times when they are alone. I went to great lengths to avoid crying publicly. In fact, I found the extended periods of sobbing over which I seemed to have little control distressing and repeatedly forced myself to accept friends' invitations to dinner in order to avoid succumbing to my grief.

While much of a widow's grief during this stage of bereavement involves yearning or searching for the lost object, anger or protest is also a common reaction. Parkes found that the most frequent form of anger reported by the widows in his study was a general irritability or bitterness. Among those women who directed their anger toward a specific target, most reported feeling angry with members of their families, clergy, or doctors. A few admitted feeling angry toward their husbands for leaving them behind. Most of us are taught from an early age to speak well of the dead. Although at times I was overwhelmed with anger toward the man who had left me to "carry on," I never mentioned these feelings to anyone. I knew my anger was irrational, and I was embarrassed as well. Parkes found that the intensity of yearning and protest diminishes considerably by the end of the second month. As the anger and the restlessness or hyperactivity that often accompany it dissipate, aimlessness and apathy take their place.

According to Parkes, the disinclination to plan or look ahead is characteristic of the disorganization that often accompanies grief. The majority of widows interviewed by Parkes were still expressing little interest in the future by the end of their first year of bereavement. During the first few months this general apathy extends even to a lack of interest in eating. Although the appetite for food usually does return by the end of the third month, many widows find it difficult to maintain interest in day-to-day activities or relationships for a much longer period. Grief work is a painful and time-consuming process; but, in order to regain a sense of independent identity and recover, it must be worked through. Fortunately, the distress engendered by bereavement is not continuous. Even during the early months, when the pain is most intense, there are periods of relative calm when that pain is mitigated.

Each of the widows interviewed by Parkes seemed to have her own pattern of mitigation. These included (1) blocking out or denial of affect, (2) partial disbelief in the reality of external events, (3) inhibition of painful thoughts by avoiding reminders, and (4) evocation of pleasant or neutral thoughts (Parkes, 1970). In Parkes's observation, the extent to which mitigation of grief was subject to voluntary control varied. I learned very quickly that by focusing my attention on job-related matters, such as preparing lectures, I could avoid feeling for brief periods of time. However, there was a price attached to the relief obtained through mitigation, because such relief was always followed by the shock of realization. It is likely that a widow's attachment to her husband is never completely severed, although the pain associated with his memory weakens over time. One common way in which this attachment is expressed in the early months of bereavement is through identification.

The most common type of identification reported by the widows in Parkes's study was the tendency to behave or think like their husbands. I was often startled to hear myself expressing views that I knew were not my own. It was almost as if I felt compelled to make certain observations for my husband because he was not available to do it himself. Similarly, I found myself actively involved in the political activities my husband had valued. A widowed friend continued her husband's coin collection for almost two years after his death.

According to Parkes, 13 months after the death of their husbands most widows were still without plans for the future and often depressed. However, the intensity of their separation anxiety had diminished, and most were functioning relatively effectively in their new roles.

Of course, individual reactions do vary, and the results of recent research suggest that two important determinants of the needs and adjustment problems experienced by widows are age and whether the cause of the spouse's death was chronic or acute. The elderly woman who loses a spouse usually enters widowhood with independent children, has some degree of financial security, and has had the opportunity to rehearse for her role. According to Heyman and Gianturco (1973), the elderly widow is psychologically prepared to accept the death of her husband because she thinks about it often. Among the widows these researchers interviewed, most admitted to frequent thoughts even about their own death, which they viewed as inevitable.

Several recent studies comparing the physical and mental health problems of older widows with those of married controls obtained no significant differences in the symptomatology reported by the two groups (Atchley, 1975; Heyman & Gianturco, 1973; Pihlblad & Adams, 1972). Heyman and Gianturco attribute the stability of life style and generally satisfactory level of adjustment to the age of the widows in their sample (65 years and older). In their view, aging is accompanied by placidity. In a similar study, Clayton (1974) found instead significantly greater incidence of depressive symptoms among the older widows in her sample—a finding that may be attributed to the fact that most of Clayton's interviews were conducted within the first year of bereavement.

Overall, studies of the effects of bereavement on older widows suggest that the stress induced by widowhood leads to limited adjustment difficulties. Some loneliness and depression result (Kutscher, 1969; Lopata, 1973), but differences between widowed and married persons in life style and general adjustment are few.

In contrast, studies of younger widows reveal that young women find it much more difficult than older ones to adjust to their new role. The results of several studies of younger widows suggest that many of their adjustment problems are related to economic needs arising from the loss of their husbands' incomes and increased responsibility for child-care (Maddison &

Viola, 1968; Parkes, 1964). The feelings of loneliness and isolation associated with widowhood are compounded for widows with young children, who must bear the burden of assuming the responsibilities of a single parent (Abrahams, 1972; Barrett, 1973; Lopata, 1973; Schlesinger, 1969; Wynn, 1964). The typical married couple with children derives mutual satisfaction from sharing the joys and concerns of parenthood. The widowed mother soon learns that others are not similarly interested in her children's antics.

The fact that among younger women the transition from wife to widow is frequently accompanied by increased financial and child-rearing responsibilities may provide a partial explanation for young widows' propensity to severe depressive reactions to bereavement (Clayton, 1975). One means of alleviating the loneliness and responsibilities associated with widowhood is to remarry. It is not surprising, therefore, that Butler and Lewis (1973) found that physical attractiveness is a major concern to young widows. As we shall see, attempts to reestablish oneself as a candidate for marriage represent another source of stress for the younger widow.

Despite the intuitive appeal of the suggestion that the impact of the death of a spouse is less severe if it has been anticipated (Lindemann, 1944), there is little evidence to suggest that prior knowledge of impending death reduces subsequent grieving (Glick et al., 1974). Women who have watched their husbands suffer for extended periods may view death as a merciful release, but they do not appear to be any less desolate.

However, there does appear to be a positive correlation between advance warning and eventual satisfactory adjustment to widowhood (Glick et al., 1974). The effects of forewarning are most apparent in the widow's ability to cope after her husband's death, despite the fact that preparation for loss does not seem to stimulate realistic planning. Forewarning allows some emotional preparation for the loss and diminishes the sense of overwhelming grief characteristically expressed by widows who have had no advance preparation. In the absence of such forewarning, the period of intense grieving and disorganization may be extended (Glick et al., 1974). Nevertheless, by the end of the first year of bereavement most of the widows in Parkes's study agreed that they were "beginning to feel like themselves again" and expressed some confidence in their ability to cope with their new roles.

Learning to accept and work through the death of a spouse is just one aspect of widowhood. The transition from wife to widow also involves the assumption of a new female role, one for which most women are ill prepared. Most married couples divide domestic tasks along traditional lines. Following the death of their husbands, many widows find it difficult to cope with the added responsibilities of home and car maintenance. Decisions regarding investments and other financial matters may provide an additional source of stress. On the other hand, learning to handle these responsibilities successfully is often a source of satisfaction for the newly bereaved, and such success may aid the widow to establish an independent sense of identity.

In America adult society is couple-oriented. The transition from wife to widow involves a change in status (Lopata, 1973) as well as a change in roles. For the traditionally oriented woman, whose self-identity is based primarily on the role of wife, the difficulties involved in achieving an independent sense of self may be particularly acute. Of course, one means of reestablishing self-identity is through remarriage. This may appear to be a particularly attractive alternative to widows with dependent children who feel obligated to provide a father for their offspring. And others often encourage younger widows to seek remarriage as a solution for their feelings of loneliness and social isolation. The fact that many widows report feeling alienated from their married friends—a feeling exaggerated by the perception that the wives of married friends discourage social contacts in fear of competition for their own husbands (Kutscher, 1969; Lopata, 1973)—may encourage widows to establish new social ties. However, the decision of whether (and when) to reenter the marriage market is not an easy one.

With time, many widows emerge from their experience stronger, more self-sufficient, and more vital than they were before. The consequences of bereavement need not be negative.

Divorce

The divorce rate in the United States has risen steadily during the last 50 years. In 1975 more than one million American couples were divorced (U. S. Bureau of the Census, 1975a). This figure represents an increase of over 6% from 1974. Of the 6.5 million Americans who are currently divorced, 4 million are women.[3]

As we have noted, the transition from wife to widow is accompanied by psychological distress and changes in both status and roles. Similar changes occur with the transition from wife to divorcée. A number of writers have drawn parallels between the loss of a spouse by divorce and the loss of a spouse by death (Bohannon, 1970; Rose & Price-Bonham, 1973; Weiss, 1976). Certainly both types of loss are accompanied by the disruption of the attachment bond (Weiss, 1976).

You will recall that the natural reaction to the loss of attachment is emotional distress. And this is true in the case of divorce, too, despite the fact that most people who decide to separate are influenced by the expectation that the outcome will be positive (Levinger, 1976). A sense of bonding to the spouse appears to persist after the end of marriage (Weiss, 1976); the individuals involved may no longer trust, idealize, or even like (love) each other, but attachment seems to persist (Weiss, 1976), and the loss of that attachment is accompanied by grieving. Just as the bereaved engage in grief work, so do the divorced engage in "divorce work" (Hunt, 1966).

The symptoms of "separation distress" found by Parkes to be charac-

[3]The majority of divorced persons remarry, particularly the men. However, the probability of remarriage is influenced by an individual's age and sex. Young divorced women (under age 30) are more likely to marry than single men and women, widows and widowers, and divorced men (Carter & Glick, 1970). After 30, divorced men are more likely to remarry than divorced women. Overall, the remarriage rate among men (either divorced or widowed) is higher than that among women.

teristic of bereavement (for example, yearning and protest, guilt, and alarm) have all been observed by Weiss (1976) in his work with the newly sepa- rated. For example, Weiss quotes a woman of 30 who made the remark "that when the idea she could live without her husband and be happier occurred to her she was terrified" (p. 137). Another stated that, although she did not like her ex-husband and found him boring, she was still attracted to him. In Weiss's view, the attachment bond, once formed, is difficult to dissolve.

Although Weiss found evidence that separation is accompanied by emotional stress, he also found that separated people reported periods of enhanced self-confidence and self-esteem, which he characterized as euphoria. In his view, the expression of euphoria often accompanies the demonstration that "one can manage alone" and may be reassuring.

As we noted in our discussion of bereavement, anger is one component of grief. However, the newly bereaved are less likely to direct their anger toward the lost spouse than the newly separated (Weiss, 1976). Among the separated, anger may be directed toward the spouse for initiating the dissolu- tion of the marriage, either because the person made the first move or because he or she proved an inadequate husband or wife. And yet, attach- ment appears to persist despite the anger, giving rise to feelings of ambiva- lence.

No matter what the circumstances surrounding it, divorce is usually a source of stress for both parties.[4] The loss of attachment appears to be one source of stress that widows share with divorcées. There are, however, some notable differences between the two types of experience. First, com- pared to divorcées, widows generally receive greater sympathy and support from others (Goode, 1956). Second, although society provides in- stitutionalized means for handling the early stages of grief after the death of a loved one, there is no recognized way to mourn a divorce (Bernard, 1970; Bohannon, 1970). Third, the involuntary loss of a spouse by divorce "in- volves a purposeful and active rejection by another person who, merely by living, is a daily symbol of rejection" (Bohannon, 1970, p. 42). As Bohannon observes, one reason why it feels so good to be engaged or newly married is the belief that out of all the possibilities *you* have been selected. The oppo- site feeling may accompany divorce, because it implies that *you* have been deselected (Bohannon, 1970).

Divorce involves changes in status and roles and typically leads to reexaminations of identity (Troll, 1975). The stresses associated with di-

---

[4]Any major change, even a pleasant one, produces stress (Holmes & Rahe, 1967), and too many changes occurring in a relatively short period of time can produce serious illnesses or severe depression. Holmes and Rahe (1967) devised a scale to assign numerical values to 40 changes that frequently affect people. According to this scale, the death of a spouse is the most stressful (100 points), but divorce is second (73 points), followed by marital separation, impris- onment, death of a close family member, personal injury or illness, and marriage (50 points). The results of a survey conducted by Holmes revealed that 80% of the people who experienced life changes totaling 300 or more points during a single year became pathologically depressed, had heart attacks, or developed other serious ailments.

vorce may be particularly acute for traditionally oriented women, whose sense of identity is contingent on the role of wife. For them the difficulties of establishing an independent sense of identity may be compounded by feelings of failure and inadequacy in the only role they know. Also, the general expectations associated with the role of "formerly married" (Hunt, 1966) are not well articulated. As we noted earlier in this chapter, role ambiguity is often detrimental to adjustment. Society's view of the divorcée is far from reassuring. Divorced women are commonly regarded as sexually deprived (and thus fair game), financially irresponsible, and psychologically depleted (Weiss, 1973). If a divorced father takes custody of his children, he is praised; a divorced mother is "expected" to live up to her responsibilities (George & Wilding, 1972). The stigma of divorce is more readily attributed to women with children, who must also contend with discrimination as a result of their roles as single parents and heads of household (Bradwein, Brown, & Fox, 1974).

It is generally assumed that the status of single mother following divorce is a difficult and transitory period that will end in remarriage (Brown, Feldberg, Fox, & Kohen, 1976). And most divorced persons do remarry eventually. Bell (1968) found that the majority of divorced persons in her sample viewed remarriage as the best way to obtain postdivorce adjustment. Certainly remarriage is one way to resolve the ambiguous role associated with divorce (Goode, 1956). In Hunt's (1966) study, even among those persons who considered themselves to be reasonably successfully divorced, most felt that only remarriage could signify full success.

Goode (1956) found a higher degree of adjustment after divorce among women who (1) had been the first to suggest divorce, (2) felt indifferent toward their former spouse, (3) received regular child-support payments, (4) had a full-time job (affording economic security, independence, and opportunities to meet people), and (5) had greater opportunities to date and develop new social relationships.

Indeed, opportunities to meet (and date) new people appear to be especially important to postdivorce adjustment (Rose & Price-Bonham, 1973). According to Goode (1956), "dating signifies a willingness to start a new life and serves as both an introduction and stimulus to that new life" (p. 258). Hunt (1966) suggests that among divorced persons dating represents a reevaluation of self and may renew self-esteem. However, beginning to date again may be awkward (Troll, 1975), particularly if the divorced person's children disapprove.

Children are involved in the majority of divorces. Nearly all divorcing parents are concerned about the possible harmful effects of divorce on their children. According to the results obtained by Goode (1956), most mothers interviewed felt that divorce had not affected their children adversely; almost all believed that their children were no worse off after the divorce than before. Kay (1970) and Bernard (1970) agree that research indicates that children of divorced parents suffer less than children living in homes torn by conflict.

Despite the fact that the dissolution of marriage is painful, the results of a recent study by Brown et al. (1976) suggest that for increasing numbers of women with children divorce may be "the chance of a new lifetime" (p. 119). Brown and her colleagues interviewed 30 mothers of dependent children (under 16) who had been either divorced or separated for at least one year. In response to the question "Are things easier or harder than when you were with your husband?" 17 said that things were "easier now" and only 3 said "harder." The remaining 10 said that things were "different"—some better (for example, freedom and emotional growth) and others worse (for example, finances and increased responsibility). Most of the women interviewed agreed that divorce or separation had "cost" them something, but they also felt that they had benefited from the dissolution of the marriages.

Among the costs identified by Brown and her colleagues were increased responsibility and financial burdens. Single mothers (either widowed or divorced) must add home and car maintenance to their routine household chores. Furthermore, the shift from sharing the responsibilities for major decisions with someone to making those decisions alone may be difficult. Two-thirds of the women interviewed mentioned the burden of these increased responsibilities. For example, one woman observed "The hard part is having to make important decisions alone—not having anyone to share these with. . . . There's the constancy of the burden—no one else to take over" (Brown et al., 1976, p. 123).

Among those single mothers who worked, the pressures of meeting the demands of both a family and a job were often a source of conflict. For example, one woman said "The situation has real conflicts. I feel I should be in two places at the same time. After work I come home, fix dinner, shop. I don't have the energy to do things. . . Everyone gets short changed" (Brown et al., 1976, p. 124). Working mothers also mentioned the difficulty of finding adequate child care and the expense of such care. Indeed, most of the women had experienced some financial strain, whether they were working or not. Twenty-five were dependent on either their ex-husbands or welfare, and over half of them felt that there were "strings attached" to that income.

Despite the recognition that independence from their husbands was costly, the majority of the women interviewed by Brown et al. (1976) also acknowledged some benefits. Eighteen women regarded the freedom from their husbands' demands and the opportunity to rear their children without interference as worth the price of their single-parent status. Others valued their increased sense of personal autonomy and competence. Although some women were financially worse off than before, several felt better off because they were free to control the resources that were available. Overall, most of the women expressed satisfaction with their newly found ability to control many aspects of their lives. They felt free to schedule household chores, rear their children, choose their friends, and regulate their sexual activity.

Of the 30 women interviewed, all of whom had been living without a husband for at least a year, only 4 were seriously interested in remarrying. However, despite the fact that these women were not interested in marriage, most felt that they could achieve a long-term relationship with a man outside the confines of a traditional marriage.

Middle Adulthood

As we have seen, the dissolution of marriage (through death or divorce) forces many women to assume new roles and establish a more independent sense of identity. Similar changes occur in the normal process of adult development. These changes are related to life-cycle stages.

Entry into adulthood may coincide with the decade of the 20s, but as a developmental period it extends into the 30s and 40s as well. Most adults are doing what they "should" by the time they reach their 30s; men have established careers, and women have established families. Having done what society said they "should," they begin to ask themselves what they "want" out of life (Sheehy, 1974).

Women who have devoted their young adulthood to caregiving may enter their 30s with the feeling that their only claim to identity is as someone's wife or someone's mother. They may envy their husbands, whom they view as having achieved a sense of independent identity (Sheehy, 1974), and long for the day when all the children are in school, so they can pursue their own interests (Neugarten, 1968; Thurnher, 1971).

The average mother is 35 when her last child enters school (Sheehy, 1974). Many women, even those who intended to remain caregivers all their lives, enter (or reenter) the labor force at this time (Troll, 1975). Others return to school to start or continue a college education prevented or interrupted by marriage and childbearing when they were younger. Still others become actively involved in community service or politics.

Bardwick (1971) suggests that, once women have successfully achieved their affiliative goals through marriage and child rearing, they may then feel free to develop independent interests outside the home. There is also some evidence that 10 to 15 years after marriage the achievement motives that many females developed during childhood reemerge.

Baruch (1966) compared the achievement-motivation scores of Radcliffe graduates who had been out of school from 5 to 25 years and found a significant relationship between the number of years since graduation, achievement motivation, and labor-force participation. Most of the women in her sample who had been out of school less than 10 years and whose children were young scored low on the fantasy-based measure of achievement motivation and were not employed. The achievement-motivation scores of women who had graduated 15 years before were higher, but few of these women were working. However, many of the women who had been out of school for 20 years or more and scored high in achievement motivation were employed. Unfortunately, since Baruch's study was not longitudinal, fluctuations in the achievement-motive scores of individual women over time cannot be assessed.

Even among those college-educated women who enter (or reenter) the labor force when their children are older, most do not commit themselves to pursuing careers in high-status, highly skilled jobs (Sheehy, 1974; Troll, 1975). As Bardwick (1971) suggests, bright and academically capable women who feared that success would reduce their chances of marrying may fear failure 15 years later. Yet, the number of women employed outside the home has increased dramatically in recent years; by the end of the decade of the 1960s there were more working women in the 35-to-54 age range than younger women (U. S. Department of Labor, 1969). Furthermore, the number of institutions of higher education sponsoring continuing education programs for older students, particularly women, continues to grow. Most faculty agree that these women are stimulating students and that their comments in class provide a mature perspective that is particularly valuable to their younger classmates.

It has been suggested that women are more disadvantaged than men by the approach of middle age. In American society there is a tendency to evaluate a woman's desirability as a sexual and marriage partner in terms of her age and physical attractiveness (Sontag, 1972). Women may "age gracefully" or appear "well preserved," but neither of these accolades has a comforting ring. In contrast, older men are often described as "mature and distinguished" (both positive evaluations), and they may be further advantaged by their claim to wealth, fame, and power.

Yet, contrary to what one might expect, younger women express more concern about aging than do middle-aged women (Neugarten, Wood, Kraines, & Loomis, 1968). Neugarten and her colleagues found that middle-aged men were more concerned about their bodies than middle-aged women. Indeed, there is some evidence to suggest that, overall, men view the prospect of middle age less positively than women (Neugarten, 1968; Sheehy, 1974).

As we have seen, many women view the decline in their domestic responsibilities as a welcome opportunity to assert their independence as persons. In contrast, many men who appeared to relish the challenge of the competitive economic marketplace enter middle adulthood longing to retreat to the security of their families (Sheehy, 1974).

Of course, some women do react to the "empty nest," or postparental stage of the life cycle, with depression (Bart, 1970). Typically, such a mother is unable to relinquish the mothering role, presumably not because she found it inordinately satisfying but, rather, because she demanded that her children meet *her* needs. Bart (1970) labels this kind of mother a "supermother," by which she means not only a woman who is overinvolved or overidentified with her children but also a woman who sees her children as "helpless" without mother's direction and "powerful" enough to destroy her very being. Obviously, "supermothers" take the mothering role seriously, but it is difficult to characterize them as passive and nonaggressive.

Most mothers are proud of their adult children's independence, and may regard that trait as a positive reflection on their own "successful" mothering. It should also be noted that motherhood does not end when the children leave home; in most cases interactions with adult children and their families continue throughout life (Hill, Foote, Aldous, Carlson, & Macdonald, 1970; Kahana & Kahana, 1972; Sussman & Burchinal, 1962; Streib, 1975).

In the United States and in other cultures as well, grandmothers tend to show more active involvement with their grandchildren than grandfathers (Kahana & Kahana, 1972; Kahana, Perez, Tagore, & Kahana, 1973). According to Benedek (1970), for many women grandmotherhood provides an opportunity to relive the early phase of their own parenthood as they observe the growth and development of their grandchildren. Older women who do not have grandchildren of their own often find the role of foster-grandparent rewarding (Troll, 1971).

However, the typical grandmother of the 1970s is not a gray-haired old lady. Rather, she is likely to be a middle-aged, or even younger, woman (Troll, 1975), who may show little interest in performing the traditional grandmother role. She has a full, busy life of her own and may resent her children's attempts to cast her into the role of babysitter. Lopata (1973) found this to be a common complaint of women widowed in middle age.

The care of small children may be a full-time job, but increasing numbers of women are recognizing the importance of establishing an independent sense of identity, apart from that of wife and mother. As we have seen, many contemporary women outlive their marriages. The ability to adjust to either widowhood or divorce depends in part on one's resources before the occurrence of such a major life crisis. But for most women personal growth represents more than an insurance policy. It is valuable in its own right.

Aging

The average life expectancy of the American woman is 75 years (Waldron, 1976). By age 65, women outnumber men by 39% (Brotman, 1972). Not only do women live longer than men,[5] but recent evidence suggests that psychologically women are remarkably well equipped to cope with the life changes associated with aging (Kahana, 1976). Many older women are widowed, and, contrary to the stereotype of the dependent, aging female, most opt to maintain residences separate from their children's or relatives' (Pihlblad & Rosencranz, 1968; Shanas, Townsend, Wedderburn, Friis, Milhoj, & Stehouwer, 1968). Also, women appear to adjust to the loss of a spouse more readily than men. Both Berardo (1970) and Lopata (1971) report

---

[5]According to Waldron (1976), mortality rates are 60% higher for males than for females. Of the excess male mortality 40% is due to arteriosclerotic heart disease. Men appear more prone than women to suffer from coronary heart disease, because they smoke more and they are more likely to develop the competitive, aggressive Coronary Prone Behavior Pattern. An additional 33% of the sex differential in mortality is due to men's higher rates of suicide, accidents, cirrhosis of the liver, and emphysema. These causes of death are linked to behaviors considered more male- than female-appropriate.

that widows are less likely than widowers to remain socially isolated or severely depressed after their spouse's death. Streib (1975) notes that throughout the life cycle women regard the maintenance of kinship ties as more important than men do. As a result, older women may have access to a supportive kin network not enjoyed by older men.

Interestingly, when Neugarten and Gutmann (1968) compared the TAT responses of a cross section of older women and men, they found that, as women aged, they tended to become more tolerant of their aggressive and egocentric impulses. In contrast, men appeared to become more tolerant of their nurturant and affiliative impulses. These results suggest that with advancing age the presumably sex-typed psychological orientations of men and women tend to merge or even reverse. In American society males are generally expected to and do assume a dominant social role throughout most of their adult lives. However, older women are seen as more dominant than older men by 55- to 70-year-olds of both sexes (Neugarten & Gutmann, 1968). Similar findings are reported by Kahana and Kahana (1970), who found that older men rated older women as more active, involved, hardy, and stable than themselves. Aging was generally considered undesirable by both women and men, but, as age increased, women were perceived as having an advantage over men.

As we have seen, even in its traditional definition the role of a woman is not a unitary one. Women play many roles throughout the life cycle. For many women, the tendency to define themselves and their roles exclusively in terms of their relationships with significant others (husband and children) diminishes as they mature. Feminine development does not end with the acquisition of a wedding ring or the arrival of children. Indeed, it appears that the departure of children from the home provides many women with the opportunity to establish a new (and more independent) sense of identity and encourages continued personal growth into later life.

Summary

American females continue to be encouraged to accept the clearly defined traditional female role, which is really a constellation of roles that women play at given stages in their lives. The demands and responsibilities associated with these traditional feminine roles shift throughout the life cycle.

The early identification of girls appears to be "bisexual," while social pressure encourages boys to earn their masculinity early. As a result, for girls the tasks of searching for identity, achieving autonomy, and developing internal criteria for self-esteem are delayed. It has been suggested that the adolescent girl is encouraged to remain flexible enough in her identity to allow for adaptation to the value system of a future spouse. This can lead to a gap between her sense of "self as I am" and "self as others (male) want me to be."

The transition from adolescence to adulthood may be defined as the time at which an individual leaves home and becomes economically independent. For many women marriage defines maturity within the family. For others the choice lies in an alternative life style, that of the single woman. A significant portion of single women are highly educated and successful career persons, who may value other goals more than marriage.

Despite increasing divorce rates, marrying couples assume that their commitment will be lasting and mutually satisfying. It appears, however, that, as time passes, women find their marriages less satisfying than men do. For many women the transition from wife to mother is stressful. Furthermore, the traditional roles of wife and mother are neither well defined nor highly valued—a role ambiguity that makes it difficult to evaluate one's success and causes stress.

Although statistically three out of four women can expect to spend some portion of their lives as widows, very few women are prepared to assume that role. Much of what we know about the effects of bereavement is based on the research of Collin Murray Parkes, who divides the grieving process into five phases: numbness, yearning and protest, disorganization, mitigation or defense, and identification. Learning to accept and work through the death of a spouse is just one aspect of widowhood. The transition from wife to widow involves a change in status as well as a change in roles. A woman can emerge from the experience of widowhood a stronger, more vital individual, but time is required for recovery to be complete.

Another type of bereavement is that which follows divorce—another situation in which the person suffers the loss of a loved one. One difference between the two types of experience is that widows generally receive more sympathy and support than divorcées; also, while there is an awareness of the grief that follows death, there is no recognized way to mourn a divorce. Divorce, too, involves changes in status and roles and typically leads to reexaminations of identity. The stresses associated with divorce may be particularly acute for traditionally oriented women whose sense of identity was dependent on the role of wife.

Changes similar to those forced upon many women by the dissolution of marriage occur during middle age, when women are likely to assume new roles and establish a more independent identity. A woman whose self-identity is based exclusively on her roles as wife and mother can find middle age threatening; but increasing numbers of women are recognizing the importance of establishing an independent identity and are continuing or beginning further education and work after rearing their children.

Not only do women live longer than men, but there is evidence that women are better equipped than men to cope with the life changes of aging. One important reason could be that, because women place more importance on kinship ties during their lifetime, they usually enjoy the support of their kin in later years much more than men do. Studies indicate that, although aging is seen as undesirable by both women and men, as people get older, women are perceived as having an advantage over men.

Chapter Ten

Conclusion

At the beginning of the decade of the 1970s, when the issue of job discrimination had emerged as a central theme in the women's movement, I was keenly aware of the difficulties faced by women who attempted to enter male-dominated professions. I had been employed as a full-time academic psychologist for over a year. The demands of preparing class lectures, which in my first year of teaching had seemed so overwhelming, had diminished with experience. The time had come to select an area of research and to attempt to build a professional reputation. In 1971 I discovered the literature relevant to the psychology of women. Once again, I was hooked.

It was apparent that society was guilty of having relegated women to a secondary political status. Within psychology, the study of women had also been relegated to a secondary status. As I began to explore the literature, I was disturbed and, at the same time, excited. I was disturbed by psychology's lack of knowledge about the behavior of women and girls and excited by the possibility that I might help fill that void. Although I was not aware of it at the time, many women psychologists were having experiences similar to mine.

There was nothing new in the observation that psychological theories of human behavior explained the behavior of males better than that of females. Psychologists had long been aware that data gathered from samples of males consistently supported their theories while data gathered from samples of females did not. The assumption that men and women are fundamentally different, both biologically and psychologically, was widely held by most members of the society. Psychologists shared these assumptions but did not regard empirical demonstrations of the obvious as scientifically valuable or even interesting.

However, as increasing numbers of feminist women and men began to question the legitimacy of the inferior social and political status assigned to women on the basis of their biological sex, many psychologists (most of them women) began to question the assumption that differences in the behavior of women and men and of girls and boys, so apparent to the casual observer, reflected the obvious and natural "order of the universe." The growing recognition within psychology that understanding female behavior is integral to understanding human behavior was new.

Some researchers interested in the study of women turned their attention to demonstrating the existence of fundamental biological and psychological differences between the sexes. As we have seen, many of these postulated differences proved to be more illusory than real. Others challenged the applicability of existing psychological theories to the study of women, on the grounds that these theories reflected male values and biases. They called for new theories and models that would more accurately reflect the reality of the female experience. Empirical studies relevant to the psychology of women accumulated rapidly, and controversy began to rage.

There are, of course, obvious and universal biological differences between women and men. Some of these biological differences, such as menstruation, pregnancy, and ejaculation, result in psychological phenomena that are uniquely female or male. To the extent that these fundamental biological differences affect human behavior, they must be studied as sex-specific phenomena. But in other areas, in which the differences between sexes appear to be only partially biological in origin (for example, visual-spatial abilities and aggression), the magnitude of observed differences is small and need not limit the behavioral potential of either women or men. As we have seen, at the human level most biological predispositions are subject to modification through experience and learning.

Indeed, most of the behaviors traditionally assumed to be more characteristic of one sex than of the other reflect social learning and values. Within the confines of these values, the female experience is different from the male experience. But the extent of the psychological similarities between the sexes indicates that these differences are not immutable.

As Grady (1975) has recently suggested, there are two loci of sex differences: *subject sex differences*, or differences that are located within the individual, and *stimulus sex differences*, or differences that arise in response to the sex of the stimulus person. The failure of researchers to obtain compelling evidence for subject sex differences in many of the areas in which they were assumed to exist forced many psychologists to reevaluate the significance of their predilection for dichotomies and reliance on the scientific method to ensure objectivity. As the work of Bem and others on psychological androgyny illustrates, simple dichotomous explanations (such as male versus female) are seldom adequate to account for the complexities of human behavior. Furthermore, psychology as a science is not value-free. Psychologists' values enter into their decisions to study a given phenomenon and influence the interpretation of the results they obtain. The fact that traditional psychology has been dominated by men and male values does not invalidate the significance of knowledge about human behavior gained from that perspective. However, the dangers inherent in failing to recognize the influence of those values should be apparent.

Interestingly, in many of the areas in which hypothesized subject sex differences have not been substantiated by empirical research, stimulus sex differences have been found. As we have seen, the results of recent studies of sex-role stereotypes suggest that men and women continue to believe that members of the opposite sex want them to be more different from the other sex than they themselves believe they are. Similarly, stimulus sex differences have been found in studies in which subjects of both sexes are asked to attribute the cause of identical behaviors performed by a woman and by a man. To the extent that males and females share expectations regarding behavioral differences between the sexes, the expression of such differences may constitute a self-fulfilling prophecy. But the expectations for and beliefs in sex differences appear to be stronger than the behavioral potential of females and males warrants.

By now it should be clear that attempts to locate the origins of sex differences either within individuals (whether or not these differences are primarily biological or cultural) or within the sex of the stimulus will necessarily result in an oversimplified view of human behavior. Human beings are social animals, and they do not behave in a vacuum. Their behavior cannot be adequately explained apart from the political-social context in which it occurs.

The importance of combining political-social analyses with psychological ones in an effort to better understand human behavior has been persuasively argued by advocates of the feminist perspective within psychology (see Vaughter, 1976). For example, Unger (1976, in press) has recently proposed a model of status/gender identity to account for the well-documented fact that women are rarely afforded dominance, or even equality, in contemporary society. In her view, male dominance in interpersonal relationships is due to the fact that maleness is almost uniformly and universally considered higher in status than femaleness. There are, of course, societies in which the expectations regarding the appropriate behavior of females and males are, by our standards, reversed. However, despite considerable variation in the roles and activities assigned to women, in every human culture women are in some way considered subordinate to men (Rosaldo, 1974).

Feminist therapists, cognizant of the impact that the political and social environment has on the behavior and psychological well-being of women, have pointed to the inadequacies of the hierarchical (male) authority model of the therapist-client relationship. Their point is well taken. Alternative approaches to the traditional models that have so long dominated the study and understanding of human behavior are needed. However, the current tendency to equate traditional modes of psychological inquiry with an exclusively masculine perspective and to replace it with the ethological approach as a feminine alternative (Hyde & Rosenberg, 1976) does little more than reify dichotomies that have proved inadequate.

Psychologists have learned more about the behavior and experience of women and girls in the last decade than they had in the previous six. The focus on the study of women as separate and distinct from men has been both a political and a scientific necessity. It is likely to continue for some time. But we do not seem to need a separate psychology of women, postulating different laws and theories. We do need to be aware of the extent to which the behavior of both women and men is affected by the political and social environment. As psychology moves toward a better understanding of women, it has the potential to move toward a better understanding of humankind.

References

Abrahams, R. B. Mutual help for the widowed. *Social Work*, September 1972, *17*, 54–61.

Ainsworth, M. D. S. The development of infant-mother attachment. In B. M. Caldwell & H. N. Reciuti (Eds.), *Review of child development research* (Vol. 3). Chicago: University of Chicago Press, 1973, 1–94.

Aldridge, D. Black women in the economic marketplace: A battle unfinished. *Journal of Social and Behavioral Sciences*, 1975, *21*(1), 48–62.

Alexson, L. The working wife: Differences in perception among negro and white males. *Journal of Marriage and the Family*, 1970, *32*, 457–464.

Alkire, A. A., Collum, M. E., Kaswan, J., & Love, L. R. Information exchange and accuracy of verbal communication under social power conditions. *Journal of Personality and Social Psychology*, 1968, *9*(4), 301–308.

Almquist, E. M., & Angrist, S. S. Role model influences on college women's career aspirations. In A. Theodore (Ed.), *The professional woman*. Cambridge, Mass.: Schenkman, 1971, 301–323.

Alper, T. G. The relationship between role orientation and achievement motivation in college women. *Journal of Personality*, 1973, *41*, 9–31.

Anastasi, A. *Differential psychology: Individual and group differences in behavior* (3rd ed.). New York: Macmillan, 1958.

Anderson, J. E. *The young child in the home*. New York: Appleton-Century, 1936.

Angelini, A. L. Um novo metodo para aviar a motivacao [A new method of evaluating human motivation]. In J. W. Atkinson (Ed.), *Motives in fantasy, action, and society*. Princeton, N. J.: Van Nostrand, 1958.

Angrist, S. The study of sex roles. *Journal of Social Issues*, 1969, *25*(1), 215–232.

Aries, E. *Interaction patterns and themes of male, female, and mixed groups*. Paper presented at the annual convention of the American Psychological Association, New Orleans, September 1974.

Armon, V. Some personality variables in overt female homosexuality. *Journal of Projective Techniques*, 1960, *24*, 292–309.

Aronson, E., & Cope, V. My enemy is my friend. *Journal of Personality and Social Psychology*, 1968, *8*, 8–12.

Astin, H. S. Career development of girls during high school years. *Journal of Counseling Psychology*, 1968, *15*, 536–540.

Astin, H. S. *The woman doctorate in America*. New York: Russell Sage Foundation, 1969.

Atchley, R. *The sociology of retirement*. Cambridge, Mass.: Schenkman, 1975.

Atkinson, J. W. (Ed.). *Motives in fantasy, action, and society*. Princeton, N. J.: Van Nostrand, 1958.

Atkinson, J. W. An approach to the study of subjective aspects of achievement motivation. In J. Nuttin (Ed.), Motives and consciousness in man. *Proceedings of the 18th International Congress in Psychology,* Symposium 13, Moscow, 1966, 21–32.

Atkinson, J. W., & Litwin, G. H. Achievement motive and test anxiety conceived as motive to approach success and motive to avoid failure. *Journal of Abnormal and Social Psychology,* 1960, *60*, 52–63.

Avery, A. W., & Ridley, C. A. *Interpersonal correlates of sexual intimacy*. Paper presented at the annual convention of the American Psychological Association, New Orleans, September 1974.

Bachtold, L. M., & Werner, E. E. Personality profiles of women psychologists. *Developmental Psychology,* 1971, *5*, 273–278.

Backman, M. E. Patterns of mental abilities: Ethnic, socioeconomic, and sex differences. *American Educational Research Journal,* 1972, *9*, 1–12.

Bakan, D. *The duality of human existence*. Chicago: Rand McNally, 1966.

Baker, L. The personal and social adjustment of the never-married woman. *Journal of Marriage and the Family,* 1968, *30*, 473–479.

Baker, S. W., & Ehrhardt, A. A. Prenatal androgen, intelligence, and cognitive sex differences. In R. C. Friedman, R. M. Richart, & R. L. VandeWiele (Eds.), *Sex differences in behavior*. New York: Wiley, 1974.

Baltes, P. B., & Nesselroade, J. R. Cultural change and adolescent personality development. *Developmental Psychology,* 1972, *7*, 244–256.

Bandura, A. Influence of models and reinforcement contingencies on the acquisition of imitative responses. *Journal of Personality and Social Psychology,* 1965, *1*, 589–595.

Bandura, A. Social learning theory and identification processes. In D. A. Goslin (Ed.), *Handbook of socialization theory and research*. Chicago: Rand McNally, 1969, 213–262.

Bandura, A. *Aggression: A social learning analysis*. Englewood Cliffs, N. J.: Prentice-Hall, 1973.

Bandura, A., & Huston, A. C. Identification as a process of incidental learning. *Journal of Abnormal and Social Psychology,* 1961, *63*, 311–318.

Bandura, A., Ross, D., & Ross, S. A. Transmission of aggression through imitation of aggressive models. *Journal of Abnormal and Social Psychology,* 1961, *63*, 575–582.

Bandura, A., Ross, D., & Ross, S. A. A comparative test of status envy, social power, and secondary reinforcement theories of identificatory learning. *Journal of Abnormal and Social Psychology,* 1963, *67*, 527–534.

Bardwick, J. M. *The psychology of women: A study of bio-cultural conflicts*. New York: Harper & Row, 1971.

Bardwick, J. M. The sex hormones, the central nervous system and affect variability in humans. In V. Franks & V. Burtle (Eds.), *Women in therapy: New psychotherapies for a changing society*. New York: Brunner/Mazel, 1974, 27–50.

Bardwick, J. M., & Douvan, E. Ambivalence: The socialization of women. In V. Gornick & B. K. Moran (Eds.), *Women in a sexist society*. New York: Basic Books, 1971, 147–159.

Barkley, R. A., Ullman, D. G., Otto, L., & Brecht, J. M. *The effects of sex-typing and sex-appropriateness of modeled behavior on children's imitation.* Paper presented at the meeting of the Midwestern Psychological Association, Chicago, May 1976.

Barnes, E. J. The black community as the source of positive self-concept. In R. L. Jones (Ed.), *Black psychology.* New York: Harper & Row, 1972.

Barraclough, C. A., & Gorski, R. A. Studies on mating behavior in the androgen-sterilized female rat in relation to the hypothalamic regulation of sexual behavior. *Journal of Endocrinology,* 1962, *25,* 175–182.

Barrett, C. J. A comparison of therapeutic intervention for widows. *The Gerontologist,* 1973, *13*(3), 66–67.

Bart, P. Mother Portnoy's complaints. *Trans-Action,* November–December 1970, 69–74.

Bar-Tal, D., & Frieze, I. H. *Achievement motivation and gender as determinants of attributions for success and failure.* Unpublished manuscript, University of Pittsburgh, 1973.

Bartold, K. M. Male versus female leaders: The effect of leader need for dominance on follower satisfaction. *Academy of Management Journal,* 1974, *17*(2), 225–233.

Baruch, G. K. Maternal influences upon college women's attitudes toward women and work. *Developmental Psychology,* 1972, *6,* 32–37.

Baruch, R. *The interruption and resumption of women's careers.* Harvard Studies in Career Development, Report 50. Cambridge, Mass.: Center for Research in Careers, 1966.

Battle, E. S. Motivational determinants of academic task persistence. *Journal of Personality and Social Psychology,* 1965, *2,* 209–218.

Baughman, E. E. *Black Americans.* New York: Academic Press, 1971.

Baumrind, D. Harmonious parents and their preschool children. *Developmental Psychology,* 1971, *4*(1), 99–102.

Beale, F. Double jeopardy: To be black and female. In T. Cade (Ed.), *The black woman.* New York: Signet, 1970, 90–100.

Bell, R. Relations between behavior manifestations in the human neonate. *Child Development,* 1960, *31,* 463–477.

Bell, R. The lower class negro mother's aspirations for her children. *Social Forces,* 1965, *43*(4), 493–500.

Bell, R. (Ed.), *Studies in marriage and the family.* New York: Crowell, 1968.

Bell, R., Weller, G. M., & Waldrop, M. F. Newborn and preschooler: Organization of behavior and relations between periods. *Monographs of the Society for Research in Child Development,* 1971, *36* (1–2, Serial No. 142).

Bem, D. J. Self perception theory. In L. Berkowitz (Ed.), *Advances in experimental social psychology* (Vol. 6). New York: Academic Press, 1972, 2–61.

Bem, S. L. *Psychology looks at sex roles: Where have all the androgynous people gone?* Paper presented at the U.C.L.A. Symposium on Women, May 1972.

Bem, S. L. The measurement of psychological androgyny. *Journal of Clinical and Consulting Psychology,* 1974, *42,* 155–162.

Bem, S. L. Sex role adaptability: One consequence of psychological androgyny. *Journal of Personality and Social Psychology,* 1975, *31,* 634–643.

Bem, S. L. Probing the promise of androgyny. In A. G. Kaplan & J. P. Bean (Eds.), *Beyond sex-role stereotypes.* Boston: Little, Brown, 1976, 47–62.

Bem, S. L., & Bem, D. J. Case study of a non-conscious ideology: Training the woman to know her place. In D. J. Bem (Ed.), *Beliefs, attitudes, and human affairs.* Monterey, Calif.: Brooks/Cole, 1970, 80–99.

Bem, S. L., & Lenney, E. Sex typing and avoidance of cross-sex behavior. *Journal of Personality and Social Psychology,* 1976, *33*(1), 48–54.

Bem, S. L., Martyna, W., & Watson, C. Sex typing and androgyny: Further exploration of the expressive domain. *Journal of Personality and Social Psychology,* in press.

Benedek, T. *Studies in psychosomatic medicine: Psychosexual functions.* New York: Ronald Press, 1952.

Benedek, T. Sexual functions in women and their disturbance. In S. Arieti (Ed.), *American handbook of psychiatry.* New York: Basic Books, 1959, 726–748.

Benedek, T. Parenthood during the life cycle. In E. J. Anthony (Ed.), *Parenthood.* Boston: Little, Brown, 1970.

Berardo, J. Survivorship and social isolation. *The Family Coordinator,* 1970, *19,* 11–25.

Berman, C. L. Study finds why Suzy snubs math. *Detroit Free Press,* November 1975.

Bernard, J. *The sex game.* Englewood Cliffs, N. J.: Prentice-Hall, 1968.

Bernard, J. No news, but new ideas. In P. Bohannon (Ed.), *Divorce and after.* Garden City, N. Y.: Doubleday, 1970, 3–29.

Bernard, J. *The future of marriage.* New York: World (Bantam Books), 1973.

Berry, J. W. Temne and Eskimo perceptual skills. *International Journal of Psychology,* 1966, *1,* 207–229.

Berzins, J. I. *New perspectives on sex roles and personality dimensions.* Paper presented at the annual convention of the American Psychological Association, Chicago, September 1975.

Bieber, I. Clinical aspects of male homosexuality. In J. Marmor (Ed.), *Sexual inversion.* New York: Basic Books, 1965.

Biller, H. B. *Adults' conceptions of masculinity and femininity in children.* Unpublished study, Emma Pendleton Bradley Hospital, Riverside, R. I., 1966.

Biller, H. B. Paternal and sex-role factors in cognitive and academic functioning. In J. K. Cole & R. Dienstbier (Eds.), *Nebraska Symposium on Motivation* (Vol. 21). Lincoln: University of Nebraska Press, 1973.

Billingsley, A. *Black families in white America.* New Jersey: Prentice-Hall, 1968.

Billingsley, A. The treatment of negro families in American scholarship. In R. Staples (Ed.), *The black family: Essays and studies.* Belmont, Calif.: Wadsworth, 1971.

Birnbaum, J. A. *Life patterns, personality style and self-esteem in gifted family oriented and career committed women.* Unpublished doctoral dissertation, University of Michigan, 1971.

Blair, G. E. The relationship of selected ego functions and academic achievement of negro students. *Dissertation Abstracts,* 1972, *28,* 3031A.

Block, J. H. Conceptions of sex role: Some cross-cultural and longitudinal perspectives. *American Psychologist,* 1973, *28*(6), 512–526.

Block, J., Van der Lippe, A., & Block, J. H. Sex-role and socialization patterns: Some personality concomitants and environmental antecedents. *Journal of Consulting and Clinical Psychology,* 1973, *41*(3), 321–341.

Blood, R., & Wolfe, D. M. *Husbands and wives: The dynamics of married living.* New York: Macmillan, 1960.

Blood, R., & Wolfe, D. M. Negro-white differences in blue-collar marriage in a northern metropolis. In R. Staples (Ed.), *The black family: Essays and studies.* Belmont, Calif.: Wadsworth, 1971.

Bock, R. D., & Kolakowski, D. Further evidence of sex-linked major-gene influence on human spatial visualizing ability. *American Journal of Human Genetics,* 1973, *25,* 1–14.

Bohannon, P. The six stations of divorce. In P. Bohannon (Ed.). *Divorce and after.* Garden City, N.Y.: Doubleday, 1970.

Bonner, F. Black women and white women: A comparative analysis of perceptions of sex roles for self, ideal-self, and the ideal male. *Journal of Afro-American Issues,* 1974, *2*(3), 237–247.

Bordon, R. J. Influence of an observer's sex and values on aggressive responding. *Journal of Personality and Social Psychology,* 1975, *31,* 567–573.

Bowlby, J. *Attachment and loss. 1: Attachment.* New York: Basic Books, 1969.

Bowlby, J., & Parkes, C. M. Separation and loss. In E. J. Anthony & C. Koupernik (Eds.), *International yearbook for child psychiatry and allied disciplines. 1: The child and his family.* New York: Wiley, 1970.

Bradwein, R. A., Brown, C. A., & Fox, E. M. Women and children last: The social situation of divorced mothers and their families. *Journal of Marriage and the Family,* 1974, *36,* 498–514.

Brannon, R. The male sex role: Our culture's blueprint of manhood, and what it's done for us lately. In D. David & R. Brannon (Eds.), *The forty-nine percent majority: The male sex role.* Reading, Mass.: Addison-Wesley, 1976.

Brannon, R. Measuring attitudes (toward women, and otherwise): A methodological critique. In J. A. Sherman & F. L. Denmark (Eds.), *The futures of women: Issues in psychology.* New York: Psychological Dimensions, in press.

Brinkman, E. H. Programmed instruction as a technique for improving spatial visualization. *Journal of Applied Psychology,* 1966, *50,* 179–184.

Broderick, C. B. Social heterosexual development among urban negroes and whites. *Journal of Marriage and the Family,* 1965, *27,* 200–203.

Bronson, F. H., & Dejardins, C. Aggression in adult mice: Modification by neonatal injections of gonadal hormones. *Science,* 1968, *161,* 705–706.

Brotman, H. *Facts and figures on older Americans* (5, An overview, 1971). Washington, D.C.: U.S. Department of Health, Education & Welfare, Administration on Aging, 1972.

Broverman, D. M., Klaiber, E. L., Kobayashi, Y. P., & Vogel, W. Roles of activation and inhibition in sex differences in cognitive abilities. *Psychological Review,* 1968, *75*(1), 23–50.

Broverman, I. K., Broverman, D. M., Clarkson, F. E., Rosenkrantz, P., & Vogel, S. R. Sex-role stereotypes and clinical judgments of mental health. *Journal of Consulting Psychology,* 1970, *34,* 1–7.

Broverman, I. K., Vogel, R. S., Broverman, D. M., Clarkson, T. E., & Rosenkrantz, P. S. Sex-role stereotypes: A current appraisal. *Journal of Social Issues,* 1972, *28,* 59–78.

Brown, C. A., Feldberg, R., Fox, E. M., & Kohen, J. Divorce: Chance of a new lifetime. *Journal of Social Issues,* 1976, *32*(1), 119–133.

Brown, H. G. *Sex and the single girl.* Greenwich, Conn.: Fawcett World Library, Crest Books, 1970.

Brown, J. B. Urinary excretion of oestrogens during pregnancy, lactation, and reestablishment of menstruation. *The Lancet,* 1956, *1,* 704–707.

Brown, J. B., & Matthew, D. G. Application of urinary estrogen measurements to the problems of gynecology. *Recent Progress in Hormone Research,* 1962, *18,* 337–385.

Brown, L. S. *Investigating the stereotypic picture of lesbians in the clinical literature*. Paper presented at the annual convention of the American Psychological Association, Chicago, September 1975.

Bryson, R. B., Bryson, J. B., Licht, M. H., & Licht, B. G. The professional pair: Husband and wife psychologists. *American Psychologist*, 1976, *31*(1), 10–16.

Buckingham, B. R., & Maclatchy, J. The number abilities of children when they enter grade one. *Yearbook of the National Society for the Study of Education*, 1930, *29*, 473–549.

Buffery,A. W. H., & Gray, J. A. Sex differences in the development of spatial and linguistic skills. In C. Ounsted & D. C. Taylor (Eds.), *Gender differences: Their ontogeny and significance*. Baltimore: Williams & Wilkins, 1972, 123–175.

Burgess, E., & Wallin, P. *Engagement and marriage*. Philadelphia: Lippincott, 1953.

Burnstein, E. Fear of failure, achievement motivation, and aspiring to prestigeful occupations. *Journal of Abnormal and Social Psychology*, 1963, *67*, 189–193.

Burr, W. R. Satisfaction with various aspects of marriage over the life cycle. *Journal of Marriage and the Family*, 1970, *32*, 26–37.

Buss, A. H. Instrumentality of aggression, feedback, and frustration as determinants of physical aggression. *Journal of Personality and Social Psychology*, 1966, *3*, 153–162.

Butler, R. N., & Lewis, M. I. *Aging and mental health: Positive psychosocial approaches*. St. Louis: Mosby, 1973.

Campbell, A., Converse, P. E., & Rodgers, W. L. *The quality of American life*. Ann Arbor, Mich. : ISR Social Science Archive, 1975.

Campus queens. *Ebony*, April 1975, pp. 78–86.

Caprio, F. S. *Female homosexuality: A psychodynamic study of lesbianism*. New York: Citadel Press, 1954.

Carlson, E. R., & Carlson, R. Male and female subjects in personality research. *Journal of Abnormal and Social Psychology*, 1961, *61*, 482–483.

Carlson, R. Stability and change in the adolescent's self image. *Child Psychology*, 1965, *36*, 659–666.

Carlson, R. Sex differences in ego functioning: Exploratory studies of agency and communion. *Journal of Consulting & Clinical Psychology*, 1971, *37*, 267–277.

Carlson, R. Understanding women: Implications for personality theory and research. *Journal of Social Issues*, 1972, *28*(2), 17–32.

Carter, H., & Glick, P. C. *Marriage and divorce: A social and economic study*. Cambridge, Mass.: Harvard University Press, 1970.

Chance, J. E., & Goldstein, A. G. Internal-external control of reinforcement and embedded-figures performance. *Perception and Psychophysics*, 1971, *9*, 33–34.

Chappelle, Y. The black woman on the negro college campus. *The Black Scholar*, January–February 1970, pp. 36–39.

Cherry, L. The preschool teacher-child dyad: Sex differences in verbal interaction. *Child Development*, 1975, *46*, 532–535.

Cherry, L., & Lewis, M. Mothers and two-year-olds: A study of sex-differentiated aspects of verbal interaction. *Developmental Psychology*, 1976, *12*(4), 278–282.

Chesler, P. Women psychiatric and psychotherapeutic patients. *Journal of Marriage and the Family*, 1971, *33*, 746–759.

Chesler, P. *Women and madness*. Garden City, N.Y.: Doubleday, 1972.

Chesser, E. *The sexual, marital, and family relationships of the English woman*. Waterford, England: Hutchinson's Medical Publications, 1956.

Child, I., Potter E., & Levine, E. Children's text books and personality development: An exploration in the social psychology of education. *Psychological Monographs*, 1946, *60*, (3, Whole No. 279).

Clark, G. R., Tefler, M. A., Baker, D., & Rosen, M. Sex chromosomes, crime and psychosis. In A. Bandura (Ed.), *Aggression: A social learning analysis*. Englewood Cliffs, N. J.: Prentice-Hall, 1973, 25.

Clark, K. *Dark ghetto: Dilemmas of social power*. New York: Harper & Row, 1965.

Clark K., & Clark, M. P. Racial identification and preference in negro children. In E. Maccoby, T. M. Newcomb, & E. L. Hartley (Eds.), *Readings in social psychology*. New York: Holt, Rinehart & Winston, 1947, 602–611.

Clay, W. L. The socio-economic status of blacks. *Ebony*, September 1975, p. 29.

Clayton, P. Mortality and morbidity in the first year of widowhood. *Archives of General Psychiatry*, 1974, *30*, 747–750.

Clayton, P. The effects of living alone on bereavement symptoms. *American Journal of Psychiatry*, 1975, *132*(2), 133–137.

Coates, S. Sex differences in field independence among preschool children. In R. C. Friedman, R. M. Richart, R. L. Vande Wiele (Eds.), *Sex differences in behavior*. New York: Wiley, 1974, 259–274.

Cohen, M. B. Personal identity and sexual identity. *Psychiatry*, 1966, *29*, 1–14.

Cohen, Y. A. Adolescent conflict in a Jamaican community. *Samiksa: Journal of the Indian Psychoanalytic Institute*, 1955, *9*, 139–172.

Collins, B. E. Four components of the Rotter internal-external scale: Belief in a difficult world, a just world, a predictable world, and a politically responsive world. *Journal of Personality and Social Psychology*, 1974, *29*(3), 381–391.

Conn, J. H. Children's reactions to the discovery of genital differences. *American Journal of Orthopsychiatry*, 1940, *10*, 747–754.

Constantinople, A. Masculinity-femininity: An exception to a famous dictum. *Psychological Bulletin*, 1973, *80*(5), 389–407.

Cooley, C. H. *Human nature and the social order*. Glencoe, Ill.: Free Press, 1956.

Coppen, A. The biochemistry of affective disorders. *British Journal of Psychiatry*, 1967, *113*(504), 1237–1264.

Coppen, A., & Kessel, N. Menstruation and personality. *British Journal of Psychiatry*, 1963, *109*, 711–721.

Corter, C. M., Rheingold, H. L., & Eckerman, C. O. Toys delay the infant's following his mother. *Developmental Psychology*, 1972, *6*, 138–145.

Cosentino, F., & Heilbrun, A. B. Sex-role identity and aggression anxiety. *Psychological Reports*, 1964, *14*, 729–730.

Costrich, N., Feinstein, J., Kidder, L., Marecek, J., & Pascale, L. When stereotypes hurt: Three studies of penalties for sex-role reversals. *Journal of Experimental Social Psychology*, 1975, *11*, 520–530.

Crandall, V. C. Sex differences in expectancy of intellectual and academic reinforcement. In C. P. Smith (Ed.), *Achievement-related motives in children*. New York: Russell Sage Foundation, 1969.

Crandall, V. C., & Battle, E. S. The antecedents and adult correlates of academic and intellectual achievement effort. In J. P. Hill (Ed.), *Minnesota Symposia on Child Psychology* (Vol. 4). Minneapolis: University of Minnesota Press, 1970.

Crandall, V. C., Katkovsky, W., & Crandall, V. J. Children's belief in their own control of reinforcement in intellectual-academic achievement situations. *Child Development*, 1965, *36*, 91–109.

Crandall, V. J. Achievement. In H. W. Stevenson (Ed.), *Child psychology: The 62nd yearbook of the National Society for the Study of Education* (Pt. 1). Chicago: University of Chicago Press, 1963.

Crandall, V. J., Dewey, R., Katkovsky, W., & Preston, A. Parents' attitudes and behaviors and grade school children's academic achievements. *Journal of Genetic Psychology,* 1964, *104,* 53–66.

Crandall, V. J., Katkovsky, W., & Preston, A. Motivational and ability determinants of young children's intellectual achievement behaviors. *Child Development,* 1962, *33,* 643–661.

Crandall, V. J., & Rabson, A. Children's repetition choices in an intellectual achievement situation following success and failure. *Journal of Genetic Psychology,* 1960, *97,* 161–168.

Croke, J. A. *Sex differences in causal attributions and expectancies for success as a function of the sex-role appropriateness of the task.* Unpublished manuscript, University of California at Los Angeles, 1973.

Dalton, K. *The premenstrual syndrome.* Springfield, Ill.: Charles C. Thomas, 1964.

Dalton, K. The influence of mother's menstruation on her child. *Proceedings of the Royal Society of Medicine,* 1966, *59,* 1014.

Dan, A. J., & Beekman, S. Male versus female representation in psychological research. *American Psychologist,* 1972, *27,* 1078.

Dansby, P. G. *A comparison of ratings of degree of freedom of blacks and whites in the United States by race and sex.* Paper presented at the meeting of the National Convention of Black Women in America, Louisville, Ky., March 1974.

Dansby, P. G. Perceptions of role and status of black females. *Journal of Social and Behavioral Sciences,* 1975, *21*(1), 31–47.

Davis, J. H., Laughlin, P. K., & Komorita, S. S. The social psychology of small groups: Cooperative and mixed motive interaction. *Annual Review of Psychology,* 1976, *27,* 501–542.

Dawson, J. L. M. Cultural and physiological influences upon spatial-perceptual processes in West Africa. *International Journal of Psychology,* 1967, *2,* 115–128, 171–185.

Deaux, K. *The behavior of women and men.* Monterey, Calif.: Brooks/Cole, 1976.

Deaux, K., & Emswiller, T. Explanations of successful performance on sex-linked tasks: What's skill for the male is luck for the female. *Journal of Personality and Social Psychology,* 1974, *29,* 80–85.

Deaux, K., & Farris, E. *Attributing causes for one's performance: The effects of sex, norms,, and outcome.* Unpublished manuscript, Purdue University, 1974.

Deaux, K., & Taynor, J. Evaluation of male and female ability: Bias works two ways. *Psychological Reports,* 1973, *32,* 261–262.

Deaux, K., White, L., & Farris, E. Skill versus luck: Field and laboratory studies of male and female preferences. *Journal of Personality and Social Psychology,* 1975, *32*(4), 629–636.

Deci, E. L. Intrinsic motivation, extrinsic reinforcement and inequity. *Journal of Personality and Social Psychology,* 1972, *22,* 113–120.

Deci, E. L., Cascio, W. F., & Krusell, J. *Sex differences, verbal reinforcement, and intrinsic motivation.* Paper presented at the meeting of the Eastern Psychological Association, Washington, D.C., May 1973.

Deckard, B. S. *The women's movement.* New York: Harper & Row, 1975.

Depner, C. E. *An analysis of motivational factors which contribute to sex differences in the expression of achievement motivation.* Unpublished manuscript, University of Michigan, 1974.

Depner, C. E., & O'Leary, V. E. Understanding female careerism: Fear of success and new directions. *Sex Roles: A Journal of Research,* 1976, *2*(3), 259–268.

Deutsch, H. *The psychology of women* (Vol. 1). New York: Grune & Stratton, 1944.

Deutsch, H. *The psychology of women* (Vol. 2). New York: Grune & Stratton, 1945.

Deykin, E. Y., Jacobson, S., Klerman, G. L., & Solomon, M. The empty nest: Psychosocial aspects of conflict between depressed women and their grown children. *American Journal of Psychiatry,* 1966, *122*(2), 1422–1426.

Dickie, J. P. Effectiveness of structured and unstructured (traditional) methods of language training. *Monographs of the Society for Research in Child Development,* 1968, *33* (8, Serial No. 124), 62–79.

Dobson, J. *To define black womanhood: A study of black female graduate students.* Atlanta: The Institute of the Black World, 1970.

Doering, C. H., Brodie, H. K. H., Kraemer, H., Becker, H., & Hamburg, D. A. Plasma testosterone levels and psychologic measures in men over a 2-month period. In R. C. Friedman, R. M. Richart, & R. L. VandeWiele (Eds.), *Sex differences in behavior.* New York: Wiley, 1974, 413–432.

Douvan, E. Sex differences in adolescent character processes. *Merrill-Palmer Quarterly,* 1960, *6*, 203–211.

Douvan, E. New sources of conflict in females at adolescence and early adulthood. In J. M. Bardwick, E. Douvan, M. S. Horner, & D. L. Gutmann (Eds.), *Feminine personality and conflict.* Monterey, Calif.: Brooks/Cole, 1970, 31–44.

Douvan, E. *Modeling in women's development.* Paper presented at the annual convention of the American Psychological Association, New Orleans, September, 1974.

Douvan, E. Personal communication, August 1976.

Douvan, E., & Adelson, J. *The adolescent experience.* New York: Wiley, 1966.

Droege, R. C. Sex differences in aptitude maturation during high school. *Journal of Counseling Psychology,* 1967, *14*, 407–410.

Dubanoski, R. A., & Parton, D. A. Effect of the presence of a human model on imitative behavior in children. *Developmental Psychology,* 1971, *4*, 463–468.

Duberman, M. The bisexual debate. In C. Gordon & G. Johnson (Eds.), *Readings in human sexuality: Contemporary perspectives* (1976–1977 ed.). New York: Harper & Row, 1976, 169–174.

Duvall, E. M. *Family development* (4th ed.). Philadelphia: Lippincott, 1971.

Edwards, D. A. Early androgen stimulation and aggressive behavior in male and female mice. *Physiology and Behavior,* 1969, *4*, 333–338.

Ehrhardt, A. A., Epstein, R., & Money, J. Fetal androgens and female gender identity in the early treated androgenital syndrome. *Johns Hopkins Medical Journal,* 1968, *122*, 160–167.

Ehrhardt, A. A., & Money, J. Progestin-induced hermaphroditism: I.Q. and psychosexual identity in a study of ten girls. *Journal of Sex Research,* 1967, *3*, 83–100.

Eisenman, R. Sex differences in moral judgment. *Perceptual and Motor Skills,* 1967, *54*, 784.

Elliot, R., & McMichael, R. E. Effect of specific training on frame dependence. *Perceptual and Motor Skills,* 1963, *17*, 363–367.

Ellis, A. *Sex and the single man.* New York: Lyle Stuart, 1965.

Ellis, L. J., & Bentler, P. M. Traditional sex-determined role standards and sex stereotypes. *Journal of Personality and Social Psychology,* 1973, *25*(1), 28–34.

Elman, J. B., Press, A., & Rosenkrantz, P. S. *Sex-roles and self-concepts: Real and ideal.* Paper presented at the annual convention of the American Psychological Association, Miami, August 1970.

Emmerick, W. Structure and development of personal-social behaviors in preschool settings. In E. E. Maccoby & C. N. Jacklin, *The psychology of sex differences*. Stanford, Calif.: Stanford University Press, 1974, 449–450. (Abstract)

Entwistle, D. To dispel fantasies about fantasy-based measures of achievement motivation. *Psychological Bulletin*, 1972, 77, 377–391.

Entwistle, D., & Greenberger, E. Adolescents' views of women's work role. *American Journal of Orthopsychiatry*, 1972, 42, 648–656.

Epstein, C. F. Positive effects of the multiple negative: Explaining the success of black professional women. *American Journal of Sociology*, 1973, 78(4), 912–935.(a)

Epstein, C. F. Black and female: The double whammy. *Psychology Today*, August 1973, 1(3), p. 57.(b)

Erikson, E. H. *Childhood and society*. New York: Norton, 1950.

Erikson, E. H. *Identity: Youth and crisis*. New York: Norton, 1968.

Etaugh, C. F., Collins, G., & Gerson, A. Reinforcement of sex-typed behaviors of 2-year-old children in a nursery school setting. *Developmental Psychology*, 1975, 11(2), 255.

Fagot, B. I. Sex-related stereotyping of toddlers' behaviors. *Developmental Psychology*, 1973, 9(3), 429.

Fagot, B. I. Sex differences in toddlers' behavior and parental reaction. *Developmental Psychology*, 1974, 10(4), 554–558.

Feather, N. T. Effects of prior success and failure on expectations of success and subsequent performance. *Journal of Personality and Social Psychology*, 1966, 3, 287–298.

Feather, N. T. Attribution of responsibility and valence of success and failure in relation to initial confidence and task performance. *Journal of Personality and Social Psychology*, 1969, 13, 129–144.

Feather, N. T., & Raphelson, A. C. Fear of success in Australian and American student groups: Motive or sex-role stereotype? *Journal of Personality*, 1974, 42, 190–201.

Federman, D. D. *Abnormal sexual development*. Philadelphia: Saunders, 1967.

Feinblatt, J. A., & Gold, A. R. Sex roles and the psychiatric referral process. *Sex Roles*, 1976, 2(2), 109–122.

Feld, S. C., & Lewis, J. The assessment of achievement anxieties in children. In C. P. Smith (Ed.), *Achievement-related motives in children*. New York: Russell Sage Foundation, 1969.

Feldman, H. *Development of the husband-wife relationship: A research report*. Ithaca, N.Y.: Cornell University Press, 1964.

Feldman-Summers, S., & Kiesler, J. Those who are number two try harder: The effects of sex on attributions of causality. *Journal of Personality and Social Psychology*, 1974, 30, 846–855.

Fenichel, O. *The psychoanalytic theory of neurosis*. New York: Norton, 1945.

Fernberger, S. W. Persistence of stereotypes concerning sex differences. *Journal of Abnormal and Social Psychology*, 1948, 43, 97–101.

Feshbach, S. Aggression. In P. H. Mussen (Ed.), *Carmichael's manual of child psychology*. New York: Wiley, 1970.

Fichter, J. H. *Graduates of predominantly negro college class of 1964*. Washington, D.C.: U.S. Department of Health, Education and Welfare, 1967.

Field, W. F. The effects on thematic apperception of certain experimentally aroused needs. In D. McClelland, J. W. Atkinson, R. A. Clark, & E. L. Lowell (Eds.), *The achievement motive*. New York: Appleton-Century-Crofts, 1953.

Fish, K. D. *Paternal availability, family role structure, maternal employment, and personality development in late adolescent females.* Unpublished doctoral dissertation, University of Massachusetts, 1969.

Fisher, S. *The female orgasm.* New York: Basic Books, 1973.

Flanagan, J. C., Dailey, J. T., Shaycoft, M. G., Gorham, W. A., Orr, D. B., Goldberg, I., & Neyman, C. A., Jr. *Counselor's technical manual for interpreting test scores (Project Talent).* Palo Alto, Calif.: American Institute for Research, 1961.

Fling, S., & Manosevitz, M. Sex typing in nursery school children's play interests. *Developmental Psychology,* 1972, *7*(2), 146–152.

Ford, C. S., & Beach, F. *Patterns of sexual behavior.* New York: Harper, 1951.

Frank, L. K., & Frank, M. *How to be a woman.* New York: Bobbs-Merrill, 1954.

Frank, R. T. The hormonal causes of premenstrual tension. *Archives of Neurology and Psychiatry,* 1931, *26,* ·1053–1057.

Franks, V., & Burtle, V. *Women in therapy.* New York: Brunner/Mazel, 1974.

Freedman, M. Homosexuality among women and psychological adjustment. *The Ladder,* 1968, *12*(2), 2–3.

Freedman, M. *Homosexuality and psychological functioning.* Monterey, Calif.: Brooks/Cole, 1971.

Freeman, J. *Women: A feminist perspective.* Palo Alto, Calif.: Mayfield, 1975.

French, E. G., & Lesser, G. S. Some characteristics of the achievement motive in women. *Journal of Abnormal and Social Psychology,* 1964, *68,* 119–129.

Freud, S. *Three contributions to a theory of sex.* New York: Nervous and Mental Disease Publishing Company, 1930. (Originally published, 1905.)

Freud, S. The psychology of women. In S. Freud, *New introductory lectures on psychoanalysis.* New York: Norton, 1933, 153–185.

Freud, S. Female sexuality. In S. Freud, *Collected papers* (Vol. 5). London: Hogarth, 1950. (Originally published, 1931.)(a)

Freud, S. Some psychological consequences of the anatomical distinction between the sexes. In S. Freud, *Collected papers* (Vol. 5). London: Hogarth, 1950. (Originally published, 1925.)(b)

Friedrich, L. K. Achievement motivation in college women revisited: Implications for women, men, and the gathering of coconuts. *Sex Roles,* 1976, *2*(1), 47–61.

Frieze, I. H. *Sex differences in perceiving the causes of success and failure.* Unpublished manuscript, University of Pittsburgh, 1973.

Frieze, I. H. *Changing self images and sex-role stereotypes in college women.* Paper presented at the annual convention of the American Psychological Association, New Orleans, September 1974.

Frieze, I. H. Women's expectations for and causal attributions of success and failure. In M. T. S. Mednick, S. S. Tangri, & L. W. Hoffman (Eds.), *Women and achievement.* New York: Wiley, 1975, 158–171.

Frieze, I. H., & Bar-Tal, D. *Achievement motivation and gender as determinants of attributions for success and failure.* Unpublished manuscript, University of Pittsburgh, 1974.

Frieze, I. H., Fisher, J., McHugh, M. C., & Valle, V. A. *Attributing causes of success and failure: Internal and external barriers to achievement in women.* Paper presented at the Conference on New Directions for Research on Women, Madison, Wis., June 1975.

Fromme, A. *A woman's critical years.* New York: Grosset & Dunlap, 1972.

Furstenberg, F., Gordis, L., & Markowitz, M. Birth control knowledge and attitude among unmarried pregnant adolescents. *Journal of Marriage and the Family,* 1969, *31*(1), 34–42.

Gagnon, J. H. Scripts and the coordination of sexual conduct. In J. K. Cole & R. Dienstbier (Eds.), *Nebraska Symposium on Motivation* (Vol. 21). Lincoln: University of Nebraska Press, 1973.

Gagnon, J. H., & Simon, W. Youth, sex, and the future. In D. Gottlieb (Ed.), *Youth in contemporary society*. Beverly Hills, Calif.: Sage Publications, 1973.

Gallatin, J. E. *Adolescence and individuality*. New York: Harper & Row, 1975.

Garai, J. E., & Scheinfeld, A. Sex differences in mental and behavioral traits. *Genetic Psychology Monographs*, 1968, 77, 169–299.

Garcia, M., & Dingman, J. H. *Sex-role stereotypes among Latinos: They work only one way*. Paper presented at the annual convention of the American Psychological Association, Chicago, September 1975.

Garrison, K. C. A study of the aspirations and concerns of ninth-grade pupils from the public schools of Georgia. *Journal of Social Psychology*, 1966, 69, 245–252.

Garron, D. C. Sex-linked, recessive inheritance of spatial and numerical abilities, and Turner's syndrome. *Psychological Review*, 1970, 77, 147–152.

Garske, J. P. *Motive to avoid success, sensitivity to rejection and male feedback as determinants of female performance in a cross-sexed competition*. Paper presented at the meeting of the Eastern Psychological Association, New York, April 1975.

Gebhard, P. Factors in marital orgasm. *Journal of Social Issues*, 1966, 22, 88–95.

George, V., & Wilding, P. *Motherless families*. London: Routledge & Kegan Paul, 1972.

Gerall, A. A., Hendricks, S. E., Johnson, L. L., & Bounds, T. W. Effects of early castration in male rats on adult sexual behavior. *Journal of Comparative Physiological Psychology*, 1967, 64, 206.

Gerbner, G. Violence in television drama: Trends and symbolic functions. In G. A. Comstock & E. A. Rubinstein (Eds.), *Television and social behavior. 1: Media content and control*. Washington, D.C.: U.S. Government Printing Office, 1972.

Gessell, A., Halverson, H. M., Thompson, H., Ilg, F. L., Castner, B. M., Ames, L. B., & Amatruda, C. S. *The first five years of life: A guide to the study of the preschool child*. New York: Harper, 1940.

Gewirtz, J. L. Mechanisms of social learning: Some roles of stimulation and behavior in early human development. In D. A. Goslin (Ed.), *Handbook of socialization theory and research*. Chicago: Rand McNally, 1969, 57–212.

Gibson, E. J. Improvement in perceptual judgments as a function of controlled practice or training. *Psychological Bulletin*, 1953, 50, 401–431.

Ginzberg, B., & Allee, W. C. Some effects of conditioning on social dominance and subordination in inbred strains of mice. *Physiological Zoology*, 1942, 15, 485–506.

Ginzberg, E. *Educated American women*. New York: Columbia University Press, 1966.

Glick, I. O., Weiss, R. S., & Parkes, C. M. *The first year of bereavement*. New York: Wiley, 1974.

Glick, P. C., & Parkes, R. New approaches in studying the life cycle of the family. *Demography*, 1965, 2, 187–202.

Goldberg, M. *Medical management of the menopause* (Modern Medical Monographs). New York: Grune & Stratton, 1959.

Goldberg, P. H. Are women prejudiced against women? *Trans-action*, 1968, 5, 28–30.

Goldberg, S., & Lewis, M. Play behavior in the year-old infant: Early sex differences. *Child Development*, 1969, 40, 21–31.

Goldstein, A. G., & Chance, J. E. Effects of practice on sex-related differences in performance on Embedded Figures. *Psychonomic Science*, 1965, 3, 361–362.

Goode, W. J. *Women in divorce*. New York: Free Press, 1956.

Goodenough, E. Interest in persons as an aspect of sex differences in the early years. *Genetic Psychology Monographs, 1957, 55,* 287–323.

Gordon, F. E., & Hall, D. T. Self-image and stereotypes of femininity: Their relationship to women's role conflict and coping. *Journal of Applied Psychology, 1974, 59,* 241–243.

Gordon, M., & Shankweiler, P. J. Different equals less: Female sexuality in recent marriage manuals. *Journal of Marriage and the Family, 1971, 33*(3), 459–466.

Gordon, R. E., & Gordon, K. K. Social factors in the prediction and treatment of emotional disorders of pregnancy. *American Journal of Obstetrics and Gynecology, 1959, 77,* 1074–1083.

Gottheil, E., & Freedman, A. Sexual beliefs and behavior of single, male medical students. *Journal of the American Medical Association, 1970, 212,* 1327–1332.

Gottschalk, L. A., Kaplan, S. M., Gleser, G. C., & Winget, C. M. Variations in magnitude of emotions: A method applied to anxiety and hostility during phases of the menstrual cycle. *Psychosomatic Medicine, 1962, 24,* 300–311.

Gough, H. G. *Manual for the California Psychological Inventory*. Palo Alto, Calif.: Consulting Psychologists Press, 1957.

Gove, W. R. Relationship between sex roles, marital status, and mental illness. *Social Forces,* September 1972, 34–44.

Gove, W. R., & Tudor, J. F. Adult sex roles and mental illness. *American Journal of Sociology, 1973, 78,* 812–835.

Goy, R. W. Early hormonal influences on the development of sexual and sex-related behavior. In F. O. Schmitt (Ed.), *The neurosciences: Second study program.* New York: Rockefeller University Press, 1970.

Grady, K. *Androgyny reconsidered*. Paper presented at the meeting of the Eastern Psychological Association, New York, April 1975.

Grady, K. L., Phoenix, C. H., & Young, E. C. Role of the developing rat testes in differentiation of the neural tissues mediating mating behavior. *Journal of Comparative and Physiological Psychology, 1965, 59,* 176–182.

Graham, P. A. Women in academe. *Science, 1970, 169,* 1284–1290.

Grant, C., & Pryse-Davies, J. Effects of oral contraceptives on depressive mood changes and on endometrial monoamine oxidase and phosphates. *British Medical Journal, 1968, 1,* 777–780.

Grayson, H. T., Jr. *Psychosexual conflict in adolescent girls who experienced early parental loss by death.* Unpublished doctoral dissertation, Boston University Graduate School, 1967. (Cited in S. M. Fisher, *The female orgasm.* New York: Basic Books, 1973, 99–100.)

Greenblatt, R. Metabolic and psychosomatic disorders in menopausal women. *Geriatrics, 1955, 10,* 165–169.

Gregor, A. J., & McPherson, D. A. Racial attitudes among white and negro children in a Deep South standard metropolitan area. *Journal of Social Psychology, 1966, 68,* 95–106.

Grier, W. H., & Cobb, P. *Black rage*. New York: Basic Books, 1968.

Grozsko, M., & Morgenstern, R. *Institutional discrimination: The case of achievement-oriented women in higher education.* Paper presented at the annual convention of the American Psychological Association, Honolulu, 1972.

Gruder, C. L., & Cook, T. D. Sex, dependency, and helping. *Journal of Personality and Social Psychology, 1971, 19,* 290–294.

Gundlach, R., & Riess, B. F. Self and sexual identity in the female: A study of female homosexuals. In B. F. Riess (Ed.), *New directions in mental health.* New York: Grune & Stratton, 1968.

Gurin, G., Veroff, J., & Feld, S. *Americans view their mental health*. New York: Basic Books, 1960.

Gurin, P., & Epps, E. G. *Black consciousness, identity, and achievement*. New York: Wiley, 1975.

Gurin, P., Gurin, G., Lao, R., & Beattie, M. Internal-external control in the motivational dynamics of negro youth. *Journal of Social Issues*, 1969, *25*(3), 29–53.

Gurin, P., & Katz, D. *Motivation and aspiration in the negro college*. Ann Arbor, Mich.: Survey Research Center, 1966.

Hacker, H. M. Women as a minority group. *Social Forces*, 1951, *30*, 60–69.

Hall, C. S., & Van de Castle, R. L. An empirical investigation of the castration complex in dreams. *Journal of Personality*, 1965, *33*(1), 20–29.

Hall, C. S., & Van de Castle, R. L. *The content analysis of dreams*. New York: Appleton-Century-Crofts, 1966.

Hall, D. T. A model for coping with role conflict: The role behavior of college-educated women. *Administrative Science Quarterly*, 1972, *17*(4), 471–486.(a)

Hall, D. T. *Role and identity processes in the lives of married women*. Unpublished paper, 1972.(b)

Hall, D. T., & Gordon, F. E. The career choices of married women: Effects on conflict, role behavior and satisfaction. *Journal of Applied Psychology*, 1973, *58*, 42–48.

Hamburg, D. A. Effects of progesterone on behavior. *Research Publications, Association for Research in Nervous and Mental Diseases*, 1966, *43*, 251–265.

Hamburg, D. A., Moos, R. H., & Yalom, I. D. Studies of distress in the menstrual cycle and postpartum period. In R. P. Michael (Ed.), *Endocrinology and human behaviour*. London: Oxford University Press, 1968, 94–138.

Hamilton, J. A. *Postpartum problems*. St. Louis: Mosby, 1962.

Hammer, M. Preference for a male child: Cultural factor. *Journal of Individual Psychology*, 1970, *26*(1), 54–56.

Hampson, J. L., & Hampson, J. G. The ontogenesis of sexual behavior in man. In W. C. Young (Ed.), *Sex and internal secretions* (3rd ed.). Baltimore: Williams & Wilkins, 1961.

Hannerz, V. *Soulside*. New York: Columbia University Press, 1969.

Harris, G. W., & Levine, S. Sexual differentiation of the brain and its experimental control. *Journal of Physiology*, 1965, *171*, 275–301.

Harrison, A. O. Dilemma of growing up black and female. *Journal of Social and Behavioral Sciences*, 1974, *20*(2), 28–40.

Harrison-Ross, P., & Wyden, B. *The black child—a parent's guide*. New York: Wyden, 1973.

Hartley, R. E. Sex role pressures and socialization of the male child. *Psychological Reports*, 1959, *5*, 457–468.

Hartley, R. E. Children's concepts of male and female roles. *Merrill-Palmer Quarterly*, 1960, *6*, 83–91.

Hartnagel, T. F. Father absence and self-conception among lower class white and negro boys. *Social Problems*, 1970, *18*, 152–163.

Hartup, W. A., Moore, S. G., & Sager, G. Avoidance of inappropriate sex typing by young children. *Journal of Consulting Psychology*, 1963, *27*, 467–473.

Harwood, E., & Hodge, C. C. Jobs and the negro family: A reappraisal. *The Public Interest*, 1971, *23*, 125–131.

Hatfield, J. S., Ferguson, L. R., & Alpert, R. Mother-child interaction and the socialization process. *Child Development*, 1967, *38*, 365–414.

Hattendorf, K. W. A study of the questions of young children concerning sex: A phase of an experimental approach to parent education. *Journal of Social Psychology*, 1932, *3*, 37–65.

Havighurst, R. J. *Developmental tasks and education* (3rd ed.). New York: McKay, 1972.

Hawley, P. What women think men think. *Journal of Counseling Psychology*, 1971, *3*, 193–199.

Hawley, P. Perceptions of male models of femininity related to career choice. *Journal of Counseling Psychology*, 1972, *19*(4), 308–313.

Heckhausen, H. *The anatomy of achievement motivation*. New York: Academic Press, 1967.

Heilbrun, A. B. Sex role, instrumental-expressive behavior, and psychopathology in females. *Journal of Abnormal Psychology*, 1968, *73*, 131–136.

Heilbrun, A. B. Identification and behavioral effectiveness during late adolescence. In E. D. Evans (Ed.), *Adolescents: Readings in behavior and development*. Hinsdale, Ill.: Dryden Press, 1970, 68–79.

Heilbrun, A. B. Parent identification and filial sex-role behavior. In J. K. Cole & R. Dienstbier (Eds.), *Nebraska Symposium on motivation* (Vol. 21). Lincoln: University of Nebraska Press, 1973.

Heilbrun, A. B. Measurement of masculine and feminine sex role identities as independent dimensions. *Journal of Consulting and Clinical Psychology*, 1976, *44*(2), 183–190.

Heilbrun, A. B., & Fromme, D. K. Parental identification of late adolescents and level of adjustment: The importance of parent model attributes, ordinal position, and sex of the child. *Journal of Genetic Psychology*, 1965, *107*, 49–59.

Heim, A. H. *Intelligence and personality*. New York: Penguin Books, 1970.

Heiman, J. *Facilitating erotic arousal: Toward sex-positive research*. Paper presented at the annual convention of the American Psychological Association, New Orleans, September 1974.

Helson, R. Women mathematicians and the creative personality. *Journal of Consulting and Clinical Psychology*, 1971, *36*(2), 210–220.

Hendricks, M., Cook, T. D., & Crano, W. D. *Sex and a prior favor as moderators of helping*. Paper presented at the meeting of the Midwestern Psychological Association, Chicago, May 1973.

Hendricks, S. E. Influence of neonatally administered hormones and early gonadectomy on rats' sexual behavior. *Journal of Comparative and Physiological Psychology*, 1969, *69*(3), 408–413.

Herman, J. B., & Kuczynski, K. A. *The professional woman: Inter and intra role conflict*. Paper presented at the annual convention of the American Psychological Association, New Orleans, September 1974.

Hetherington, E. M. A developmental study of the effects of sex of the dominant parent on sex-role preference, identification, and imitation in children. *Journal of Personality and Social Psychology*, 1965, *2*, 188–194.

Hetherington, E. M. Effects of father absence on personality development in adolescent daughters. *Developmental Psychology*, 1972, *7*, 313–326.

Hetherington, E. M., & Deur, J. The effects of father absence on child development. *Young Children*, 1971, *26*, 233–248.

Hetherington, E. M., & Frankie, G. Effects of parental dominance, warmth, and conflict on imitation in children. *Journal of Personality and Social Psychology*, 1967, *6*, 119–125.

Hetherington, E. M., & Parke, R. D. *Child psychology*. New York: McGraw-Hill, 1975.

Heyman, D. K., & Gianturco, D. T. Long-term adaptation by the elderly to bereavement. *Journal of Gerontology, 1973, 28*, 359–362.

Hilgard, E. R. *Introduction to psychology* (2nd ed.). New York: Harcourt Brace & World, 1957.

Hill, C. T., Rubin, Z., & Peplau, L. A. Breakups before marriage: The end of 103 affairs. *Journal of Social Issues, 1976, 32*(1), 147–168.

Hill, K. T., & Sarason, S. B. The relation of test anxiety and defensiveness to test and school performance over elementary school years: A further longitudinal study. *Monographs of the Society for Research in Child Development, 1966, 31*(2, Serial No. 104).

Hill, R. *The strengths of black families*. New York: Emerson Hall, 1972.

Hill, R., Foote, N., Aldous, J., Carlson, R., & Macdonald, R. *Family development in three generations*. Cambridge, Mass.: Schenkman, 1970.

Hill, R., & Rogers, R. H. The developmental approach. In H. T. Christensen (Ed.), *Handbook of marriage and the family*. Chicago: Rand McNally, 1964, 171–211.

Himes, J. Some reactions to a hypothetical premarital pregnancy by 100 negro college women. *Journal of Marriage and the Family, 1964, 26*, 344–346.

Hjelle, L. A. Internal-external control as a determinant of academic achievement. *Psychological Reports, 1970, 26*, 326.

Hoffman, L. W. Early childhood experiences and women's achievement motives. *Journal of Social Issues, 1972, 28*(2), 129–156.

Hoffman, L. W. Fear of success in males and females: 1965 and 1972. *Journal of Consulting and Clinical Psychology, 1974, 42*, 353–358. (a)

Hoffman, L. W. Effects of maternal employment on the child: A review of the research. *Developmental Psychology, 1974, 10*(2), 204–228. (b)

Hoffman, L. W., & Nye, F. I. *Working mothers*. San Francisco: Jossey-Bass, 1974.

Hokanson, J. E., & Edelman, R. Effects of three social responses on vascular processes. *Journal of Personality and Social Psychology, 1966, 3*, 442–447.

Hollander, E. P., & Marcia, J. E. Parental determinants of peer orientation and self orientation among preadolescents. *Developmental Psychology, 1970, 2*, 292–302.

Hollingsworth, L. S. Variability as related to sex differences in achievement. *American Journal of Sociology, 1914, 19*, 510–530.

Holmes, T. H., & Rahe, R. H. The social readjustment rating scale. *Journal of Psychosomatic Research, 1967, 11*, 219.

Holmstrom, L. L. *The two-career family*. Cambridge, Mass.,: Schenkman, 1972.

Hopkins, J. The lesbian personality. *British Journal of Psychiatry, 1969, 115*(529), 1433–1436.

Horner, M. S. *Sex differences in achievement motivation and performance in competitive and non-competitive situations*. Unpublished doctoral dissertation, University of Michigan, 1968.

Horner, M. S. Femininity and successful achievement: A basic inconsistency. In J. M. Bardwick, E. Douvan, M. S. Horner, & D. Guttmann (Eds.), *Feminine personality and conflict*. Monterey, Calif.: Brooks/Cole, 1970, 45–74.

Horner, M. S. Toward an understanding of achievement-related conflicts in women. *Journal of Social Issues, 1972, 28*(2), 157–176.

Horner, M. S., & Walsh, M. R. Causes and consequences of existing psychological barriers to self-actualization. In R. B. Kundsin (Ed.), *Women and success: The anatomy of achievement*. New York: Morrow, 1974, 138–144.

Hottes, J. H., & Kahn, A. Sex differences in a mixed-motive conflict situation. *Journal of Personality,* 1974, *42,* 260–275.

Hraba, J., & Geoffrey, G. Black is beautiful: A reexamination of racial preference and identification. *Journal of Personality and Social Psychology,* 1970, *16*(3), 398–402.

Hunt, M. *The world of the formerly married.* New York: McGraw-Hill, 1966.

Hunt, M. *Sexual behavior in the 1970s.* Chicago: Playboy Press, 1974.

Hutt, C. *Males and females.* Middlesex, England: Penguin Books, 1972.

Hyde, J. S., & Rosenberg, B. G. *Half the human experience.* Lexington, Mass.: Heath, 1976.

Idestrom, C. M. Reaction to horethisterone withdrawal. *The Lancet,* 1966, *1,* 718.

Ivey, M. E., & Bardwick, J. M. Patterns of affective fluctuation in the menstrual cycle. *Psychosomatic Medicine,* 1968, *30,* 336–345.

Jackson, J. J. But where are the men? *The Black Scholar,* December 1971, 30–41.

Jackson, J. J. Marital life among aging blacks. *The Family Coordinator,* 1972, *21,* 21–27.

Jackson, J. J. Black women in a racist society. In C. Willie, B. Kramer, & B. Brown (Eds.), *Racism and mental health.* Pittsburgh: University of Pittsburgh Press, 1973, 185–268.

Jacobs, P. A., Brunton, M., & Melville, M. M. Aggressive behavior, mental subnormality and the XYY male. *Nature,* 1965, *208,* 1351–1352.

Janis, I. L., & Field, P. B. Sex differences and personality factors related to persuasibility. In C. Hovland & I. L. Janis (Eds.), *Personality and persuasibility.* New Haven, Conn.: Yale University Press, 1959, 55–68.

Janowsky, D. S., Gorney, R., Castelnuovo-Tedesco, P., & Stone, C. B. Premenstrual-menstrual increase in psychiatric hospital admission rates. *American Journal of Obstetrics and Gynecology,* 1969, *103,* 189–191.

Janowsky, D. S., Gorney, R., & Kelley, B. The "curse" vicissitudes and variations of the female fertility cycle. 1: Psychiatric aspects. *Psychosomatics,* 1966, *7,* 242–247.

Jenkin, N., & Vroegh, K. Contemporary concepts of masculinity and femininity. *Psychological Reports,* 1969, *25,* 679–697.

Joesting, J., & Joesting, R. Sex differences in group belongingness as influenced by instructor's sex. *Psychological Reports,* 1972, *31,* 717–718.

Johnson, C. D., & Gormly, J. Academic cheating: The contribution of sex, personality, and situational variables. *Developmental Psychology,* 1972, *6,* 320–325.

Johnson, D. W. Racial attitudes of negro freedom school participants and negro and white civil rights participants. *Social Forces,* 1966, *45,* 266–272.

Johnson, G. B. Penis-envy? Or pencil-needing? *Psychological Reports,* 1966, *19,* 758.

Johnson, M. Sex role learning in the nuclear family. *Child Development,* 1963, *34,* 319–333.

Jost, A. Recherches sur la différenciation sexuelle de l'embryon de lapin. 1: Introduction et embryologie génitale normale. *Archives d'Anatomie Microscopique et de Morphologie Expérimentale,* 1947, *30,* 151–200.

Jost, A. Embryonic sexual differentiation. In H. W. Jones & W. W. Scott (Eds.), *Hermaphroditism, genital anomalies and related endocrine disorders.* Baltimore: Williams & Wilkins, 1958.

Kaats, G. R., & Davis, K. E. The dynamics of sexual behavior of college students. *Journal of Marriage and the Family,* 1970, *32,* 390–399.

Kagan, J. Acquisition and significance of sex typing and sex role identity. In M. L. Hoffman & L. W. Hoffman (Eds.), *Review of child development research*. New York: Russell Sage Foundation, 1964, 137–167.

Kagan, J. *Change and continuity in infancy*. New York: Wiley, 1971.

Kagan, J. The emergence of sex differences. In F. Rebelsky (Ed.), *Life: The continuous process*. New York: Knopf, 1975.

Kagan, J., & Moss, H. A. *Birth to maturity: A study in psychological development*. New York: Wiley, 1962.

Kahana, B., & Kahana, E. How different generations view each other. *Geriatric Focus*, 1970, *9*(10), 1–13.

Kahana, B., Perez, L., Tagore, E., & Kahana, E. *Crosscultural perspectives on grandparenthood*. Paper presented at the annual convention of the American Psychological Association, Montreal, August 1973.

Kahana, E. *The older woman: Implications of research for social policy*. Paper presented at the meeting of the American Sociological Association, New York, August 1976.

Kahana, E., & Kahana, B. Parenting and personality in three generational families. In T. Williams (Ed.), *Infant Care*. Washington, D.C.: U.S. Department of Health, Education and Welfare, 1972.

Kandel, D. B., Lesser, G. S., Roberts, G., & Weiss, R. S. *Adolescents in two societies: Peers, school and family in the United States and Denmark*. Final report. Washington, D.C.: U.S. Department of Health, Education and Welfare, 1968. (Bureau of Research, Office of Education, Contract No. OE-4-10-069, Project No. 2139)

Kane, F. G., Lipton, M. A., & Ewing, J. Hormonal influences in female sexual response. *Archives of General Psychiatry*, 1969, *20*, 202–209.

Kantor, H. I., Michael, C. M., Boulas, S. H., Shore, H., & Ludvigson, H. W. *The administration of estrogens to older women: A psychometric evaluation*. Paper presented at the Seventh International Congress of Gerontology, Vienna, June 1966.

Kaplan, H. S. *The new sex therapy*. New York: Brunner/Mazel, 1974.

Katchadorian, H. A., & Lunde, D. T. *Fundamentals of human sexuality* (2nd ed.). New York: Holt, Rinehart & Winston, 1975.

Katz, M. L. *Female motive to avoid success: A psychological barrier or response to deviancy?* Unpublished manuscript, 1973. (Educational Testing Service, Princeton, N.J.)

Kay, H. H. A family court: The California proposal. In P. Bohannon (Ed.), *Divorce and after*. Garden City, N.Y.: Doubleday, 1970, 243–281.

Keating, D. P., & Stanley, J. C. Extreme measures for the exceptionally gifted in mathematics and science: Study of the mathematically and scientifically precocious youth. In E. E. Maccoby & C. N. Jacklin (Eds.), *The psychology of sex differences*. Stanford, Calif.: Stanford University Press, 1972, 502. (Abstract)

Keeler, M. H., Kane, F., & Daly, R. An acute schizophrenic episode following abrupt withdrawal of Enovid in a patient with previous postpartum psychiatric disorder. *American Journal of Psychiatry*, 1964, *120*, 1123–1124.

Kemper, T. Reference groups, socialization and achievement. *American Sociological Review*, 1968, *33*, 31–45.

Kennedy, B. J. Effect of massive doses of sex hormones on libido. *Medical Aspects of Human Sexuality*, 1973, *7*, 67–78.

Kenyon, F. E. Studies in female homosexuality—Psychological test results. *Journal of Consulting and Clinical Psychology*, 1968, *32*, 510–513.

Kinsey, A. C., Pomeroy, W. B., & Martin, C. E. *Sexual behavior in the human male*. Philadelphia: Saunders, 1948.

Kinsey, A. C., Pomeroy, W. B., Martin, C. E., & Gebhard, P. H. *Sexual behavior in the human female*. Philadelphia: Saunders, 1953.

Kipnis, D. M. Inner direction, other direction and achievement motivation. *Human development*, 1974, *17*(5), 321–343.

Kirsch, B. Consciousness-raising groups as therapy for women. In F. Franks & V. Burtle (Eds.), *Women in therapy*. New York: Brunner/Mazel, 1974.

Klaiber, E., Kobayaski, Y., Broverman, D., & Hall, F. Plasma monoamine oxidase activity in regularly menstruating women and in amenorrheic women receiving cyclic treatment with estrogens and a progestin. *Journal of Clinical Endocrinology and Metabolism*, 1971, *33*, 630–638.

Knof, C. The dynamics of newly born babies. *Journal of Pediatrics*, 1946, *29*, 271–278.

Knupfer, G., Clark, W., & Room, R. The mental health of the unmarried. *American Journal of Psychiatry*, 1966, *122*, 841–851.

Koenigsknecht, R. H., & Friedman, P. Syntax development in boys and girls. *Child Development*, 1976, *47*(4), 1109–1115.

Koeske, G. F., & Koeske, R. K. *Sex stereotypes and self-perception: A new look at female devaluation*. Paper presented at the annual convention of the American Psychological Association, Chicago, September 1975.

Koeske, R. K. *Physiological, social and situational factors in the pre-menstrual syndrome*. Unpublished manuscript, University of Pittsburgh, 1973.

Koeske, R. K., & Koeske, G. F. An attributional approach to moods and the menstrual cycle. *Journal of Personality and Social Psychology*, 1975, *31*(3), 473–478.

Kohlberg, L. A cognitive-developmental analysis of children's sex-role concepts and attitudes. In E. Maccoby (Ed.), *The development of sex differences*. Stanford, Calif.: Stanford University Press, 1966.

Kohlberg, L., & Ullman, D. Z. Stages in the development of psychosexual concepts and attitudes. In R. C. Friedman, R. M. Richart, & R. L. Vande Wiele (Eds.), *Sex differences in behavior*. New York: Wiley, 1974, 209–222.

Kohlberg, L., & Zigler, E. The impact of cognitive maturity on the development of sex-role attitudes in the years 4 to 8. *Genetic Psychology Monographs*, 1967, *75*, 89–165.

Komarovsky, M. Cultural contradictions and sex roles. *American Journal of Sociology*, 1946, *52*(3), 184–189.

Komarovsky, M. Cultural contradictions and sex roles: The masculine case. *American Journal of Sociology*, 1973, *78*, 873–884.

Komorita, S. S. Cooperative choice in a Prisoner's Dilemma game. *Journal of Personality and Social Psychology*, 1965, *2*, 741–745.

Korner, A. F. Neonatal startles, smiles, erection, and reflex sucks as related to state, sex, and individuality. *Child Development*, 1969, *40*, 1039–1053.

Krebs, R. L. Girls—More moral than boys or just sneakier? *Proceedings of the 76th Annual Convention of the American Psychological Association*, 1968, *3*, 607–608.

Kreitler, H., & Kreitler, S. Children's concepts of sexuality and birth. *Child Development*, 1966, *37*, 363–378.

Kreuz, L. E., & Rose, R. M. Assessment of aggressive behavior and plasma testosterone in a young criminal population. *Psychosomatic Medicine*, 1972, *34*, 321–332.

Krieger, W. G. Infant influences and the parent sex x child sex interaction in the socialization process. *JSAS Catalog of Selected Documents in Psychology,* 1976, *6*(1), 36. (Ms. No. 1234)

Kroeker, T. Coping and defensive function of the ego. In R. W. White (Ed.), *A study of lives.* New York: Atherton Press, 1963.

Kutscher, A. H. *But not to lose: A book of comfort for those bereaved.* New York: Fell, 1969.

Kuvlesky, W., & Obordo, A. A racial comparison of teenage girls' projection for marriage and procreation. *Journal of Marriage and the Family,* February 1972, *34,* 75–84.

Ladner, J. *Tomorrow's tomorrow.* Garden City, N.Y.: Doubleday, 1972.

Lagerspitz, K. M. J. *Studies on the aggressive behavior of mice.* Helsinki: Suomalainen Tiedeakatemia, 1964.

Lagerspitz, K. M. J. Aggression and aggressiveness in laboratory mice. In S. Garattina & E. B. Sigg (Eds.), *Aggressive behaviour.* New York: Wiley, 1969, 77–85.

Lambert, W. E., Yakley, A., & Hein, R. N. Child training values of English Canadian and French Canadian parents. *Canadian Journal of Behavioral Science,* 1971, *3,* 217–236.

Landis, C., Landis, A., & Bolles, M. M. *Sex in development.* New York: Hoeber, 1940.

Landy, E. E. Sex differences in some aspects of smoking behavior. *Psychological Reports,* 1967, *20*(2), 575–580.

Lansdell, H. The use of factor scores from the Wechsler-Bellevue Scale of Intelligence in assessing patients with temporal lobe removals. *Cortex,* 1976, *4,* 257–268.

Lansky, L. M. The family structure also affects the model: Sex-role attitudes in parents of preschool children. *Merrill-Palmer Quarterly,* 1967, *13,* 139–150.

Lesser, G. S., Krawitz, R., & Packard, R. Experimental arousal of achievement motivation in adolescent girls. *Journal of Abnormal and Social Psychology,* 1963, *66*(1), 59–66.

Levenson, H. Distinctions within the concept of internal-external control: Development of a new scale. *Proceedings of the 80th Annual Convention of the American Psychological Association,* 1972, *1,* 261–262.

Levin, R. J., & Levin, A. Sexual pleasure: The surprising preferences of 100,000 women. *Redbook,* September 1975, pp. 51–57.

Levine, S., & Mullins, R. Estrogen administered neonatally affects adult sexual behavior in male and female rats. *Science,* 1964, *144,* 185–187.

Levinger, G. A social-psychological perspective on marital dissolution. *Journal of Social Issues,* 1976, *32*(1), 21–47.

Lewis, M., & Freedle, R. Mother-infant dyad: The cradle of meaning. In P. Pliner, L. Kramer, & T. Alloway (Eds.), *Communication and affect: Language and thought.* New York: Academic Press, 1973.

Lewis, M., Kagan, J., & Kalafat, J. Patterns of fixation in the young infant. *Child Development,* 1966, *37,* 331–341.

Lewis, M., Myers, W., Kagan, J., & Grossberg, R. Attention to visual patterns in infants. Paper presented at the annual convention of the American Psychological Association, Philadelphia, August 1963.

Liddicoat, R. Untitled article in *British Medical Journal,* 1957, *2* (November 9), 1110–1111.

Liebow, E. *Tally's corner.* Boston: Little, Brown, 1967.

Life is more exciting with my new bustline: An interview with Cathy Neal of San Francisco, California. *Glamour,* 1976, *74*(21), p. 195.

Lindemann, E. Symptomatology and management of acute grief. *American Journal of Psychiatry*, 1944, *101*, 141–148.

Littig, L. W. Effect of anxiety on real and ideal vocational aspirations among grammar school boys. *Nature*, 1963, *199*(4899), 1214–1215.

Litwin, G. H. *Motives and expectancies as determinants of preference for degrees of risk*. Unpublished honors dissertation, University of Michigan, 1958.

Loevinger, J. The meaning and measurement of ego development. *American Psychologist*, 1966, *21*, 195–206.

Loevinger, J., & Wessler, R. *Measuring ego development* (Vol. 1). San Francisco: Jossey-Bass, 1970.

Loo, C., & Wenar, D. Activity level and motor inhibition: Their relationship to intelligence-test performance in normal children. *Child Development*, 1971, *42*, 967–971.

Lopata, H. Z. The life cycle of the social role of the housewife. *Sociology and Social Research*, 1966, *51*, 5–22.

Lopata, H. Z. *Occupation: Housewife*. London: Oxford University Press, 1971.

Lopata, H. Z. *Widowhood in an American city*. Cambridge, Mass: Schenkman, 1973.

Luckey, E. B. Perceptual congruence of self and family concepts as related to marital interaction. *Sociometry*, 1961, *24*, 234–250.

Lundgren, D. C., & Schaub, M. R. *Sex differences in the social bases of self esteem*. Paper presented at the annual convention of the American Psychological Association, New Orleans, September 1974.

Lunneborg, P. W. Stereotypic aspects in masculinity-femininity measurement. *Journal of Consulting and Clinical Psychology*, 1970, *34*, 113–118.

Lynn, D. B. *Parent and sex-role identification: A theoretical formulation*. Berkeley, Calif.: McCutchan, 1969.

Lyon, P., & Martin, D. The realities of lesbianism. In C. Gordon & G. Johnson (Eds.), *Readings in human sexuality: Contemporary perspectives* (1976–1977 ed.). New York: Harper & Row, 1976, 166–168.

MacArthur, R. Sex differences in field dependence for the Eskimo. *International Journal of Psychology*, 1967, *2*, 139–140.

Maccoby, E. E. *The development of sex differences*. Stanford, Calif.: Stanford University Press, 1966.

Maccoby, E. E. The meaning of being female (Review of *Psychology of women* by J. M. Bardwick). *Contemporary Psychology*, 1972, *17*(7), 369–372.

Maccoby, E. E., & Jacklin, C. N. *Sex differences and their implications for sex roles*. Paper presented at the annual convention of the American Psychological Association, Washington, D.C., September 1971.

Maccoby, E. E., & Jacklin, C. N. *The psychology of sex differences*. Stanford, Calif.: Stanford University Press, 1974.

Maccoby, E. E., & Masters, J. C. Attachment and dependence. In P. Mussen (Ed.), *Carmichael's manual of child psychology* (3rd ed.). New York: Wiley, 1970, 73–157.

Maddison, D., & Viola, A. The health of widows in the year following bereavement. *Journal of Psychosomatic Research*, 1968, *12*,(4), 297–306.

Madsen, C. Nurturance and modeling in preschoolers. *Child Development*, 1968, *39*, 221–236.

Mahone, C. H. Fear of failure and unrealistic vocational aspiration. *Journal of Abnormal and Social Psychology*, 1960, *60*, 253–261.

Makosky, V. P. *Fear of success, sex-role orientation of the task, and competitive conditions as variables affecting women's performance in achievement-oriented situations.* Paper presented at the meeting of the Midwestern Psychological Association, Cleveland, May 1972.

Mandler, G., & Sarason, S. B. A study of anxiety and learning. *Journal of Abnormal and Social Psychology,* 1952, *47,* 166–173.

Mannion, K. Female homosexuality: A comprehensive review of theory and research. JSAS *Catalogue of Selected Documents in Psychology,* 1976, *6*(1), 44.

Marshall, P. Reena. In T. Case (Ed.), *The black woman.* New York: Signet, 1970, 20–37.

Martin, D., & Lyon, P. *Lesbian/woman.* New York: Bantam, 1972.

Masters, W. H., & Johnson, V. E. *Human sexual response.* Boston: Little, Brown, 1966.

Masters, W. H., & Johnson, V. E. *Human sexual inadequacy.* Boston: Little, Brown, 1970.

McAdoo, H. *Race and sex-typing in young black children.* Paper presented at the annual meeting of the National Conference of Social Welfare, Cincinnati, May 1974.

McCandless, B. R., Bilous, C. B., & Bennett, H. L. Sex differences in aggression and its correlates in middle-class adolescents. *Child Development,* 1962, *32,* 45–58.

McCarthy, D. Language development of the preschool child. In R. G. Barker, J. S. Kounin, & R. F. Wright (Eds.), *Child behavior and development.* New York: McGraw-Hill, 1943.

McClelland, D. C. Risk-taking and children with high and low need for achievement. In J. W. Atkinson (Ed.), *Motives in fantasy, action and society.* Princeton: Van Nostrand, 1958, 306–321.

McClelland, D. C., Atkinson, J. W., Clark, R. A., & Lowell, E. L. *The achievement motive.* New York: Appleton-Century-Crofts, 1953.

McClintock, M. K. Menstrual synchrony and suppression. *Nature,* 1971, *37,* 571–605.

McGlone, J. *Sex differences in functional brain asymmetry* (Research Bulletin No. 378). Unpublished manuscript, University of Western Ontario, 1976.

McIntyre, A. Sex differences in children's aggression. *Proceedings of the 80th Annual Convention of the American Psychological Association,* 1972, *7,* 93–94.

McKee, J. P., & Sherriffs, A. C. The differential evaluation of males and females. *Journal of Personality,* 1957, *25,* 356–371.

McKee, J. P., & Sherriffs, A. C. Men's and women's beliefs, ideals, and self concepts. *American Journal of Sociology,* 1959, *65,* 356–363.

McKenna, W., & Kessler, S. J. *Differential treatment of males and females as a source of bias in social psychology.* Paper presented at the annual convention of the American Psychological Association, New Orleans, September 1974.

McMahan, I. D. *Sex differences in causal attribution following success and failure.* Paper presented at the meeting of the Eastern Psychological Association, New York, April 1971.

McMahan, I. D. *Sex differences in expectancy of success as a function of task.* Paper presented at the meeting of the Eastern Psychological Association, New York, April 1972.

McMahan, I. D. Sex-role stereotypes of cognitive task performance. JSAS *Catalogue of Selected Documents in Psychology,* 1976, *6*(1), 39.

Mead, M. *Male and female.* London: Morrow, 1949.

Mednick, M. *Motivational and personality factors related to career goals of black women*. Final report. Washington, D.C.: Howard University, 1973. (ERIC Document Reproduction Service No. ED 081 408)

Mednick, M. "Review essay: Psychology." *Signs,* 1976, *1*(3, Pt. 1), 763–770.

Mednick, M., & Puryear, G. Motivational and personality factors related to career goals of black women. *Journal of Social and Behavioral Sciences,* 1975, *21*(1), 1–30.

Mednick, M., Tangri, S. S., & Hoffman, L. W. *Women and achievement.* Washington, D.C.: Hemisphere, 1975.

Mednick, M., & Weissman, H. J. The psychology of women—Selected topics. *Annual Review of Psychology,* 1975, *26,* 1–18.

Megargee, E. I. Influence of sex-roles on the manifestation of leadership. *Journal of Applied Psychology,* 1969, *53,* 377–382.

Mehrabian, A. Measures of vocabulary and grammatical skills for children up to age six. *Developmental Psychology,* 1970, *2,* 439–446.

Mendelsohn, R., & Dobie, S. *Women's self conception: A block to career development.* Unpublished manuscript, Lafayette Clinic, Department of Mental Health, Detroit, 1970.

Milton, G. A. *Five studies of the relationship between sex-role identification and achievement in problem solving* (Tech. Rep. 3). New Haven, Conn.: Yale University, Department of Industrial Administration and Department of Psychology, December 1958.

Minton, D., Kagan, J., & Levine, J. A. Maternal control and obedience in the two-year-old. *Child Development,* 1971, *42,* 1873–1894.

Mischel, W. Sex-typing and socialization. In P. H. Mussen (Ed.), *Carmichael's manual of child psychology* (3rd ed., Vol. 3). New York: Wiley, 1970, 3–72.

Monahan, L., Kuhn, D., & Shaver, P. Intrapsychic versus cultural explanations of the "fear of success" motive. *Journal of Personality and Social Psychology,* 1974, *29,* 60–64.

Money, J. Prenatal hormones and intelligence: A possible relationship. *Impact of Science on Society,* 1971, *21,* 285–290.

Money, J., Prenatal hormones and postnatal socialization in gender identity differentiation. In J. K. Cole & R. Dienstbier (Eds.), *Nebraska Symposium on Motivation* (Vol. 21). Lincoln: University of Nebraska Press, 1974.

Money, J., & Ehrhardt, A. A. *Man and woman, boy and girl: Differentiation and dimorphism of gender identity.* Baltimore: Johns Hopkins University Press, 1972.

Monks, F. Future time perspective in adolescents. *Human Development,* 1968, *11,* 107–123.

Montanelli, D. S., & Hill, K. T. Children's expectations of performance as a function of two consecutive reinforcements. *Journal of Personality and Social Psychology,* 1969, *13,* 115–128.

Moore, T. Language and intelligence: A longitudinal study of the first eight years. 1: Patterns of development in boys and girls. *Human Development,* 1967, *10,* 88–106.

Moos, R. H. The development of a menstrual distress questionnaire. *Psychosomatic Medicine,* 1968, *30,* 853–867.

Moos, R. H. Assessment of psychological concomitants of oral contraceptives. In H. A. Salhanick et al. (Eds.), *Metabolic effects of gonadal hormones and contraceptive steroids.* New York: Plenum, 1969, 676–705.

Morgan, S. W., & Mausner, B. Behavioral and fantasied indicators of avoidance of success in men and women. *Journal of Personality,* 1973, *41,* 457–469.

Morland, K. J. Racial recognitions by nursery school children in Hynchleburg, Virginia. *Social Forces,* 1958, *37,* 132–137.

Mosher, D. L. Sex differences, sex experience, sex guilt, and explicitly sexual films. *Journal of Social Issues,* 1973, *29*(3), 95–112.

Moss, H. A. Sex, age, and state as determinants of mother-infant interaction. *Merrill-Palmer Quarterly,* 1967, *13,* 19–36.

Moss, H. A., & Robson, K. S. The relationship between the amount of time infants spend at various states and the development of visual behavior. *Child Development,* 1970, *41,* 509–517.

Mowrer, O. H. *Learning theory and personality dynamics.* New York: Ronald Press, 1950.

Moynihan, D. P. *The negro family: The case for national action.* Washington, D.C.: U.S. Department of Labor, Office of Policy Planning and Research, 1965.

Mussen, P. H., & Rutherford, E. Parent-child relations and parental personality in relation to young children's sex role preferences. *Child Development,* 1963, *34,* 589–607.

Myers, L. Black women: Selectivity among roles and reference groups in the maintenance of self-esteem. *Journal of Social and Behavioral Sciences,* 1975, *21*(1), 39–47.

Myrdal, G. *An American dilemma.* New York: Harper & Row, 1944.

Nadelman, L. Sex identity in American children: Memory, knowledge and preference tests. *Developmental Psychology,* 1974, *10*(3), 413–417.

Naditch, S. F. *Experimental demand characteristics and sex differences on the rod-and-frame test.* Paper presented at the annual convention of the American Psychological Association, Washington, D.C., September 1976.

Nadler, R. D. Masculinization of female rats by intracranial implantation of androgen in infancy. *Journal of Comparative and Physiological Psychology,* 1968, *66,* 157–167.

Nadler, R. D. Differentiation of the capacity for male sexual behavior in the rat. *Hormones and Behavior,* 1969, *1,* 53–63.

Nash, S. C. The relationship among sex-role stereotyping, sex-role preference, and the sex difference in spatial visualization. *Sex Roles,* 1975, *1*(1), 15.

Neufeld, E., Langmeyer, D., & Seeman, W. Some sex-role stereotypes and personal preferences, 1950 and 1970. *Journal of Personality Assessment,* 1974, *38,* 247–254.

Neugarten, B. L. (Ed.). *Middle age and aging.* Chicago: University of Chicago Press, 1968.

Neugarten, B. L., & Associates (Eds.). *Personality in middle and late life.* New York: Atherton, 1964.

Neugarten, B. L., & Gutmann, D. L. Age-sex roles and personality in middle age: A thematic apperception study. In B. L. Neugarten (Ed.), *Middle age and aging.* Chicago: University of Chicago Press, 1968, 58–70.

Neugarten, B. L., & Kraines, R. J. Menopausal symptoms in women of various ages. *Psychosomatic Medicine,* 1967, *27,* 266–273.

Neugarten, B. L., & Moore, J. W. The changing age-status system. In B. L. Neugarten (Ed.), *Middle age and aging.* Chicago: University of Chicago Press, 1968, 5–21.

Neugarten, B. L., Wood, V., Kraines, R. J., & Loomis, B. Women's attitudes toward the menopause. In B. L. Neugarten (Ed.), *Middle age and aging.* Chicago: University of Chicago Press, 1968.

Neulinger, J. Perceptions of the optimally integrated person: A redefinition of mental health. *Proceedings of the 76th Annual Convention of the American Psychological Association,* 1968, *3,* 553–554.

Neumann, F., & Elger, W. Permanent changes in gonadal function and sexual behavior as a result of early feminization of male rats by treatment with an antiandrogenic steroid. *Endokrinologie,* 1966, *50,* 209–225.

Neumann, F., Elger, W., & Kramer, M. Development of a vagina in male rats by inhibiting androgen receptors with an anti-androgen during the critical phase of organogenesis. *Endocrinology,* 1966, *78,* 628.

Newson, J., & Newson, E. *Four years old in an urban community.* Harmondworth, England: Pelican Books, 1968.

Norris, R. V., & Lloyd, C. W. Psychosexual effects of hormone therapy. *Medical Aspects of Human Sexuality,* 1971, *5,* 129–146.

Norton, A. J., & Glick, P. C. Marital instability: Past, present, and future. *Journal of Social Issues,* 1976, *32*(1), 5–20.

Oakley, A. *Sex, gender and society.* South Melbourne, Australia: Sun Books, 1972.

Oakley, A. *The sociology of housework.* Bath, England: Pitman, 1974.

O'Brien, P. *The woman alone.* New York: Quadrangle, 1973.

Oetzel, R. M. Annotated bibliography. In E. E. Maccoby (Ed.), *The development of sex differences.* Stanford, Calif.: Stanford University Press, 1966.

Offer, D. Attitudes toward sexuality in a group of 1500 middle class teen-agers. *Journal of Youth and Adolescence,* 1972, *1*(1), 81–90.

O'Leary, V. E. *The motive to avoid success: Antecedents, correlates, and arousal contexts. Some speculative results.* Paper presented at the First Annual Spring Conference of the Michigan Psychological Association, April 1974. (a)

O'Leary, V. E. Some attitudinal barriers to occupational aspirations in women. *Psychological Bulletin,* 1974, *81*(11), 809–816. (b)

O'Leary, V. E., & Braun, J. S. Antecedents and personality correlates of academic careerism in women. *Proceedings of the 80th Annual Convention of the American Psychological Association,* 1972, *7*(1), 277–278.

O'Leary, V. E., & Braun, J. S. *Antecedents and personality correlates of professional careerism in women.* Paper presented at the annual convention of the American Psychological Association, New Orleans, September 1974.

O'Leary, V. E., & Depner, C. E. College males' ideal female: Changing sex-role stereotypes. *Journal of Social Psychology,* 1975, *95,* 139–140.

O'Leary, V. E., & Depner, C. E. Alternative gender roles among women: Masculine, feminine, androgynous. *Intellect,* 1976, *104*(2371), 313–315.

O'Leary, V. E., & Hammack, B. Sex-role orientation and achievement context as determinants of the motive to avoid success. *Sex Roles,* 1975, *1*(3), 225–234.

O'Leary, V. E., & Harrison, A. O. *Sex role stereotypes as a function of race and sex.* Paper presented at the annual convention of the American Psychological Association, Chicago, September 1975.

Omark, D. R., Omark, M., & Edelman, M. Dominance hierarchies in young children. In E. E. Maccoby & C. N. Jacklin (Eds.), *The psychology of sex differences.* Stanford, Calif.: Stanford University Press, 1974, 533.

O'Niel, A., & O'Niel, G. Open marriage: A conceptual framework. In J. R. Smith & L. G. Smith (Eds.), *Beyond monogamy.* Baltimore: Johns Hopkins University Press, 1974, 56–67.

Paige, K. E. Effects of oral contraceptives on affective fluctuations associated with menstrual cycle. *Psychosomatic Medicine,* 1971, *33*(6), 515–537.

Paige, K. E. Women learn to sing the menstrual blues. *Psychology Today,* 1973, *7*(4), pp. 41–46.

Pappo, M. *Fear of success: A theoretical analysis of the construction and validation of a measuring instrument.* Unpublished manuscript, Community Research Program, Washington, D.C., 1973.

Parkes, C. M. Effects of bereavement on physical and mental health: A study of the medical records of widows. *British Medical Journal*, 1964, *2*, 274–279.

Parkes, C. M. The first year of bereavement. *Psychiatry*, 1970, *33*(4), 444–467.

Parkes, C. M. *Bereavement*. New York: International Universities Press, 1972.

Parlee, M. B. Comments on "Roles of activation and inhibition in sex differences in cognitive abilities." *Psychological Reports*, 1972, *79*, 180–184.

Parlee, M. B. The premenstrual syndrome. *Psychological Bulletin*, 1973, *80*, 454–465.

Parlee, M. B. Stereotypic beliefs about menstruation: A methodological note on the Moos Menstrual Distress Questionnaire and some new data. *Psychosomatic Medicine*, 1974, *36*, 229–240.

Parlee, M. B. Review essay: Psychology. *Signs*, 1975, *1*(1), 119–138.

Parsons, T., & Bales, R. F. *Family, socialization, and interaction process*. Glencoe, Ill.: Free Press, 1955.

Pederson, F., & Robson, K. Father participation in infancy. *American Journal of Orthopsychiatry*, 1969, *39*, 466–472.

Peplau, L. A. Impact of fear of su ess and sex-role attitudes on women's competitive achievement. *Journal of Personality and Social Psychology*, 1976, *34*(4), 561–568.

Perloff, W. H. Hormones and homosexuality. In J. Marmor (Ed.), *Sexual inversion*. New York: Basic Books, 1965, 44–69.

Persky, H., Smith, K. D., & Basu, G. K. Relation of psychologic measures of aggression and hostility to testosterone production in man. *Psychosomatic Medicine*, 1971, *33*, 265–277.

Petersen, A. C. Physical androgyny and cognitive functioning in adolescence. *Developmental Psychology*, 1976, *12*(6), 524–533.

Pfeiffer, E., & Davis, G. Determinants of sexual behavior in middle and old age. *Journal of the American Geriatric Society*, 1972, *20*, 151–158.

Phares, E. G. Differential utilization of information as a function of internal-external control. *Journal of Personality*, 1968, *36*, 649–662.

Pheterson, G. I., Kiesler, S. G., & Goldberg, P. A. Evaluation of the performance of women as a function of their sex, achievement, and personal history. *Journal of Personality and Social Psychology*, 1971, *19*, 114–118.

Phoenix, C. H., Goy, R. W., Gerall, A. A., & Young, W. C. Organizing action of prenatally administered testosterone propionate on the tissues mediating mating behavior in the female guinea pig. *Endocrinology*, 1962, *65*, 369–382.

Pihlblad, T., & Adams, C. Widowhood, social participation and life satisfaction. *Aging and Human Development*, 1972, *3*(4), 323–330.

Pihlblad, T., & Rosencranz, H. *Social participation of older women in the small town*. Unpublished manuscript, University of Missouri, 1968.

Piskin, V. Psychosexual development in terms of object and role preferences. *Journal of Clinical Psychology*, 1960, *16*, 238–240.

Pleck, J. H. Males' traditional attitudes toward women: Conceptual contexts in research. In J. A. Sherman & F. L. Denmark (Eds.), *The futures of women: Issues in psychology*. New York: Psychological Dimensions, in press.

Pleshette, N., Asch, S. S., & Chase, J. A study of anxieties during pregnancy, labor, the early and late puerperium. *Bulletin of the New York Academy of Medicine*, 1965, *32*, 436–456.

Pohlman, E. H. *Psychology of birth planning*. Cambridge, Mass.: Schenkman, 1969.

Polani, P. E. Abnormal sex chromosomes and mental disorder. *Nature*, 1969, *223*(5207), 680–686.

Poloma, M. M. Role conflict and the married professional woman. In C. Safilios-

Rothschild (Ed.), *Towards a sociology of women*. Lexington, Mass.: Xerox College Publishing, 1972, 187–198.

Poloma, M. M., & Garland, T. N. The myth of the egalitarian family: Familial roles and the professionally employed wife. In A. Theodore (Ed.), *The professional woman*. Cambridge, Mass.: Schenkman, 1971.

Pomazal, R. J., & Clore, G. L. Helping on the highway: The effects of dependency on sex. *Journal of Applied Social Psychology*, 1973, *3*, 150–164.

Powell, G. J. Self-concept in white and black children. In C. V. Willie, B. M. Kramer, & B. S. Brown (Eds.), *Racism and mental health*. Pittsburgh: University of Pittsburgh Press, 1973.

Prather, J. Why can't women be more like men? A summary of the sociopsychological factors hindering women's advancement in the professions. *Behavioral Scientist*, 1971, *15*(2), 39–47.

Prendergass, V. E., Kimmel, E., Joesting, J., Peterson, J. E., & Bush, E. Sex discrimination counseling. *American Psychologist*, 1976, *31*(1), 36–46.

Prescott, S., & Foster, K. *Why researchers don't study women: The responses of 67 researchers*. Paper presented at the annual convention of the American Psychological Association, New Orleans, September 1974.

Prociuk, T. J., & Breen, L. J. Internal-external control, test anxiety, and academic achievement: Additional data. *Psychological Reports*, 1973, *33*, 563–566a.

Protheroe, C. Puerperal psychosis: A long-term study, 1927–1961. *British Journal of Psychiatry*, 1969, *115*, 9–30.

Puryear, G. R., & Mednick, M. S. Black militancy, affective attachment, and fear of success in black college women. *Journal of Consulting and Clinical Psychology*, 1975, *38*, 343–347.

Rainwater, L. Some aspects of lower class sexual behavior. *Medical Aspects of Human Sexuality*, 1966, *2*, 15.

Rainwater, L. Crucible of identity. In T. E. Parsons & K. B. Clark (Eds.), *The negro American*. Boston: Beacon, 1967.

Rainwater, L. *Behind ghetto walls: Black family life in federal slums*. Chicago: Aldine, 1970.

Ramey, E. Men's cycles (they have them too you know). *Ms.* Spring 1972, pp. 8–14.

Rapaport, A., & Chammah, A. M. Sex differences in factors contributing to the level of cooperation in the prisoner's dilemma game. *Journal of Personality and Social Psychology*, 1965, *2*(6), 831–838.

Rapaport, R., & Rapaport, R. N. The dual career family: A variant pattern and social change. In C. Safilios-Rothschild (Ed.), *Towards a sociology of women*. Lexington, Mass.: Xerox College Publishing, 1972, 216–244.

Rebelsky, F., & Hanks, C. Father's verbal interaction with infants in the first three months of life. *Child Development*, 1971, *42*, 63–68.

Reed, J. Marriage and fertility in black female teachers. *The Black Scholar*, January–February 1970, *1*(3–4), 22–28.

Reiss, I. *The social context of premarital sexual permissiveness*. New York: Holt, Rinehart & Winston, 1967.

Rhodes, R. The changing role of the black woman. In R. Staples (Ed.), *The black family: Essays and studies*. Belmont, Calif.: Wadsworth, 1971.

Riess, B. F. New viewpoints on the female homosexual. In V. Franks & V. Burtle (Eds.), *Women in therapy: New psychotherapies for a changing society*. New York: Brunner/Mazel, 1974.

Rim, Y. Risk-taking and need for achievement. *Acta Psychologica*, 1963, *21*, 108–115.

Robin, A. A. The psychological changes of normal parturition. *Psychiatric Quarterly,* 1962, *36,* 129–150.

Roff, M. Intra-family resemblances in personality characteristics. *Journal of Psychology,* 1950, *30,* 199–227.

Romm, M. E. Sexuality and homosexuality in women. In J. Marmor (Ed.), *Sexual inversion.* New York: Basic Books, 1965, 282–301.

Roper, E. The Fortune survey: Women in America (Pt. 1). *Fortune,* 1946, *34,* pp. 5–12.

Rosaldo, M. Z. Women, culture, and society: A theoretical overview. In M. Z. Rosaldo & L. Lamphere (Eds.), *Women, culture, and society.* Stanford, Calif.: Stanford University Press, 1974, 17–42.

Rose, R. M., Gordon, T. P., & Bernstein, I. S. Plasma testosterone levels in the male rhesus: Influences of sexual and social stimuli. *Science,* 1972, *178,* 643–645.

Rose, R. M., Holaday, J. W., & Bernstein, I. S. Plasma testosterone, dominance rank, and aggressive behavior in male rhesus monkeys. *Nature,* 1971, *231,* 366–368.

Rose, V. L., & Price-Bonham, S. Divorce adjustment: A woman's problem? *The Family Coordinator,* 1973, *22,* 291–297.

Rosen, B. C. The achievement syndrome. *American Sociological Review,* 1956, *21,* 203–211.

Rosen, D. H. *Lesbianism: A study of female homosexuality.* Springfield, Ill.: Charles C Thomas, 1974.

Rosenberg, B. G., & Sutton-Smith, B. Family interaction effects on masculinity-femininity. *Journal of Personality and Social Psychology,* 1968, *8,* 117.

Rosenkrantz, P. S., Vogel, S. R., Bee, H., Broverman, I. K., & Broverman, D. M. Sex-role stereotypes and self-concepts in college students. *Journal of Consulting and Clinical Psychology,* 1968, *32,* 287–295.

Rosenteur, P. *The single woman.* New York: Popular Library, 1961.

Rosenthal, R., & Rosnow, R. L. *The volunteer subject.* New York: Wiley, 1975.

Rosenthal, S. H. The involutional depressive syndrome. *American Journal of Psychiatry,* 1968, *124,* 128–131.

Ross, S. A. A test of generality of the effects of deviant preschool models. *Developmental Psychology,* 1971, *4,* 262–267.

Rossi, A. S. Equality between the sexes: An immodest proposal. *Daedalus,* 1964, *93,* 607–652.

Rossi, A. S. Barriers to the career choice of engineering, medicine or science among American women. In J. A. Mattfeld & C. G. VanAker (Eds.), *Women and the scientific professions.* Cambridge, Mass.: M.I.T. Press, 1965.

Rothbart, K., & Rothbart, M. K. Birth order, sex of child, and maternal help-giving. *Sex Roles,* 1976, *2*(1), 39–46.

Rothbart, M. K., & Maccoby, E. E. Parents' differential reactions to sons and daughters. *Journal of Personality and Social Psychology,* 1966, *4*(3), 237–245.

Rotter, J. Generalized expectancies for internal versus external control of reinforcement. *Psychological Monographs,* 1966, *80*(1, Whole No. 609).

Rotter, J. Some problems and misconceptions related to the construct of internal versus external control of reinforcement. *Journal of Consulting and Clinical Psychology,* 1975, *43*(1), 56–67.

Rubin, Z. *Liking and loving.* New York: Holt, Rinehart & Winston, 1973.

Rubin, Z., Provenzano, F. J., & Luria, Z. Social and cultural influences on sex-role development. The eye of the beholder: Parents' views on sex of newborns. *American Journal of Orthopsychiatry,* 1974, *44*(4), 512–519.

Russo, N. F. The motherhood mandate. *Journal of Social Issues,* 1976, *32*(3), 143–153.

Sacks, B. D., Pollack, E. I., Kreiger, M. S., & Barfield, R. J. Sexual behavior: Normal male patterning in androgenized female rats. *Science,* 1973, *181,* 770–772.

Saghir, M. T., & Robins, E. *Male and female homosexuality: A comprehensive investigation.* Baltimore: Williams & Wilkins, 1973.

Sandidge, S., & Friedland, S. J. *Sex role-taking and aggressive behavior in children.* Paper presented at the meeting of the Society for Research in Child Development, Philadelphia, March 1973.

Santos, J. F., & Murphy, G. An odyssey in perceptual learning. *Bulletin of the Menninger Clinic,* 1960, *24,* 6–17.

Sarason, S. B., Lighthall, F. F., Davidson, K. S., Waite, R. R., & Ruebush, B. K. *Anxiety in elementary school children.* New York: Wiley, 1960.

Scanzoni, J. *The black family.* Boston: Allyn & Bacon, 1971.

Schaefer, L. *Sexual experiences and reactions of 30 women.* Unpublished doctoral dissertation, Columbia University, 1964.

Schlesinger, B. *The one-parent family.* Toronto: University of Toronto Press, 1969.

Schrader, S. L., Wilcoxon, L. A., & Sherif, C. W. *Daily self-reports on activities, life events, moods, and somatic changes during the menstrual cycle.* Paper presented at the annual convention of the American Psychological Association, Chicago, September 1975.

Schulz, D. *Coming up black: Patterns of ghetto socialization.* Englewood Cliffs, N.J.: Prentice-Hall, 1969.

Schwenn, M. *Arousal of the motive to avoid success.* Unpublished junior honors thesis, Harvard University, 1970.

Seaman, B. *Free and female.* New York: Coward, McCann & Geoghegan, 1972.

Sears, R. R. Relation of early socialization experiences to aggression in middle childhood. *Journal of Abnormal and Social Psychology,* 1961, *63,* 466–492.

Sears, R. R., Maccoby, E. E., & Levin, H. *Patterns of child rearing.* Evanston, Ill.: Row, Peterson, 1957.

Sears, R. R., Rau, L., & Alpert, R. *Identification and child rearing.* Stanford, Calif.: Stanford University Press, 1965.

Seavey, C. A., Katz, P. A., & Zalk, S. R. Baby X: The effect of gender labels on adult responses to infants. *Sex Roles,* 1975, *1*(2), 103–109.

Serbin, L. A., O'Leary, K. D., Kent, R. N., & Tonick, I. S. A comparison of teacher response to the pre-academic and problem behavior of boys and girls. *Child Development,* 1973, *44,* 796–804.

Shah, S. A. *Report on the XYY chromosomal abnormality.* Washington, D.C.: U.S. Government Printing Office, 1970.

Shainess, N. A re-evaluation of some aspects of femininity through a study of menstruation: A preliminary report. *Comprehensive Psychiatry,* 1961, *2,* 20–26.

Shanas, E., Townsend, P., Wedderburn, D., Friis, H., Milhoj, P., & Stehouwer, Y. *Old people in three industrial societies.* New York: Atherton, 1968.

Sheehy, G. *Passages: Predictable crises of adult life.* New York: Dutton, 1974.

Shepard, W., & Peterson, J. Are there sex differences in infancy? JSAS *Catalogue of Selected Documents in Psychology,* 1973, *3,* 121.

Sherfey, M. J. *The nature and evaluation of female sexuality.* New York: Vintage Books, 1972.

Sherif, C. W. *Orientation in social psychology.* New York: Harper & Row, 1976.

Sherif, M. A study of some social factors in perception. *Archives of Psychology,* 1935, *27*(187).

Sherman, J. A. Problem of sex differences in space perception and aspects of intellectual functioning. *Psychological Review,* 1967, *74,* 290–299.

Sherman, J. A. *On the psychology of women.* Springfield: Charles C Thomas, 1971.

Sherman, J. A. Field articulation, sex, spatial visualization, dependency, practice, laterality of the brain, and birth order. *Perceptual and Motor Skills,* 1974, *38,* 1223–1235.

Sherman, J. A. Freud's "theory" and feminism: A reply to Juliet Mitchell. In A. H. Cantor (Chair), *Feminism's impact on psychoanalysis.* Symposium presented at the annual convention of the American Psychological Association, Chicago, September 1975.

Sherriffs, A. C., & Jarrett, R. F. Sex differences in attitudes about sex differences. *Journal of Psychology,* 1953, *35,* 161–168.

Sherriffs, A. C., & McKee, J. P. Qualitative aspects of beliefs about men and women. *Journal of Personality,* 1957, *25,* 451–464.

Shields, S. A. Functionalism, Darwinism, and the psychology of women: A study in social myth. *American Psychologist,* 1975, *30*(7), 739–754.

Shope, D. F. The orgastic responsiveness of selected college females. *Journal of Sex Research,* 1968, *4,* 206–219.

Shope, D. F. Sexual responsiveness in single girls. In J. Henslin (Ed.), *Studies in the sociology of sex.* New York: Appleton-Century-Crofts, 1971.

Shope, D. F. *Interpersonal sexuality.* Philadelphia: Saunders, 1975.

Shope, D. F., & Broderick, C. B. Level of sexual experience and predicted adjustment in marriage. *Journal of Marriage and the Family,* 1967, *29,* 424–427.

Shortell, J. R., & Biller, H. B. Aggression in children as a function of sex of subject and sex of opponent. *Developmental Psychology,* 1970, *3,* 143–144.

Siegel, A. E., & Curtis, E. H. Familial correlates of orientation toward future employment among college women. *Journal of Educational Psychology,* 1963, *44,* 33–37.

Siegelman, M. Adjustment of homosexual and heterosexual women. *British Journal of Psychiatry,* 1972, *30,* 477–481.

Siguisch, V., Schmidt, G., Reinfeld, A., & Weidemann-Sutor, I. Psychosexual stimulation: Sex differences. *The Journal of Sex Research,* 1970, *6*(1), 10–24.

Siiter, R., & Unger, R. K. *Ethnic differences in sex-role stereotyping.* Paper presented at the annual convention of the American Psychological Association, Chicago, September 1975.

Silberman, C. E. *Crisis in black and white.* New York: Random House, 1964.

Simon, J. G., & Feather, N. T. Causal attributions for success and failure at university examinations. *Journal of Educational Psychology,* 1973, *64,* 46–56.

Simon, W., Gagnon, J., & Carns, D. *Sexual behavior of the college student.* Paper presented at the meeting of the American Academy of Psychoanalysis, New York, June 1968.

Simpson, M. *Parent preferences of young children.* New York: Bureau of Publications, Teachers College, Columbia University, 1935.

Simpson, R. L., & Simpson, I. Occupational choice among career-oriented college women. *Marriage and Family Living,* 1963, *33,* 377–383.

Sintchak, G., & Geer, J. A vaginal plethysmograph system. *Psychophysiology,* 1975, *12*(1), 113–115.

Sistrunk, F., & McDavid, J. W. Sex variable in conforming behavior. *Journal of Personality and Social Psychology,* 1971, *17,* 200–207.

Slater, J. Suicide: A growing menace to black women. *Ebony,* September 1973, pp. 152–160.

Small, A., Nakamura, C. Y., & Ruble, D. N. *Sex differences in children's outer directedness and self perceptions in a problem-solving situation.* Unpublished manuscript, University of California at Los Angeles, 1973.

Smith, J. R., & Smith, L. G. Introduction. In J. R. Smith & L. G. Smith (Eds.), *Beyond monogamy.* Baltimore: Johns Hopkins University Press, 1974.

Smith, S. Age and sex differences in children's opinions concerning sex differences. *Journal of Genetic Psychology,* 1939, 54, 17–25.

Sontag, S. The double standard of aging. *Saturday Review of the Society,* September 1972, *50,* pp. 29–38.

Sorrentino, R. M., & Short, J. A. Effects of fear of success on women's performance of masculine versus feminine tasks. *Journal of Research in Personality,* 1974, 8, 277–290.

Spence, J. T. The Thematic Apperception Test and attitudes toward achievement in women: A new look at the motive to avoid success and a new method of measurement. *Journal of Consulting and Clinical Psychology,* 1974, *42*(3), 427–437.

Spence, J. T., & Helmreich, R. Who likes competent women: Sex-role congruence of interests and subjects' attitudes toward women as determinants of interpersonal attraction. *Journal of Applied Social Psychology,* 1972, *2*(3), 197–213.

Spence, J. T., Helmreich, R., & Stapp, J. The personal attributes questionnaire: A measure of sex role stereotypes and masculinity-femininity. JSAS *Catalog of Selected Documents in Psychology,* 1974, 4, 43.

Spence, J. T., Helmreich, R., & Stapp, J. Ratings of self and peers on sex-role attributes and their relation to self-esteem and conception of masculinity and femininity. *Journal of Personality and Social Psychology,* 1975, *32,* 29–39.

Sprenger, J., & Krämer, H. *Malleus Maleficarum* (M. Summers, trans.; P. Hughes, Ed.). London: Folio Society, 1968. (Originally published, 1486.)

Stack, C. B. Sex roles and survival strategies in an urban black community. In M. Z. Rosaldo & L. Lamphere (Eds.), *Woman, culture and society.* Stanford, Calif.: Stanford University Press, 1974.

Stafford, R. E. Sex differences in spatial visualization as evidence of sex-linked inheritance. *Perceptual and Motor Skills,* 1961, *13,* 428.

Staines, G., Tavris, C., & Jayarante, T. The queen-bee syndrome. *Psychology Today,* 1974, 7(8), pp. 55–60.

Stake, J. E. The effect of information regarding group-performance norms on goal-setting in males and females. *Sex Roles,* 1976, *2*(1), 23–28.

Staples, R. The myth of the black matriarchy. *The Black Scholar,* 1970, *1*(3–4), 8–16.

Staples, R. Research on black sexuality: Its implication for family life, education and public policy. *The Family Coordinator,* 1972, *21,* 183–188.

Staples, R. *The black woman in America.* Chicago: Nelson-Hall, 1973.

Stayton, D. J., Hogan, R., & Ainsworth, M. D. S. Infant obedience and maternal behavior: The origin of socialization reconsidered. *Child Development,* 1971, *42,* 1057–1069.

Stein, A. H. The effects of sex role standards for achievement and sex role preference on three determinants of achievement motivation. *Developmental Psychology,* 1971, *4,* 219–231.

Stein, A. H., & Bailey, M. M. The socialization of achievement orientation in females. *Psychological Bulletin,* 1973, *80*(5), 345–366.

Stein, A. H., Pohly, S. R., & Mueller, E. The influence of masculine, feminine and neutral tasks on children's achievement behavior, expectancies of success and attainment values. *Child Development,* 1971, *42,* 195–207.

Stein, A. H., & Smithells, J. Age and sex differences in children's sex role standards about achievement. *Developmental Psychology,* 1969, *1,* 252–259.

Steinmann, A. *Male-female concepts of sex roles: Twenty years of cross-cultural research.* Paper presented at the annual convention of the American Psychological Association, Chicago, September 1975.

Steinmann, A., & Fox, D. J. Male-female perceptions of the female role in the United States. *Journal of Psychology,* 1966, *64,* 265–276.

Steinmann, A., & Fox, D. J. Attitude toward women's family role among black and white undergraduates. *The Family Coordinator,* 1970, *19,* 363–368.

Steinmann, A., & Fox, D. J. *The male dilemma.* New York: Aronson, 1974.

Sternglanz, S., & Serbin, L. Sex role stereotyping in children's television programs. *Developmental Psychology,* 1974, *10,* 710–715.

Stouwie, R. J. Inconsistent verbal instructions and children's resistance to temptation behavior. *Child Development,* 1971, *42,* 1517–1531.

Stouwie, R. J. An experimental study of adult dominance and warmth, conflicting verbal instructions, and children's moral behavior. *Child Development,* 1972, *43,* 959–971.

Streib, G. *Mechanisms for change-viewed in a sociological context.* Paper presented at the annual conference of the Institute of Gerontology, Ann Arbor, June 1975.

Strodtbeck, F. L., James, R. M., & Hawkins, C. H. Social status in jury deliberations. *American Sociological Review,* 1957, *22,* 713–719.

Sussman, M. B., & Burchinal, L. Kin family network: Unheralded structure in current conceptualizations of family functioning. *Marriage and Family Living,* 1962, *24*(3), 231–240.

Svensson, A. Relative achievement. In E. E. Maccoby & C. N. Jacklin (Eds.), *The psychology of sex differences.* Stanford: Calif.: Stanford University Press, 1974, 601.

Swanson, H. H. Effects of castration at birth in hamsters of both sexes on luteinization of ovarian implants, oestrous cycles and sexual behavior. *Journal of Reproduction and Fertility,* 1970, *21,* 183–186.

Tangri, S. S. Determinants of occupational role innovation among college women. *Journal of Social Issues,* 1972, *28*(2), 177–199.

Tanner, J. M. *Growth at adolescence* (2nd ed.). Springfield, Ill.: Charles C Thomas, 1962.

Taylor, S. P., & Epstein, S. Aggression as a function of the interaction of the sex of the aggressor and the sex of the victim. *Journal of Personality,* 1967, *35,* 474–496.

Taynor, J., & Deaux, K. When women are more deserving than men: Equity, attribution, and perceived sex differences. *Journal of Personality and Social Psychology,* 1973, *28*(3), 360–367.

Terman, L. M. *Psychological factors in marital happiness.* New York: McGraw-Hill, 1938.

Terman, L. M., & Miles, C. C. *Sex and personality.* New York: McGraw-Hill, 1936.

Thompson, H. B. *The mental traits of sex.* Chicago: University of Chicago Press, 1903.

Thorndike, E. L. *Educational psychology* (2nd ed.). New York: Teachers College, Columbia University, 1910.

Thoye, C. B. Status, race, and aspirations: A study of the desire of high school students to enter a professional or a technical occupation. *Dissertation Abstracts,* 1969, *2*(10-A), 3672.

Throop, W. F., & MacDonald, A. P., Jr. Internal-external locus of control: A bibliography. *Psychological Reports,* 1971, Monograph Supplement 1-V28.

Thurber, S. D. Defensive externality and academic achievement by women. *Psychological Reports*, 1972, *30*, 454.

Thurnher, M. I. *Values and goals in later middle age*. Paper presented at the annual meeting of the Gerontological Society, Houston, October 1971.

Torgoff, I. *Parental developmental time table: Parental field effects on child's compliance*. Paper presented at biennial meeting of the Society for Research in Child Development, State College, Pa., 1961.

Touhey, J. C. Effects of additional women professionals on ratings of occupational prestige and desirability. *Journal of Personality and Social Psychology*, 1974, *29*, 86–89.(a)

Touhey, J. C. Effects of additional men on prestige and desirability of occupations typically performed by women. *Journal of Applied Social Psychology*, 1974, *4*(4), 330–335.(b)

Treadway, C. R., Kane, F. J., Jarrahi-Zadeh, A., & Lipton, M. A. A psychoendocrine study of pregnancy and puerperium. *American Journal of Psychiatry*, 1969, *125*(10), 1380–1386.

Tresemer, D. Fear of success: Popular but unproven. In C. Travis (Ed.), *The female experience*. Delmar, Calif.: CRM, 1973.

Tresemer, D. Do women fear success? *Signs*, 1976, *1*(4), 863–874.

Tresemer, D., & Pleck, J. Sex-role boundaries and resistance to social change. *Women's Studies*, 1974, *2*, 61–78.

Trigg, L. J., & Perlman, D. Social influences on women's pursuit of a nontraditional career. *Psychology of Women Quarterly*, 1976, *1*(2), 138–150.

Troll, L. E. Family in later life: A decade review. *Journal of Marriage and the Family*, May 1971, *33*, 263–290.

Troll, L. E. *Early and middle adulthood*. Monterey, Calif.: Brooks/Cole, 1975.

Troll, L. E., Neugarten, B. L., & Kraines, R. J. Similarities in values and other personality characteristics in college students and their parents. *Merrill-Palmer Quarterly*, 1969, *15*(4), 323–336.

Turner, B. F. *Socialization and career orientation among black and white college women*. Paper presented at the annual convention of the American Psychological Association, Honolulu, September 1972.

Turner, R. H. Some aspects of women's ambition. *American Journal of Sociology*, 1964, *70*(3), 271–285.

Tyler, F. B., Rafferty, J., & Tyler, B. Relationships among motivations of parents and their children. *Journal of Genetic Psychology*, 1962, *101*, 69–81.

Tyler, L. E. *The psychology of human differences*. New York: Appleton-Century-Crofts, 1965.

Unger, R. K. Male is greater than female: The socialization of status inequality. *The Counseling Psychologist*, 1976, *6*(2), 2–9.

Unger, R. K. Status, power and gender: An examination of parallelisms. In J. A. Sherman & F. L. Denmark (Eds.), *The futures of women: Issues in psychology*. New York: Psychological Dimensions, in press.

Unger, R. K., & Denmark, F. L. *Women: Dependent or independent variable?* New York: Psychological Dimensions, 1975.

Unger, R. K., & Siiter, R. *Sex-role stereotypes: The weight of a "grain of truth."* Paper presented at the meeting of the Eastern Psychological Association, Philadelphia, April 1974.

U.S. Bureau of the Census. *Census of the population: General social and economic characteristics, 1970*. Final report. Washington, D.C.: U.S. Government Printing Office, 1972.

U.S. Bureau of the Census. *Marital status and living arrangements, March 1975*.

Current population reports, population characteristics, Series P-20, No. 287. Washington, D.C.: U.S. Government Printing Office, 1975.(a)

U.S. Bureau of the Census. *The social and economic status of the Black population in the U.S., 1974*. Current population reports special studies, Series P-23, No. 54. Washington, D.C.: U.S. Government Printing Office, 1975.(b)

U.S. Department of Commerce, Council of Economic Advisors. *Where women stand in the professions*. Washington, D.C.: U.S. Government Printing Office, 1973.

U.S. Department of Health, Education and Welfare. *Monthly vital statistics report,* Vol. 23, No. 13. Washington, D.C.: U.S. Government Printing Office, 1975.

U.S. Department of Labor, Women's Bureau. *1969 handbook on women workers*. Washington, D.C.: U.S. Government Printing Office, 1969.

Vaughter, R. Review essay: Psychology. *Signs,* 1976, *2*(1), 120–146.

Vaughter, R., Gubernick, D., Matassian, J., & Haslett, B. *Sex differences in academic expectations and achievement*. Paper presented at the annual convention of the American Psychological Association, New Orleans, September 1974.

Veevers, J. E. Voluntarily childless wives: An exploratory study. *Sociology and Social Research,* 1973, *57,* 356–366.

Veroff, J. Social comparison and the development of achievement motivation. In C. P. Smith (Ed.), *Achievement-related motives in children*. New York: Russell Sage Foundation, 1969.

Veroff, J. How general is the achievement motive? In W. Edelstein (Ed.), *Conditions of the educational process*. Stuttgart: Klett, 1973.

Veroff, J., & Feld, S. *Marriage and work in America: A study of motives and roles*. New York: Van Nostrand Reinhold, 1970.

Veroff, J., McClelland, L., & Ruhland, D. Varieties of achievement motivation. In M. T. S. Mednick, S. S. Tangri, & L. W. Hoffman (Eds.), *Women and achievement*. New York: Wiley, 1975, 172–205.

Veroff, J., Wilcox, S., & Atkinson, J. W. The achievement motive in high school and college-age women. *Journal of Abnormal and Social Psychology,* 1953, *48,* 108–119.

Vogel, S. R., Rosenkrantz, P. S., Broverman, I. K., Broverman, D. M., & Clarkson, F. E. Sex-role self-concepts and life style plans of young women. *Journal of Consulting and Clinical Psychology,* 1975, *43*(3), 427.

Vroegh, K. *Young children's sex role and knowledge of sex stereotypes*. Paper presented at the annual convention of the American Psychological Association, Chicago, September 1975.

Waber, D. P. Sex differences in cognition: A function of maturation rate? *Science,* 1976, *192* (4239), 572–574.

Walberg, H. J. Physics, femininity and creativity. *Developmental Psychology,* 1969, *1,* 47–54.

Waldron, I. Why women live longer than men. *Journal of Human Stress,* 1976, *2*(1), 2–13.

Wallach, E. F., & Garcia, C. R. Psychodynamic aspects of oral contraception: A review. *Journal of the American Medical Association,* 1968, *203,* 927–931.

Wallach, M. A., & Kogan, N. *Modes of thinking in young children*. New York: Holt, Rinehart & Winston, 1965.

Wallin, P. A study of orgasm as a condition of women's enjoyment of intercourse. *Journal of Social Psychology,* 1960, *51,* 191–198.

Ward, I. L. Differential effect of pre- and post-natal androgen on the sexual behavior of intact and spayed female rats. *Hormones and Behavior,* 1969, *1,* 25–36.

Ward, I. L. Prenatal stress feminizes and demasculinizes the behavior of males. *Science,* 1972, *175,* 82–84.

Ward, I. L., & Renz, F. J. Consequences of perinatal hormone manipulation on the adult sexual behavior of female rats. *Journal of Comparative Physiological Psychology,* 1972, *78*(3), 349–355.

Ward, W. D. Variance of sex-role preference among boys and girls. *Psychological Reports,* 1968, *23,* 467–470.

Warren, J. Time: Resource or utility? *Journal of Home Economics,* 1968, *49,* 20–21.

Watson, V. Self-concept formation and the Afro-American woman. *Journal of Afro-American Issues,* 1974, *2*(3), 226–236.

Weideger, P. *Menstruation and menopause.* New York: Knopf, 1976.

Weiner, B., Frieze, I., Kukla, A., Reed, L., Rest, S., & Rosenbaum, R.M. Perceiving the causes of success and failure. In E.E. Jones, R.E. Kanouse, H.H. Kelley, R.E. Nisbett, S. Valins, & B. Weiner (Eds.), *Attribution: Perceiving the causes of behavior.* Morristown, N.J.: General Learning Press, 1971.

Weiner, B., & Kukla, A. An attributional analysis of achievement motivation. *Journal of Personality and Social Psychology,* 1970, *15,* 1–20.

Weiner, B., & Potepan, P. Personality characteristics and affective reactions toward exams of superior and failing college students. *Journal of Educational Psychology,* 1970, *61,* 144–151.

Weiss, R. S. *Loneliness.* Cambridge, Mass.: M.I.T. Press, 1973.

Weiss, R. S. The emotional impact of marital separation. *Journal of Social Issues,* 1976, *32*(1), 135–145.

Weisstein, N. Psychology constructs the female, or the fantasy life of the male psychologist. In M. H. Garskof (Ed.), *Roles women play: Readings toward women's liberation.* Monterey, Calif.: Brooks/Cole, 1971, 68–83.

Weston, P., & Mednick, M. Race, social class, and the motive to avoid success in women. In J. Rosenblith, W. Allinsmith, & J. Williams (Eds.), *Readings in child development.* Boston: Allyn & Bacon, 1973, 308–312.

White, K. Social background variables related to career commitment of women teachers. *Personnel and Guidance Journal,* 1967, *45,* 48–52.

Whiting, B., & Edwards, C. P. A cross-cultural analysis of sex differences in the behavior of children aged three through eleven. *The Journal of Social Psychology,* 1973, *91,* 171–188.

Williams, J. H. Sexual role identification and personality functioning in girls: A theory revisited. *Journal of Personality,* 1973, *41*(1), 1–8.

Williamson, N. E. Sex preferences, sex control, and the status of women. *Signs,* 1976, *1* (4), 847–862.

Wilson, G. D. An electrodermal technique for the study of phobia. *New England Medical Journal,* 1966, *85,* 696–698.

Wilson, M., & Greene, R. Personality characteristics of female homosexuals. *Psychological Reports,* 1971, *28,* 407–412.

Winokur, G. Depression in the menopause. *American Journal of Psychiatry,* 1973, *130,* 92–93.

Witkin, H. A. Origins of cognitive style. In C. Sheerer (Ed.), *Cognition: Theory, research, promise.* New York: Harper & Row, 1964.

Witkin, H. A. Social influences in the development of cognitive style. In D. A. Goslin (Ed.), *Handbook of socialization theory and research.* Chicago: Rand McNally, 1969.

Witkin, H. A., Dyk, R. B., Faterson, H. F., Goodenough, D. R., & Karp, S. A. *Psychological differentiation.* New York: Wiley, 1962.

Witkin, H. A., Lewis, H. B., Hertzman, M., Machover, K., Meissner, P. B., & Wapner, S. *Personality through perception.* New York: Harper, 1954.

Wittig, M. A. Sex differences in intellectual functioning: How much of a difference do genes make? *Sex Roles,* 1976, *2*(1), 63–74.

Wolf, T. M. Effects of live modeled sex-inappropriate play behavior in a naturalistic setting. *Developmental Psychology,* 1973, *9,* 120–123.

Wolff, C. *Love between women.* New York: Harper & Row, 1971.

Work, M. S., & Rogers, H. Effect of estrogen on food-seeking dominance among male rats. *Journal of Comparative and Physiological Psychology,* 1972, *79,* 414–418.

Wright, B., & Taska, S. The nature and origin of feeling feminine. *British Journal of Social and Clinical Psychology,* 1966, *5*(2), 140–149.

Wright, M. *Self-concept and the coping process of black undergraduate women at a predominantly white university.* Unpublished doctoral dissertation, University of Michigan, 1975.

Wynn, M. *Fatherless families.* London: Michael Joseph, 1964.

Yalom, I. D., Lunde, D. T., Moos, R. H., & Hamburg, D. A. "Postpartum blues" syndrome: A description and related variables. *Archives of General Psychiatry,* 1968, *18,* 16–27.

Yates, J. F., & Collins, W. *Self-confidence and motivation among black and white college freshmen: An exploration.* Unpublished manuscript, 1974. (Available from the University of Michigan)

Young, V. H. Family and childhood in a southern negro community. *American Anthropologist,* 1970, *72,* 269–288.

Youssef, Z. I. The role of race, sex, hostility, and verbal stimulus in inflicting punishment. *Psychonomic Science,* 1968, *12,* 285–286.

Zander, A., Fuller, R., & Armstrong, W. Attributed pride or shame in group and self. *Journal of Personality and Social Psychology,* 1972, *23*(3), 346–352.

Zuckerman, M., & Wheeler, L. To dispel fantasies about the fantasy-based measure of fear of success. *Psychological Bulletin,* 1975, *82*(6), 932–946.

Author Index

Subject Index

Toward Understanding Women

Lawrence S. Wrightsman

Consulting Editor

The Environment and Social Behavior: Privacy,
Personal Space, Territory, and Crowding
Irwin Altman, The University of Utah

Contemporary Issues in Social Psychology, 3rd Edition
John C. Brigham, Florida State University
Lawrence S. Wrightsman, University of Kansas

The Behavior of Women and Men
Kay Deaux, Purdue University

Research Projects in Social Psychology:
An Introduction to Methods
Michael King, California State University, Chico
Michael Ziegler, York University

Evaluating Research in Social Psychology:
A Guide for the Consumer
Clara Mayo, Boston University
Marianne LaFrance, Boston College

Toward Understanding Women
Virginia E. O'Leary, Oakland University

Three Views of Man: Perspectives from Sigmund Freud,
B. F. Skinner, and Carl Rogers
Robert D. Nye, State University of New York, College at New Paltz

Theories of Personality
Duane Schultz, The American University

Interpersonal Behavior
Harry C. Triandis, University of Illinois at Urbana-Champaign

Social Psychology, 2nd Edition
Lawrence S. Wrightsman, University of Kansas